Argentine Sugar Politics:

TUCUMÁN AND THE GENERATION OF EIGHTY

Lules Factory of Clodomiro Hileret, 1882.
From *Memoria histórica y descriptiva*.

Lules Factory of Clodomiro Hileret, 1882.
From *Memoria histórica y descriptiva*.

Argentine Sugar Politics:

TUCUMÁN AND THE GENERATION OF EIGHTY

By Donna J. Guy

Published by
The Center for Latin American Studies
Arizona State University
Tempe, Arizona

Library of Congress Cataloging in Publication Data

Guy, Donna J
    Argentine sugar politics.

    Bibliography: p.
    Includes index.
    1. Sugar trade--Argentine Republic--Tucumán
(Province)--History. 2. Tucumán, Argentine Republic
(Province)--History. I. Title
HD9114.A73T785   338.4'7'66411509824   79-22922
ISBN 0-87918-043-9

Copyright © 1980 -- Arizona Board of Regents
Arizona State University
Center for Latin American Studies
Tempe, Arizona 85281

Published in the United States of America.

Typing by Lynnette Winkelman

Printed by Contempo Graphics

Bookbinding by Roswell Bookbinding

Bureau of Publications · 90127

TO

MY

PARENTS

ARGENTINA

Showing Location
of Tucumán Province

CONTENTS

LIST OF ILLUSTRATIONS

(Frontispiece)

Lules Factory of Clodomiro Hileret

(Following Page 88)

President Carlos Pellegrini

Lt. Coronel Lucas A. Córdoba, governor of Tucumán

Pedro G. Méndez

Juan Posse, 1904

President Nicolás Avellaneda, 1874–1880

Teodoro De Bary, 1907

Otto Bemberg

President Julio A. Roca, 1880–1886, 1898–1904

Ernesto Tornquist

Marco Avellaneda

Clodomiro Hileret

Salón de Maquinara, Lules Factory, 1882

PREFACE

Argentina's desire to foment a modern sugar industry in Tucumán was not an isolated incident in the late nineteenth century. In the early years of that century the introduction of beet sugar in Europe, along with the adaptation of modern industrial technology to sugar processing, resulted in a tremendous expansion of cane and beet cultivation throughout the world. Soon countries interested in developing their own sugar industries adopted preferential tariffs and domestic legislation to encourage local sugar production, protect national refiners, prevent the entry of cheap sugar, or a combination of these tactics. By 1900 sugar had become one of the most competitive commodities in the world due to political intrigues as well as abundant supplies. [1]

In Latin America sugarcane had been one of the first plantation crops sanctioned by colonial officials because it brought high prices in European markets. Sugar became the principal export of British, French and Spanish colonies in the Caribbean, and of Portuguese Brazil. Sugarcane was also grown on a smaller scale for local consumption in other regions of the Spanish colonies. After independence new European inventions such as steam engines, centrifuges and hydraulic cane crushers were imported to Latin America and applied mostly to the production of unrefined sugar for export to refineries in Europe and the United States.

The application of modern technology to the sugar industries of Latin America differed greatly from the European and North American experiences. Unlike the situation in highly urban, industrialized societies, Latin American countries did not have large consumer markets until immigrants from Europe swelled the capital cities of Brazil, Argentina and Chile in the late nineteenth century, and two world wars stimulated internal migration from rural to urban areas throughout Latin America in the twentieth century. Without increased domestic sugar consumption, Latin American sugar suppliers continued to focus on the export market. Under these circumstances many industrialists and plantation owners found they could not afford the tremendous investment needed to construct modern processing plants and refineries; even if they could raise the capital, tariff policies in Europe blocked the entry of Latin American made refined sugar. Similarly, political protection of sugar refineries in the United States forced Latin American exporters to trade in unrefined sugar if they wanted to enter U.S. markets. The only other markets open to Latin American producers were in neighboring countries that did not have a domestic sugar industry; yet most of these countries purchased cheap European refined sugar or constructed local refineries. Only government subsidies, protective tariffs and increased local sugar consumption could temporarily alleviate these problems. [2]

In addition to unfavorable tariff conditions in Europe and the United States, Latin American exporters also confronted a rapid decrease in the world price of sugar at the same time that the abolition of slavery first in the British Caribbean and later in Brazil and Cuba forced basic and often costly readjustments in the labor recruitment patterns within the labor-intensive agricultural sector of the sugar industry. Low selling prices and added production costs made purchase of expensive machinery particularly difficult and financially unsound. Consequently, many established sugar processers in Latin America did not--often were unable to--modernize all phases of sugar production and even were unable to revise the basic methods of making unrefined sugar unless they received direct government aid or attracted new private sources of investment. In this way the Latin American sugar industry became dependent upon supplies of inexpensive labor, political protection and accessible foreign markets.[3]

The apparent reluctance of Latin American sugar producers to adopt modern techniques to this industry has often been seen as part of a larger tradition of underdevelopment that has been defined in cultural, structural and economic terms.[4] Yet in this case, as well as in other examples of underdevelopment, modernization has been impeded by a series of circumstances both internal and external that have little to do with the inflexible factors often applied to these problems. Industrialists in most sugar producing countries tried to improve the amount and quality of sugar production, some lost their fortunes because they unwisely invested in new machines. The market structure of the modern sugar industry, as well as business practices, thus often blocked the benefits of progress. Further, politics, in the form of international diplomacy, favors to individual industrialists, tariffs, taxation and other forms of direct government intervention in the national economy, even in nineteenth-century Latin America, had a great impact on the uneven advancement of the sugar industry in the nineteenth and twentieth century.[5]

Although the Argentine sugar industry of the late nineteenth century does not fit precisely into the general pattern of Latin American sugar industries, it experienced all the tribulations that beset the cane sugar industry at that time. Equally important for the study of the modern sugar industry in Latin America, the Argentine sugar industry was one of the first to become integrated into the domestic economy. The evolution of the non-export economy in the nineteenth century has often been neglected by economic historians of Latin America more interested in the powerful export sectors. Yet without import substitutions of staple consumer items, rapidly growing countries like Argentina, Brazil and Chile would have had an even worse balance of payments problems than what they faced with this limited base of national industry. Moreover, they would have been completely unprepared for the increased urban growth and general expansion of the domestic market in the twentieth century. Thus early non-export industries were crucial to the creation of a local bourgeoisie and in the adaptation of export-oriented business practices to the internal market. Due to their political and industrial links, Argentine sugar producers were highly visible participants in this process and their actions reveal new dimensions of this relatively unexplored topic.

Just as the Tucumán sugar industry illustrates many facets of the Latin American sugar industry, it also sheds light on aspects of Argentine political and economic history in the late nineteenth century. The sugar industry helped integrate the Argentine northwest into the national economy at the same time sugar and its politics resolved a series of political dilemmas left over from years of civil war and personal rivalries. Thus sugar elites, along with other representatives of regional industry, helped expand the political and economic dimensions of Argentina at a crucial moment.[6]

The move to develop the sugar industry in Argentina was as much a grassroots campaign as it was imposed from above by interested national politicians. In fact, the strength of local sugar oligarchs, as well as certain provincial governments like Tucumán, was remarkable in a time of increased centralization and control through the presidency. The resulting struggle between local and national politicians for control of sugar politics--the intervention of government in the sugar business—helped force national government to be responsive to local interests.

The successful protection and development of regional agroindustry like sugar thus became a key component in the domestic plans of the eighties and nineties, the era of the "Generation of Eighty." Yet the example of the sugar industry showed that success often brought with it a set of problems as grave as the original difficulties. Uneven distribution of industrial benefits, market crises and uncontrolled sugar politics eventually threatened to destroy the benefits sugar originally brought to Argentina and to the northwest. Further, economic depression after 1890 encouraged industrial conservatism that curbed further participation in politics by national industrialists until the twentieth century. Thus short-term success brought long-term failure.

In order to reconstruct and analyze the political economy of the sugar industry in Tucumán, a variety of issues had to be discussed before the complete picture of sugar's impact on Argentina could emerge. Consequently the organization of this study consists of a partly thematic, partly chronological approach. Chapters One through Three examine factors such as national and local political and economic conditions, banking and credit mechanisms, elite family politics and the renovation of the sugar industry by old and new groups. After Chapter Three, these various themes begin to interact in a manner that warrants chronological as well as topical treatment.

The research for this study began in 1968 when the Latin American Studies Department of Indiana University sponsored my first research trip to Argentina to see if the topic was feasible. Since then the Midwest Universities Consortium for International Activities, the Foreign Area Fellowship Program and the University of Arizona have all sponsored additional field trips, and I thank them for their financial support.

Many people have offered advice, comfort and their skills during the preparation of this manuscript. Professor James R. Scobie directed the original dissertation research. Professors Robert Schulzinger, Peter Smith, Michael Meyer, Michael Passi, Felicity Nussbaum, Jorge Balán and Carlos Waisman have all critiqued various drafts. In Argentina Dr. Fernando Tornquist, Dr. Elio Rodríguez Marquina, Dr. Ernesto E. Padilla (h), José María Nougués, Lauro Fagalde, Ramón Leoni Pinto, Alejandro Hugo Costa and Carlos Páez de la Torre (h) lent their aid in tracking down letters and documents vital to my research. Employees of the Biblioteca del Congreso, the Biblioteca Tornquist, the Archivo General de la Nación, the Museo Roca, the Archivo Histórico de la Provincia de Tucumán, the Estación Experimental Agrícola of Tucumán, the Biblioteca de la Honorable Legislatura de Tucumán, the Biblioteca Alberdi and the Biblioteca Nacional helped me locate the necessary archival papers, books and journals. I also want to thank Professors Hebe Clemente and Carlos Segreti, Dr. Víctor M. Vázquez, Dr. Robert Fourcaud, Marta Moia and the Julio C. Ramos family of Tucumán for their help. Finally, I would like to thank Mrs. Wiladene Stickel and Mrs. Marilyn Bradian for typing the final drafts and Professor Sidonie Smith for her editorial advice. The final responsibility for the book, of course, is mine.

ENDNOTES TO PREFACE

1. For a general history of the nineteenth-century sugar industry
    see Hedrick C. Prinsen Geerligs, *The World's Cane Sugar Indus-
    try Past and Present* (Manchester: N. Rodger, 1912), and Noel
    Deerr, *The History of Sugar*. 2 vols. (London: Chapman and Hall
    Ltd., 1949.

2. Peter L. Eisenberg, *The Sugar Industry in Pernambuco, 1840-1910;
    Modernization Without Change* (Berkeley: University of California,
    1974); Alfred S. Eichner, *The Emergence of Oligopoly. Sugar
    Refining as a Case Study* (Baltimore, Md.: Johns Hopkins Press,
    1969); Eric Williams, *Capitalism and Slavery* (Chapel Hill: Univer-
    sity of North Carolina, 1944); and Alan H. Adamson, *Sugar With-
    out Slaves; the Political Economy of British Guiana, 1838-1904*
    (New Haven: Yale University Press, 1972).

3. Williams, *Capitalism and Slavery*; Adamson, *Sugar Without Slaves*,
    Eisenberg, *Pernambuco*; Sidney Mintz, Foreword to Ramiro Guerra
    y Sánchez, *Sugar and Society in the Caribbean; an Economic His-
    tory of Cuban Agriculture*; trans. Marjory M. Urquidi (New Haven:
    Yale University, 1927, 1964).

4. Stanley and Barbara Stein, *The Colonial Heritage of Latin America;
    Essays on Economic Dependence in Perspective* (New York: Oxford,
    1970); André Gunder Frank, *Capitalism and Underdevelopment in
    Latin America; Historical Studies of Chile and Brazil* (New York:
    Monthly Review Press, 1967); Richard Graham, *Britain and the
    Onset of Modernization in Brazil 1850-1914* (London: Cambridge
    University Press, 1968); and "Confronting Theory and Practice,"
    special issue of *Latin American Perspectives*, Issue 4, 2:1 (Spring,
    1975).

5. William P. Glade, *The Latin American Economies, a Study of their
    Institutional Evolution* (New York: American Book Company, 1969),
    pp. 232-247.

6. Other studies of Argentine elites include Peter H. Smith, *Politics
    and Beef in Argentina, Patterns of Conflict and Change* (New York:
    Columbia University Press, 1969); Darío Canton, *El Parlamento
    argentino en épocas de cambio: 1890, 1916 y 1946* (Buenos Aires:
    Editorial del Instituto di Tella, 1966); Juan Carlos Agulla, *Eclipse
    de una aristocracia; una investigación sobre las élites dirigentes
    de la ciudad de Córdoba* (Buenos Aires: Ediciones Libera, 1968);
    and José Luis de Imaz, *Los que mandan (Those Who Rule)*, trans.
    and with an introduction by Carlos A. Astiz with Mary F. McCarthy
    (Albany: State University of New York Press, 1970).

INTRODUCTION
The Generation of Eighty

In 1869 Michael and Edward Mulhall, Englishmen living in Argentina, commented on the sorry state of Argentine agriculture: "There is, unhappily, a sad contrast between what La Plata might be, and what it actually is." Although many agricultural products such as rice, cotton, tobacco, wine and sugar were produced in the interior provinces, high transport costs prevented them from competing in coastal as well as international markets. Consequently, they noted that "exports show but three great staples in the Republic--wool, hides and tallow."[1] Yet sixteen years later, in 1885, the same men reported that "the development of agriculture in recent years has been more rapid than the growth of sheep-farming. The breadth of land under tillage, including not only grain crops, but also wine, sugar, linseed, and artificial grasses, has risen...[from 156,000 hectares in 1854 to 1,730,000 hectares in 1884]."[2] In less than a generation, agriculture and its related industries had made remarkable progress.

By 1900 major advances in railroad construction and a conscious effort to stimulate industry and agriculture in the Republic testified to the strides taken to create a new Argentina. Rails penetrated the Argentine interior and opened new opportunities for the sugar and alcohol industries of Tucumán, for the wine industry of Mendoza and for commerce and cattle in Córdoba. Similarly, rails in the littoral opened the pampas to extensive cultivation that added wheat, corn and other cereals to the list of exports. Economic activity based upon agricultural products had become an integral part of the Argentine economy.

The first two national censuses, taken in 1869 and 1895, confirmed the rapid growth of agroindustries. In 1869 industrial development of any kind was so minimal that census takers did not examine it in depth. In sharp contrast, the 1895 census devoted a special section to industry. In addition to public services such as railroads, gas and electric companies, the census concluded that Argentina's principal industries consisted of small urban factories, flour mills, *saladeros* (salted beef factories), sugar, wine, beer and alcohol distilleries:[3]

TABLE 0.1

PRINCIPAL ARGENTINE INDUSTRIES IN 1895

Location	Industry	Number of Factories	Capital Invested in Land, Machinery and Stock (gold pesos)
Littoral	General Industry	22,204	94,700,456
Littoral, West	Flour Mills	659	12,131,174
Littoral	Saladeros	39	12,411,700
Mendoza, San Juan	Wineries	949	8,509,936
Littoral	Beer Breweries	61	2,947,863
Littoral, Tucumán	Distilleries	131	5,004,122
Tucumán	Sugar Factories	50	17,472,661

Although this census was fraught with imprecisions, it clearly demonstrated the importance of coastal industries and of Tucumán and Mendoza as industrial sites in the interior.[4]

Rails, sugar and wine meant much more to Argentina than just the possibility that the country might become self-sufficient in the production of certain commodities. Indeed, many aspirations, both economic and political, had been pinned to official encouragement of transport and industry in the interior. Economic development there might provide the solution to a number of problems that had plagued the young Argentine nation long before it achieved independence.

As early as the eighteenth century, economic grievances began to fragment the southern region of the Spanish empire. The decline of the Potosí mines severely affected the landlocked areas now known as the Argentine interior.[5] These areas had supplied the mines with livestock and agricultural products and served as important administrative centers; without the mines they faced serious economic and political setbacks. The 1776 formation of the Viceroyalty of the Río de la Plata with its seat in Buenos Aires formally acknowledged the fact that the coastal area had become more important than the heavily populated interior. Later the wars of independence, the prohibitive costs of overland transport and the insistence of the coastal area on free trade with Europe further curtailed prospects for regional economic activities. Limited primarily to local trade or to the pursuit of traditional markets in Chile and Bolivia, few interior products made their way to Buenos Aires. When they did, textiles, wines and other provincial products were met by less expensive European goods. Consequently, earlier problems were compounded by post-independence circumstances. Together they kept the interior and Buenos Aires both isolated from and hostile toward one another.[6]

These economic realities combined with serious political disputes over the structure of future government to emphasize the desire of the interior to preserve its political and economic independence from the coastal area and the equally strong desire of Buenos Aires to rule the rest of the country. Local caudillos from both regions helped perpetuate the controversy by gathering military support for their respective causes. Civil war, dictatorship and secessionist movements typified the political situation in Argentina from 1810 to 1862. When unity was restored in 1862, political leaders, instead of reconciling grievances of the interior and the littoral, completed the military pacification of the country. Only after peace was restored several years later were politicians able to tackle the question of how to improve the economic relationship between Buenos Aires and the interior.

By 1880 the encouragement of certain regional industries was seen as the most successful way to maintain peace, facilitate the economic integration of the nation and bolster the interior provinces against undue economic domination by Buenos Aires. In the short run, many of these goals were accomplished, but lasting success depended upon more than a piecemeal plan of limited industrialization. In the long run, the programs of the eighties left bitter legacies for future governments. They distributed political favors in a way that nurtured resentment and maintained regional conflicts as a feature in Argentine political life. They helped ensure the hegemony of Buenos Aires over the interior through economic and political centralization. Finally, they prevented much of the interior from sharing the prosperity of the times.

THE GENERATION OF EIGHTY

Throughout all the turmoil that preceded the final stages of national unification, Buenos Aires played a pivotal and often controversial role. It was logical that *Porteños* would seek special privileges so that their city would maintain its preeminence and a degree of autonomy in the new regime.[7] The income from its port helped Buenos Aires maintain a defiant stance. A national government, on the other hand, could not accept an independent Buenos Aires. Unable to survive without the city's wealth, national government was unwilling to subordinate national to local interests. Consequently, in 1880 the Argentine Congress finally resolved the dilemma by federalizing Buenos Aires city as the national capital. In that way the long struggle apparently ended.

The group that created a national capital and devised a workable formula for peace became known as the Generation of Eighty.[8] Comprised of provincial and Porteño elites who held power in Argentina from 1874 to 1916, the Generation of Eighty was intent upon completing the tasks of national consolidation. Although the federalization of Buenos Aires in 1880 was but one step in the overall plan, it symbolized the spirit of the movement. With Buenos Aires under its control, the Generation of Eighty turned to the interior and finished the task of pacification there. The Conquest of the Desert, aimed at eliminating the Indian menace, ended successfully. Armed insurrection by provincial caudillos was kept to a minimum by the presence of the national army in the interior and by the possibility of sending reinforcements by way of recently constructed railroads. Governments of the eighties then went on to finish railroad and telegraph construction, develop a national bank system and complete other infrastructural improvements that would spur progress. Part of this program included government encouragement of agroindustry in the interior.

The inland areas which received the most attention from the oligarchy--Tucumán, Mendoza and Córdoba provinces--were selected originally because they had been important military strongholds since the 1860s. As natural regional centers both distant and isolated from Buenos Aires, Tucumán, Mendoza and Córdoba had been provinces where loyal governments were needed to prevent secessionist movements, control Indians and quell rebellions.[9] Thus all three provinces offered attractions of a military nature independent of agricultural or industrial pursuits.

To facilitate military campaigns, a number of new railroad concessions had been granted in the 1870s. The Córdoba-Tucumán section of the North Central Railroad was authorized in 1870, and a Buenos Aires-Mendoza and San Juan line was added along with several others in 1872.

The Tucumán line opened to traffic in 1876 and rail service to Mendoza began in 1885.[10] By the time these railroads provided full service, interior provinces had little to fear from Indians or caudillos, and they welcomed the possibility of using the railroads to expand trade.

The railroad became linked with agroindustrial development after 1876, when the Argentine Congress passed a series of protective tariffs. That year general tariffs increased from twenty to twenty-five percent *ad valorem*, while certain imports had duties increased from twenty-five to forty percent *ad valorem*. A number of interior industries including tobacco, wine and sugar directly benefited from the new customs laws. The sugar industry received further symbolic aid in 1876, when Tucumán Deputy Lídoro Quinteros successfully proposed the automatic exoneration of all customs duties for machinery designed to process sugar.[11]

A brief look at the circumstances that led to the Quinteros amendment reveals the importance of the railroads to regional trade. As Quinteros noted, the North Central Railroad was about to open service to Tucumán. Without new machinery, Tucumán would not be able to take full advantage of new trade opportunities in the littoral.[12] Similar arguments were used to defend protection of other regional pursuits, and in this way the military role of the railroad soon became subordinated to its economic function.

The 1877 tariff, the most protectionist to date, marked the beginning of limited government aid to industry. Regional agriculture became the principal beneficiary, although a number of urban industries like shoes, textiles and hats were also aided by the new duties. Thus for the first time since the 1830s, Argentine government leaders advocated a federalist plan of economic development through protective tariffs.[13]

By 1880 and the election of Julio Roca as president, additional government aid to industry seemed feasible, especially if such protection would win more friends for the oligarchs in power. The focus of tariff legislation remained upon agroindustry, and the eighties brought further changes that not only raised duties but also changed the kind of tax from *ad valorem* to specific duties. This kind of modification, along with government-decreed reductions in railroad freight rates, further aided agricultural products from the interior.

The rapid period of modernization of agriculture in the 1880s affected the Argentine interior in different ways. The experiences of inland provinces varied over time and depended to a great extent upon the amount of attention national politicians lavished upon a given province. Some were more important to the political and economic programs than others and this, too, became a decisive factor. Since Tucumán, Córdoba and Mendoza provinces formed the focal points for the Generation of Eighty's domestic plans, those provinces are appropriate places from which to begin a regional investigation. This particular study will concentrate on Tucumán and its neighbors in the northwest, and how they participated in industrial politics that related to the sugar industry.

The domestic sugar industry initially helped the Generation of Eighty include the northwest within the process of nation building and integrated that region into the national economy. In return, the modern sugar industry offered the northwest new economic possibilities and perhaps a degree of autonomy. At first it seemed that sugar would free the northwest of any need to rely on Buenos Aires, and in fact, the early modernization of the industry took place without undue interference from coastal areas.

Yet once domestic sugars competed successfully in coastal markets, the political and economic center of the sugar industry shifted to Buenos Aires. Sugar brought the northwest and Buenos Aires into close contact as anticipated, but on unequal terms. Further, by the turn of the century, the domestic sugar industry posed grave problems for the northwest as well as for the littoral. To continue the economic revitalization of the northwest, Tucumán and its neighbors needed more than sugar.   In fact, other economic activities were desperately needed to counterbalance the harmful aspects of monoculture and sugar politics.   New industries needed political help and independent sources of capital.   Nevertheless, neither national nor local politicians brought forth new plans for Tucumán and its neighbors, and sugar industrialists were partly responsible for this failure.   If the Generation of Eighty could not ensure growth, prosperity and peace in places like Tucumán, its overall blueprint for a modern Argentina was doomed to fail.

ENDNOTES TO INTRODUCTION

1.   Michael George Mulhall, and Edward T. Mulhall, *Handbook of the River Plate; Comprising Buenos Ayres, the Upper Provinces, Banda Oriental, and Paraguay*, Vol. I (Buenos Ayres: Standard Printing Office, 1869), p. 4.

2.   M. G. and E.T. Mulhall, *Handbook of the River Plate, Comprising the Argentine Republic, Uruguay and Paraguay;* 5th ed. (Buenos Aires: M.G. and E.T. Mulhall, 1885), pp. 29-30.

3.   Argentine Republic, Comisión Directiva del Censo, *Segundo Censo de la República Argentina.* [El 10 de mayo de 1895], 3 vols. (Buenos Aires: Taller Tipográfico de la Penitenciaría Nacional, 1898), III: 271, 319, 322, 327, 336, 341, 353, 354. The value of distilleries in sugar factories was included in the sugar statistics. See essay on industry, which explains motives for industrial census and analyzes its contents: III, XC-CXL. Gold pesos were computed at a premium of 1 gold peso = 3 pesos m/n.

4.   Among the many imprecisions was the exclusion of the Refinería Argentina as well as modern frigoríficos, or meat packing plants. In addition several sugar factory owners failed to report the value of their factories and lands.

5.   The Argentine interior before the pacification of the Indian population consisted of the provinces of Tucumán, Salta, Jujuy, Santiago del Estero, Catamarca, San Juan, Mendoza, San Luis, La Rioja and Córdoba. Other parts of the interior were territories occupied principally by Indians.

6.   Works that deal with the colonial economy include Aldo Ferrer, *The Argentine Economy;* trans. Marjory M. Urquidi (Berkeley: University of California, 1967), pp. 22-31; Pedro Santos Martínez, *Las industrias durante el virreinato, 1776-1810* (Buenos Aires: EUDEBA, 1969); Horacio William Bliss, *Del virreinato a Rosas, ensayo de historia económica argentina* (Tucumán: Editorial Richardet, 1959), Part I; and Manfred Kossok, *El virreinato del Río de la Plata, su estructura económica social* (Buenos Aires: La Pléyade, 1972). For the post-independence period see Miron Burgin, *Economic Aspects of Argentine Federalism* (Cambridge: Harvard University Press, 1946).

7.   *Porteño* refers to inhabitants of the port city of Buenos Aires. For extensive documentation of the struggle between Buenos Aires and national government see Arturo B. Carranza, *La cuestión capital de la República. 1826 a 1887,* 6 vols. (Buenos Aires: L.J. Rosso, 1926).

8.   The term "Generation of Eighty" appears frequently in literature relating to this era of Argentine history, although the group does not necessarily conform to the usual definition of a generation. For a justification as well as an explanation of the Generation of Eighty, see Oscar Cornblit, Ezequiel Gallo (h), and Alfredo O'Connell, "La generación del 80 y su proyecto; antecedentes y consecuencias," in Torcuato di Tella, Gino Germani, Jorge Graciarena *et al., Argentina, sociedad de masas;* 3rd ed. (Buenos Aires: Jorge

Álvarez, 1966), pp. 18-58. These ruling elites, wielders of economic and political power, have also been called the oligarchy, and James Scobie bases elite identification on occupation: James R. Scobie, "Buenos Aires as a Commercial-Bureaucratic City, 1880-1910: Characteristics of a City's Orientation," *American Historical Review*, 77:4 (October, 1972), p. 1057.

9. Olga Gamboni, "La rebelión del oeste y sus proyecciones en el norte," *Trabajos y comunicaciones*, 13 (1965): 75-110; Alfredo Gargaro, "Antecedentes de la guerra del Paraguay y reacciones en las provincias," *Trabajos y comunicaciones*, 10 (1963): 83-91.

10. Winthrop R. Wright, *British-owned Railways in Argentina, Their Effect on the Growth of Economic Nationalism, 1854-1948.* Latin American Monograph No. 34 (Austin: University of Texas, 1974), pp. 50-52.

11. Law No. 751, in Argentine Republic, Congreso Nacional, Cámara de Diputados, *Diario de Sesiones, 1862-* (Buenos Aires: Imprenta del Congreso de la Nación, 1863-), 1876: 751-753. Other industrialists who wished to import machinery duty-free had to petition the president.

12. Ibid., August 23, 1876, p. 95.

13. Juan Carlos Nicolau, *Industria argentina y aduana, 1835-1854* (Buenos Aires: Devenir, 1975), pp. 27-49; Juan Álvarez, *Las guerras civiles argentinas;* 3rd ed. Colección Siglo y Medio, no. 94. (Buenos Aires: EUDEBA, 1966), pp. 81-94.

CHAPTER I
Tucumán in Transition: 1862-1880

While stationed in Tucumán in 1869, Lt. Colonel Julio Argentino Roca discovered that his native province was a land of marvels and opportunities. Overwhelmed by what he saw, the twenty-six-year-old officer wrote his brother Ataliva, who then lived in Córdoba:[1]

> Our province is a wonder without equal in all the American continent. . . . No pen can adequately describe the beauty of our eternally verdant lands, dotted with hundreds of rivers and streams; or our incredibly dense forests where . . . a multitude of . . . trees and shrubs form the kingdom whose monarch is the cedar; whose mountain ranges show off their eternally snow-covered peaks, and whose slopes are adorned with unbelievable vegetation.

> To this picture add the blessings of climate and you will agree with me that Tucumán is a paradise where life slips by in the midst of prodigious natural beauty. Here there are no poor people, no misery, and if one can not live well amidst this abundance it is because he is some slothful or stupid fool. Here everybody gets rich.

The letter might have expressed simple youthful exuberance, but it also prophesied Roca's later efforts to develop the Tucumán economy.

By the time Roca became president in 1880, Tucumán no longer resembled the idyllic memories of the young soldier. A period of economic and political change brought on by the process of national unification between 1862 and 1880, the repercussions of an international financial crisis in 1873, and the decline of traditional economic pursuits in the sixties and seventies, all left their mark in Tucumán. In order to turn these events into an advantage, Tucumán needed political aid, new sources of credit and a new economic base. Sugar and its politics helped Tucumán emerge successfully from this era of transition.

NATIONAL UNIFICATION

Long before sugar became important, politicians and caudillos had sought to control Tucumán, the most important province in the northwest. Tucumán thus played a vital role in national unification. The goals of unification--elimination of civil disorders, construction of railroads, and the creation of a national monetary system--could benefit Tucumán in three very significant ways. The first would provide the order and stability necessary to conduct daily affairs; the second would enable Tucumán trade to find new outlets in coastal markets; and the third would eliminate the disadvantages Tucumán merchants suffered by limited banking facilities and the presence of debased foreign currency in the northwest. In return the national government would be assured that a loyal Tucumán could keep watch over her neighbors and provide products unavailable in the coastal areas.

The first step towards national unity had been the elimination of civil disorder. The September 1861 battle of Pavón and the election of Bartolomé Mitre as President of Argentina had reunited Buenos Aires province with the rest of the nation, but it took much longer to make the caudillos of the interior accept the new regime.[2] Within a month of the Pavón battle Tucumán began to feel the effects of renewed civil war, and the old banners of federalism and unitarianism were raised again by regional enemies.[3]

Regional intrigue also flared up later when Antonino and Manuel Taboada, caudillos from nearby Santiago del Estero decided to help a faction of Tucumán *Liberales*, pro-Mitre unitarians and anti-Rosas federalists, who were intent upon ousting their governor, Wenceslao Posse. What bothered the malcontents had nothing to do with Wenceslao's Liberal political affiliations, but rather the fear that the Posse family would use its extensive kinship network to dominate provincial politics. Posse's enemies deposed him on June 30, 1867 and Posse responded by staging three abortive rebellions in 1868. The benefits of national government had not yet brought lasting peace to Tucumán.

By the time new presidential elections took place in 1868, the Tucumán Liberal coalition had been reduced to a number of warring factions who used the impending elections to stir up more trouble. Those who supported the candidacy of Domingo Faustino Sarmiento blamed Mitre for political dissention of earlier years, especially the invasion by the Taboada brothers. The Mitre allies in Tucumán fulminated at similar efforts by Sarmiento supporters.

After Sarmiento won the 1868 election, the pro-Mitre faction continued to rely on the outside interference of the Taboadas while Sarmiento used the national army to help his Tucumán allies. The new president thus sent federal troops under the command first of General Ignacio Rivas and later of Lt. Colonel Julio Roca to maintain peace in the northwest. With the help of the army, the Taboadas were thwarted in their attempt to influence the outcome of the 1869 gubernatorial elections in Tucumán.

Sarmiento and the national army kept the Taboadas under control temporarily, but it was left to Sarmiento's successor, Nicolás Avellaneda, to destroy the political power of Mitre's northern allies. Avellaneda's opportunity came when the Taboadas joined with Mitre in an anti-Avellaneda rebellion in 1874. Once the revolt had been quelled, Avellaneda then turned the incident over to the courts.[4] Avellaneda's successful control of the Taboadas by legal means marked the end of endemic civil wars as well as the first signs that national unification would bring benefits to the northwest. Yet even though peace was crucial to Tucumán, it could not alone solve all of Tucumán's problems.

THE CRISIS OF 1873 AND THE
DECLINE OF TRADITIONAL INDUSTRIES

Despite the political instability inside and outside the province, Tucumán managed to continue agricultural, pastoral and trading activities until the 1870s. Part of her economic vitality was due to lenient practices of purportedly ruthless Rosista governors in Tucumán. When Celedonio Gutiérrez came to power in 1841, he refused to carry out the death sentences and property confiscation orders for unitarians.[5] Consequently, after 1844 political exiles returned to Tucumán from Chile and Bolivia and they helped contribute to provincial prosperity.

The temporary political peace at mid-century helped Tucumán's principal city of San Miguel regain its former status as the commercial center of the northwest long before any other city in the region could challenge San Miguel's position.[6] Tucumán's abundant natural resources and its hard-working farmers and artisans provided the necessary economic base to revitalize trade. The dense subtropical forests that covered most of the province provided hardwoods such as *quebracho colorado*, used for cart and furniture construction, and *cebil*, whose tannin-rich bark made tanning a boom industry in the fifties. Cereal crops formed the basis of a regional flour industry while cattle, rice and tobacco satisfied local and regional markets. In addition to these products, rum and brandy, along with amounts of crude sugar, were manufactured by a growing number of cane cultivators. All these products destined for local and foreign markets were loaded up on caravans of giant ox-drawn, two-wheeled carts, the famed *carretas tucumanas*, or on the smaller mule-drawn wagons that became more popular by the early seventies.[7]

Descriptions of rural and urban Tucumán in the late 1850s and 1860s depict a bustling community that developed its markets despite uncertain conditions caused by political anarchy and isolation from coastal markets. In 1884 Vicente Quesada wrote his recollections of Tucumán in the 1850s and concluded that San Miguel, and Tucumán in general, was a place where "everything . . . revealed an aura of prosperity: its homes, clothing, even its rural customs attested to this. . . . Property was very subdivided; there were no great landowners, but then again one did not see poverty among those willing to work. The difference between this province and those of Santiago and La Rioja was enormous."[8] Quesada noted that merchants traded with Chile and Bolivia, but rarely with Buenos Aires. However, he was also quick to point out that Tucumán's impressive regional trade, as well as hopes of expanding its markets, would be limited until peace and additional credit facilities became available.[9]

Hermann N. Burmeister, a German scientist who passed through Tucumán in 1859, showed great interest in Tucumán's profitable tanning industry. Unfortunately, Burmeister reported, the tanning business already had been debilitated by two serious problems that would ultimately limit further opportunities: rising prices for cebil bark and transport. As he reported:

> At first tanning was so profitable that their leathers yielded a 200% profit, but now this has fallen to fifty percent, since hides that previously sold for 4 *reales* are now sold at 8 to 12 *reales*. This [price increase] is due to the scarcity of tannin and the increased cost of shipping the bark. Earlier tanners purchased a wagon load of bark for 12 *reales* which now costs 3 or 4 pesos.[10]

As late as the sixties tanners and merchants met rising production and shipping costs by constantly searching for new markets and eventually finding new products to sell along with their leather. According to his grandson, Miguel Padilla with the help of nine sons earned the family's fortune in the 1860s by trading as far south as La Rioja and as far north and west as Bolivia and Copiapó, Chile. They sold tobacco and cattle in Chile and purchased mules in Salta that brought good prices in Bolivia and Peru. They also sold small quantities of sugar, molasses and brandy to people in rural Tucumán and in nearby provinces.

Wenceslao Posse also engaged in tanning and trade. One of the unitarians who returned from exile in the 1840s, Posse soon became a wealthy man. He raised cattle, experimented with indigo plants and engaged in retail trading. After 1845 he also began to raise sugarcane, from which he manufactured brandy and crude sugar.

Although merchants like Posse and Padilla managed to diversify their activities, a new crisis caused by the depression of 1873, combined with the effects of a new national monetary system and other fiscal pressures in Tucumán, sounded the death knell for a number of Tucumán industries.

The national depression that resulted from the 1873 international panic finally hit Tucumán in 1875 and destroyed the already weakened tanning business. Evidence of the demise was offered in the *Memoria histórica y descriptiva de la provincia de Tucumán* of 1882, an officially sanctioned publication. The *Memoria* noted that whereas in 1874 Tucumán had boasted of forty-three tanneries, by 1880 there were only thirty-two. Official statistics for 1882 confirmed this pattern: only twenty-five tanning establishments had paid the 1882 license tax. Equally important was the fact that the productive capacity of remaining establishments had declined, as evidenced by the growing number of second- and third-class license fees and the decreased numbers of first-class fees paid. [11]

Another activity affected by the depression was cereal cultivation. As part of the 1876 tariff revisions that were passed in part as a response to the 1873 depression, national legislators had passed wheat tariffs that eventually favored the coastal pampas. Soon cheap pampa wheat discouraged cereal cultivation in Tucumán, and by 1882 parts of the province formerly devoted to cereal production switched to more remunerative sugarcane. [12]

The *Memoria* also attributed the emigration of skilled carpenters and cabinetmakers from Tucumán on the depression. Financial conditions had forced delays in most private and public construction. By the time the situation had improved, Tucumán had no way to live up to its earlier reputation for locally produced cabinets, furniture and wagons. [13]

The provincial tax structure reinforced rather than relieved the deepening business slump. According to tax records from 1870 to 1889, the cattle industry, commerce and cereal cultivation were primary sources of provincial income. Thus the license fees, branding charges, export stamps for hides, slaughtering taxes and cart fees, along with cereal taxes assessed according to the amount of land used rather than the amount of grain produced, heightened the impact of the national depression. And just as tanneries fell into disuse, of the fifty-five flour mills on tax roles in 1874, only twenty-six remained in 1880. [14]

As for the merchant class, most depended upon the sale of local goods in regional markets. As business deteriorated, they too found that the local tax system became burdensome. Their main tax consisted of a flat percentage of the total value of inventory, regardless of whether it was sold or restocked in the course of a given year. During times of economic stagnation, taxes were much higher as goods gathered dust on the shelves. Consequently it appears that merchants also began to show interest in the sugar industry, since it offered relatively high profits and almost no special taxes. [15]

BANKING AND CREDIT

The last major effect of the 1873 depression in Tucumán was to dis-courage expansion of banking and credit facilities at a critical moment. Because Tucumán had always been an important trading area, many at-tempts had been made to establish a local bank, but political instability and changing economic conditions prevented this until the 1870s.

As early as 1867 the Rosario-based Banco Argentino planned to open a series of branches in the northwest. The bank's president, José Cullen, thus responded favorably to enquiries made by Federico Helguera, Tucumán politician and cattleman, concerning a Tucumán branch. Cullen's response of September 10 indicated that the bank's directorate would consider the proposal, provided that support for such a project came from Tucumán.[16] Evidently Helguera and several associates managed to sell 728 bank shares in Tucumán by November 30, but their efforts proved fruitless. While they immediately wrote Cullen of their success, for un-known reasons the letter did not reach Rosario until June 1868 and by then conditions had changed and the Banco Argentino suspended all plans for new branches.[17]

While awaiting a response from Cullen, Helguera joined with Marco Avellaneda, brother of the future president, and several others to found a local bank. They went to the provincial legislature and petitioned suc-cessfully for a ninety-nine year contract for the Banco de Tucumán. Its authorized capital would be 300,000 *pesos fuertes*, based upon 3,000 shares of 100 pesos.[18] This bank never functioned, but that did not stop Helguera and his associates from making further plans.

By 1872 the Banco de San Juan, backed by Chilean currency, of-fered to establish a branch in San Miguel. Debates in the Tucumán legis-lature resulted in a contract for the bank that included provisions to exonerate the bank from all provincial taxes for four years. The holders of the Banco de Tucumán contract sponsored the Banco de San Juan pro-ject and newly elected Governor Helguera signed the final law on June 13, 1872.[19]

The Banco de San Juan opened and functioned on a modest level for a few years. Once again, however, national financial conditions af-fected the future of a Tucumán bank. It had not been coincidental that the metallic reserves for this were Chilean; for only foreign specie circu-lated in Tucumán. The major problems with this currency were its fluc-tuating value and the reluctance of coastal merchants to accept such specie. Under these conditions the Banco de San Juan had few hopes of continuing success, and the 1873 depression only added to its problems.

As late as 1874 the Tucumán Banco de San Juan paid fourteen per-cent profits to its shareholders.[20] By 1876 deteriorating local conditions and low exchange rates for Bolivian coins prevented the bank from ex-panding its operations. The bank was caught up in the same predicament facing merchants who felt it was impossible to trade when the value of currency changed daily. Thus the Banco de San Juan joined merchants who unsuccessfully petitioned the national government for a circulating currency equivalent to the national peso fuerte.[21]

The final blow to the Banco de San Juan came in May 1878 when the Tucumán legislature passed a special bank tax. The new tax would be a flat rate ranging from 400 to 2,000 pesos, depending upon the amount of capital owned by that bank.[22] From the moment the legislature passed this law the Banco de San Juan's managers, Benigno Barril and his suc-cessor John Fourcaud, petitioned the local courts for exoneration of all or part of the new tax. The Tucumán attorney-general (*fiscal*) recom-mended that the governor pay no heed to this request and eventually bank officials were forced to liquidate the bank's assets.[23] After 1880 the Banco de San Juan ceased to function on a regular basis.

The Banco de San Juan was not the only bank operating in Tucumán at this moment, and the fate of the other in part helps explain the downfall of the Banco de San Juan. In 1874 the Banco Nacional began to open branches in the interior, thereby hoping to bring credit to the interior and unite the nation monetarily by driving out foreign currency. The process, however, was slow and painful. The first notice of the Tucumán branch appeared in *La razón*'s issue of September 11, 1874. [24] A few days later *La razón* published an editorial that pointed out that the interior would surely suffer rather than benefit from the Banco Nacional because the bank's policies had been designed to help the export-oriented coastal areas. [25] *La razón*'s prediction soon came true for Tucumán, as the presence of the Banco Nacional helped destroy the Banco de San Juan, while the Banco Nacional's efforts to drive out Bolivian currency left Tucumán with no currency.

To be successful in its desire to unify the nation, the Banco Nacional ultimately depended upon the enforcement of an 1876 bank law that prohibited banks from using and emitting foreign currency, a provision that would ruin the Banco de San Juan. When the Tucumán branch finally began to operate full-time after May 1877, it began fierce competition with the Banco de San Juan by offering lower interest rates and disseminating national currency that was acceptable throughout the Republic. Less than a year later, besieged by the Banco Nacional and local tax collectors, the Banco de San Juan closed its doors.

Even after the closing of the Banco de San Juan, the Banco Nacional could not provide all the services Tucumán needed, so most Tucumán entrepreneurs welcomed the opening of another bank in 1881. The Banco Muñoz Rodríguez y Cía. began to operate out of the offices of the defunct Banco de San Juan. Its founders, all local merchants, began with a modest working capital of 75,000 pesos fuertes.

By the time these banks could provide useful services to Tucumán, the province had fundamentally changed and, instead of hides and flour, sugarcane cultivation became the most profitable provincial crop. Encouraged by an antiquated tax system and the linking of Tucumán to Córdoba by rail in 1876, people began to plant sugarcane and a few imported modern sugar processing machinery. Though it was not the first time Tucumán industrialists tried to make the sugar industry successful, the last part of the nineteenth century became the golden age of sugar in Tucumán.

THE SUGAR INDUSTRY PRIOR TO 1880

Unlike most of Argentina, parts of the northwest provided quite suitable conditions for the cultivation of sugarcane. Most of Tucumán as well as parts of Salta, Jujuy and Santiago were endowed with a subtropical climate, especially at lower altitudes. It provided sufficient rainfall during the rainy season (December-February) as well as a dry *zafra* season (June-August) that allowed the stalks to mature so long as frosts did not not rob the cane of its sucrose content. Although certain parts of Tucumán periodically suffered from frost or hail during the winter months, an elongated area ranging from the center of Burruyacú district in the northeast to just south of the Marapá River in Graneros ultimately defined the limits of sugarcane cultivation. [26]

Although documents indicate that some sugarcane had been planted in Tucumán as early as 1648, from 1670 on only Jesuits planted it systematically on their farm in Lules in northern Famaillá district. No evidence exists that the Jesuits actually made sugar, but inventories suggest that they produced sugar syrup (*miel de caña*) for themselves and for their Indian charges. When the Spanish government expelled the Jesuits from

FIGURE 1.1

<u>TUCUMAN PROVINCE, POST-1888 BOUNDARIES</u>

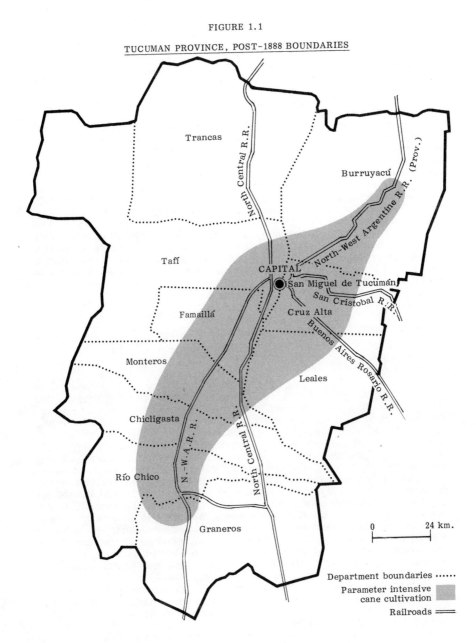

the Spanish colonies in 1767, the plantations evidently decayed and the entire mission turned into ruins before the land was auctioned off.[27]

Between 1767 and 1821 no one took interest in sugarcane cultivation until Bishop José Eusebio Colombres, a signer of Argentina's 1816 Declaration of Independence, reintroduced sugarcane cultivation in Tucumán. The Bishop distributed cane seeds and plant cuttings to other landowners in 1821 with the hope that sugar production might revive Tucumán's war-torn economy. Though these efforts turned the Bishop into a provincial hero and marked him as the father of the Argentine sugar industry, inefficiency due to poor technology, lack of inexpensive transport to the coast and civil wars all prevented Tucumán from entering the national sugar market until the 1870s.[28]

In the meantime sugar became an important secondary industry for many landowners, especially after the unofficial truce offered by Celedonio Gutiérrez. Wenceslao Posse founded the Esperanza factory in 1845. Vicente Posse established the Reducción factory in 1852. San Andrés, founded by Domingo García, began to operate by 1860. These as well as many other factories founded during this period provided farmers and cattlemen with additional products for trade.[29]

When Burmeister passed through Tucumán in 1859, he noticed that the factories were found in farming areas closest to the city of San Miguel. They produced two kinds of sugar: one an unrefined yellow which deteriorated rapidly, and the other a higher quality, nearly white sugar. The prices of these sugars, 2 reales per pound for the former and $2\frac{1}{2}$ reales per pound for the latter, were too high to compete with less expensive refined European sugars.[30] To expand their markets Tucumán merchants had to either improve their product or lower the costs of their crude sugar, or both.

AN EARLY ATTEMPT TO MODERNIZE

At that very moment an enterprising Tucumán industrialist made an abortive attempt to import more modern equipment. Balthazar Aguirre became the owner of a primitive sugar factory and plantation. He also went to Europe in the mid-fifties, when he probably saw his first examples of modern steam-driven sugar processing machinery. By 1858 Aguirre decided to order some English machinery but then discovered that his own resources could not match the tremendous expenses, and no one in Tucumán wanted to lend him the money. Consequently, he set off for San José, Entre Ríos, to speak with General Justo José de Urquiza, then president of the Confederation and a known industrial entrepreneur and speculator. Aguirre managed to persuade Urquiza to enter into a business partnership that would finance the importation of the new machinery. They worked out an agreement in March 1858 that was revised and signed in 1860. The new contract stated that each partner would contribute 45,000 pesos during a five-year period, Aguirre's share mostly in the form of real estate and existing inventory and Urquiza's share in cash.[31]

Aguirre's pioneering attempts to bring modern technology to Tucumán ultimately failed for a number of reasons. First of all, internal political events such as the battles of Cepeda and Pavón distracted Urquiza from all thoughts of industrial enterprise and temporarily interrupted the flow of promised money.[32] Second, the continued secession of Buenos Aires province from the Confederation made all international commercial transactions difficult to negotiate.[33] Third, the costs of setting up both the machinery and expanded sugar plantation turned out to be infinitely greater than Aguirre had anticipated.

The March 2, 1858, contract had estimated transport charges from the port of Rosario to Tucumán at 10,000 silver pesos, excluding installation charges. This same contract stated that the total value of these machines, including shipping costs from England, came to 21,500 silver pesos. Thus the total cost of the machines would come to 31,000 pesos. Yet by the time Aguirre actually got the machinery to Tucumán, he exceeded his earlier estimate by more than 27,000 pesos. [34]

Once Aguirre had the machinery, he discovered that the mere possession of modern machinery could not ensure success. From the outset the machinery failed to work properly and Aguirre found himself producing more alcohol products than sugar. Even if the machinery had worked properly, Aguirre would not have produced much sugar because natural calamities such as flooding ruined his sugarcane. To add to his miseries, political intrigue created problems when local residents began to suspect Aguirre's relationship with Urquiza might have led to Urquiza's takeover of Tucumán. Last, but not least, Aguirre realized that he needed local credit facilities to help him with day-to-day transactions, but no such facilities existed. By 1870 Aguirre had lost all his lands and machinery to the descendants of General Urquiza. [35]

Although the economic and political instability characteristic of Tucumán in the 1860s ultimately undermined Aguirre's attempt to import new equipment for his sugar plantation and factory, others experienced better luck by pursuing more modest improvements in sugar commerce and production. Wenceslao Posse, for example, attempted in 1865 to expand his alcohol and sugar trade to Córdoba. His copybooks reveal some of the difficulties he had to overcome in order to expand his markets without the benefits of modern transportation and packaging. In a November 1865 letter to his cousin Rudecindo Ybaceta, Posse noted that:

> From Tucumán, a trip to Córdoba is like a trip to Russia. Everything is an effort and inconvenient. Because the trade has so many problems and so few profits, no respectable man wants to get involved. To be successful you have to have an assured market and send the sugar in your own fleet of carts. Yet even with all this, the business yields few profits. In the future these problems will be resolved and finally Córdoba will be a good market for the sugar industry. [36]

Posse later noted other problems related to the sugar and alcohol trade. His letters to José Uriburu and Company of Salta dated December 1 and 28, 1866 contained typical reminders to transfer sugar brandy immediately from large wooden barrels to smaller kegs and thereby prevent seepage and evaporation. Otherwise such losses often resulted in partially empty barrels and lower prices for Posse. [37] Sugar, too, had its problems. Posse found that certain factory brands commanded higher prices than others. Thus the trader had to sell a variety of brands to find out which market prized which brand. In addition, regardless of which brand of sugar he sold, Posse insisted that purchasers transfer sugar into their own leather sacks, as the price of leather sacks was too great to be included in the price. [38] This, of course, resulted in further sugar losses above and beyond those incurred by moisture or external objects penetrating the sacks during the wagon or cart haul.

Despite all these problems and inconveniences, Posse became a rich man during the sixties and managed to divert some of this money into new equipment for his factory. When British Major Francis Rickard passed through Tucumán in 1869, he chose the Posse estate as one of the most modern of the twenty-five factories he knew operated in Tucumán:

The estate consists of 2,500 acres of splendidly
wooded and open pasture land, situated about
ten miles south of the city, and 240 acres of this
was planted with sugar cane . . . . Sr. Posse
began 24 years ago with a capital of £5,000; his
estate cost then only £75, and this together with
the works, are now worth at least £10,000, according to the local valuation, whilst the annual
income derived from it would represent about
£5,000. [39]

Rickard then went on to explain how most Tucumán factories produced
sugar and how Posse had revolutionized sugar production there:

It [sugarcane] is transported from the fields on
bullock carts and delivered at the mill, where it
is cleaned of the leaves and passed through a
powerful pair of rolls, worked by an overshot
water wheel. The syrup is received in a trough
beneath, and pumped into vats or deposits,
whence it is drawn off by pipes into boilers, or
evaporating pans, and boiled down. The fuel
used is wood, but owing to a very old and obso-
lete method of setting the pans, a great waste of
caloric takes place, and makes this operation
very costly and slow. Formerly the resulting
mass of sugar was whitened or decolorized by
being placed in earthenware jars of a conical
shape, having a hole perforated in the bottom,
on which was placed a thin layer of straw. These
were filled up to within a few inches of the top,
and the remaining space filled up with mud, when
the jars were allowed to stand and the treacle to
drain off by the perforation in the bottom. This
continued for sometimes 60 and 80 days, when
the layer of mud was removed and the sugar
found to be quite dry and white . . . . This
system required a very large amount of house
accommodation and apparatus, as well as considerable capital to enable the sugar maker to wait
for the completion of the process and realize his
profits.

Now it is different, as Señor Posse has introduced
the well known centrifugal decolorising machine
as used in the West Indies. This is driven by a
small steam engine, and performs in a few min-
utes what on the old principle required months
to effect. [40]

Rickard ended his discourse on the Tucumán sugar industry by observing that only two or three of these machines had been imported by sugar
producers.

Arsenio Granillo's 1870 study, *Provincia de Tucumán*, provided a
more systematic analysis of the sugar industry but came to similar conclusions. Of the forty-six factories reported by Granillo, only twenty-
four had iron rollers and only four factories operated with steam
engines. [41] Nevertheless, Granillo felt that the progress made in the
Tucumán sugar industry marked it as "one of the principal industries in
the nation" even though the sugar sold well only in regional markets. [42]

As it turned out, his prediction seemed to be realistic. The value of Tucumán production in 1876 was reported to be as follows:[43]

150,000	arrobas sugar	$ 370,000
25,000	barrels rum	350,000
200,000	arrobas tobacco	300,000
50,000	tanned hides	280,000
12,000	dried hides	50,000
10,000	saddle blankets	50,000
100,000	arrobas rice	80,000
	cheeses, woods, cereals,	
	citrus fruits	900,000
		$2,380,000

This showed that sugar and alcohol products made up more than thirty percent of the value of Tucumán's production. By 1884 Mulhall reported that the value of sugar production had increased to 5.9 million pesos for 24,000 tons out of a total crop value of 7.62 million pesos.[44] That same year a provincial report also noted that the number of sugar factories had been reduced to thirty-three, yet a better cane-to-sugar ratio of five and a half percent accounted for the increased production.[45]

The spectacular growth and modernization of the Tucumán sugar industry testified to the success of national unification and its attempts to stimulate the interior, as well as the ability of Tucumán to adapt to new circumstances. More people wanted to buy sugar, and while prices remained relatively constant at four to five pesos per arroba, improved technology increased the amount of sugar produced per hectare of sugarcane. If a farmer wished to plant sugarcane and then grind it with the primitive machinery available in 1872, Granillo calculated that the total investment needed was 50,000 pesos, including lands, building and machinery, and that such an establishment would yield 25,000 pesos per year.[46] Thus anyone who could muster the necessary capital could pay off his original investment in two years. Granillo was not the only person to make this kind of estimate; indeed, throughout the seventies and eighties various observers claimed yearly returns of fifty to eighty percent per year on the original plantations investment.[47]

While sugarcane cultivation began to yield these kinds of profits, the imminent initiation of passenger and cargo service on the North Central railroad from Córdoba to Tucumán promised a drastic reduction in the cost of conveying imported machinery to Tucumán. After 1876 the cost of sending one arroba of merchandise from Tucumán to Córdoba fell from two Bolivian pesos to fifteen to sixteen centavos, depending on the merchandise.[49] For large bulk items such as steam engines, boiling vats and centrifuges, the savings could be spectacular. In an 1884 interview with the *Handbook of the Argentine Republic*, Wenceslao Posse claimed that the railroad had reduced the cost of transporting one ton of machinery from Rosario to Tucumán from 220 to twenty pesos.[49] That same year the Nougués brothers, owners of the San Pablo sugar factory, itemized their total expenses for shipping and installing some modern machinery in the following manner:[50]

Cost of machinery ordered in 1881		54,395.55 francs
Packing expense and transport to Rosario from France	18%	
Expense in Rosario and transport to Tucumán	12½	
Unloading and transport to San Pablo	2	
Engineer's fee	4	
Blacksmith, copper worker and mechanics' fee	10	
Building materials and workers' salaries	18½	
	65%	
Total additional expenses		35,357.10
Total cost of 1881 order		89,752.65 francs

This useful breakdown of expenses, one that remained constant in future calculations of machine costs for the Nougués brothers, clearly contrasts fourteen and one half percent land freight rates in the mid-eighties with the ninety percent land freight rates calculated by Aguirre in the late 1850s.

The machinery delivered to Tucumán industrialists after 1876 was more sophisticated than that purchased earlier. Many industrialists, for example, ordered vacuum pans. Invented by Edward G. Howard in 1812, they allowed sugar syrup to boil at a lower temperature under pressure and thereby save fuel. Lower heat also eliminated brown stains caused by high temperatures. Although vacuum pans had been ordered by Aguirre, they were not used generally until 1876.[51] By the time the 1882 *Memoria descriptiva* had been published, eighty-seven steam engines totaling 1,181 horsepower and twenty hydraulic engines equaling 268 horsepower not only provided steam for the vacuum pans but also for modern distilleries, hydraulic cane crushers and bone charcoal factories.[52]

Perhaps the best way to describe the transformation of Tucumán from a diversified industrial and trading center to one dominated by the sugar industry would be an examination of how one Tucumán family confronted the events of the seventies. Juan Nougués, a Frenchman, had founded the San Pablo ranch and tannery in 1827 and by the early seventies his three sons, Juan, Miguel and Ambrosio, had taken control of the property. The San Pablo inventory books reveal that Juan and his sons in 1875 had expanded the family business to include grazing lands, fruit groves, a sugar house and distillery, a sawmill, two flour mills, a rice polishing machine and produce, all valued at 134,253 Bolivian pesos. Of this total B$40,967 related to the sugar establishment; B$16,964 in sugar plantation lands, B$22,743 for sugar and alcohol processing machinery and B$1,260 for sugar and alcohol stocks.[53] The Nougués family engaged in retail trade along with industrial pursuits and the younger Juan traveled the northwest selling his family's products.

That same year, one year before the North Central provided service between Tucumán and Córdoba, Juan and his brothers decided to open a series of general stores in Salta and Jujuy and delegate someone in those provinces to handle the Nougués business transactions. At least one such store, operated by another Frenchman, Urbano Lardière, opened in Salta in January 1876. Through the correspondence between Lardière and the Nougués brothers it is easy to see how the railroad credit and stable currency would eventually help Tucumán and the sugar industry.

When Lardière first opened for business, it appeared that almost anything sent from San Pablo and arriving in good condition could be sold at a profit:

As Don Juan already wrote you, business has
picked up a little and the last few days we would
have sold good sugar and rum if we had had sufficient supplies. The sugar loaves we recently
received even though disintegrated and damp still
sold for 7B $ and that is the price we will charge
for the boxes of sugar . . . loaves white and hard
would sell easily at 7.50 if you could send me a
good supply . . . . The 15 pipas of rum we're
waiting for have been sold and we are committed
to advance sales of even more . . . . The proximity of *carnaval* makes it mandatory that the
caña arrive immediately; the price has risen to
B $25 a barrel. [54]

After a few months of business, however, Lardière realized that many
San Pablo products could not be sold and that Peruvian centrifuged
sugar threatened Tucumán's control of the sugar trade in the northwest:

We have reduced the price of sugar recently received to B $6 (3rd class without the box), and
although the going price here is 6.50 we would
like to get 6.25 or 6.37, but fine Peruvian sugar
has arrived and we can not compete with it. The
flours remain unsold as usual: we will have to
sell them at 10 or 11 pesos . . . . You can see
that we must not limit ourselves to Tucumán products, ·for at this moment only caña brings us a
profit. [55]

By July even the price of brandy fell and Lardière confronted equally
serious problems of being unable to collect payments and discount promissory notes at local banks due to the shortage of currency. [56]
 Despite some good months of business, by October Lardière reported that business was so slow that he could keep his door closed without fear of losing a sale. To remain solvent he suggested closing the
store, renting an office and doing business from there. Unless they
could get more credit, run their own fleet of mules or start dealing in the
Bolivian tin business, the situation would only deteriorate. [57]
 The Nougués-Lardière business arrangement seems to have petered
out by the end of 1876, and we can only imagine how relieved people like
the Nougués family were that the railroad opened new business prospects
for them. Even though the entire Nougués establishment managed to make
a paper profit of B $35,505.24 that year out of a total capital investment
of B $92,567.23, within six years their total capital investment expanded
to B $352,021.37. In one year their profits reached almost fifty percent.
At the same time they managed to import new machines and expand their
sugar plantation. [58]
 Tucumán from 1874 to 1880 saw the confluence of local and national
factors resulting in the growth of the sugar industry. The attempts to
pacify the interior through force had eliminated provincial enemies of
Tucumán. The arrival of the first train in 1876 brought guns to arm
Tucumán's national guard. Once Tucumán was fortified militarily, passenger and freight service was inaugurated. [59] By 1881 the northwest,
along with other parts of the interior, was so peaceful and bubbling with
activity that President Roca informed Congress:

> Already the provinces have forgotten their desire
> to arm themselves and fight for local rights. They
> have discovered that protection from revolution
> and disorder can only come from political, economic
> and social reorganization, . . . from agriculture,
> irrigation, roads, banks and all those things which
> represent progress. [60]

Northwestern prosperity came from the sugar industry, and soon politicians realized that sugar could bring them peace and prosperity without force.

President Roca's comments testified to the presence of a burgeoning industrial center, one which had been nourished by political protection from the outset. His predecessor, President Avellaneda, became the first to mention the sugar industry in an annual message to Congress in 1877. In so doing he brought sugar into the political arena by confronting legislators with his views on industrial protection:

> I have heard people say that we ought to protect
> our infant industries. I truly believe that national
> industries should be protected. But in what way
> should we ensure such protection? By means of
> high protective tariffs . . . . Now is not the time
> to discuss this matter, but there is another kind
> of natural protection that is safe and does not harm
> vested interest. That is the protection that comes
> from providing markets for products, by shorten-
> ing distances and transportation costs. This is
> the best kind of protection . . . and we should
> consider ourselves fortunate if we could make this
> possible throughout the Republic. [61]

With that speech Avellaneda brought Tucumán and the sugar industry into the national political arena of the 1880s.

ENDNOTES TO CHAPTER I

1. Julio Roca to Ataliva Roca, November 19, 1869, Museo Roca, *Publicaciones del Museo Roca: documentos.* 7 vols. (Buenos Aires: Ministerio de Educación y Justicia, 1966-1967), V:38.

2. For further elaboration of this theme see James R. Scobie,*La lucha por la consolidación de la nacionalidad argentina, 1852-1862* (Buenos Aires: Solar-Hachette, 1964), passim.

3. In theory federalists advocated a loose confederation of states, whereas the unitarians insisted on a strong central government. Manuel Lizondo Borda, *Historia de Tucumán, siglo XIX.* Facultad de Ciencias Culturales, Instituto de Historia XIV, Publicación 451 (Tucumán: Universidad Nacional de Tucumán, 1948), pp. 104, 251.

4. Luis H. Sommariva, *Historia de las intervenciones federales en las provincias.* 3 vols. (Buenos Aires: El Ateneo, 1929), II:306.

5. Carlos Páez de la Torre (h), "El Gobernador Celedonio Gutiérrez y sus relaciones con los 'salvajes unitarios,' 1841-1852," in Academia Nacional de Historia, *Primer Congreso de Historia Argentina y Regional* [celebrado en San Miguel de Tucumán del 14 al 16 de agosto de 1971] (Buenos Aires: Academia Nacional de Historia, 1973), pp. 765-782.

6. Teodoro Ricardo Ricci, *Evolución de la ciudad de San Miguel de Tucumán.* Colección del Sesquicentenario de la Independencia Argentina (Tucumán: UNT, 1967), pp. 82-85.

7. Arsenio Granillo, *Provincia de Tucumán, 1872;* 2nd ed. Serie V, Vol. I (Tucumán: Archivo Histórico de Tucumán, 1947), p. 106.

8. Vicente Quesada [Víctor Gálvez], "Recuerdos de Tucumán y Salta. Las ciudades del interior hace 30 años," *La nueva revista de Buenos Aires,* 10 (1884): 456.

9. Ibid., pp. 453-454.

10. Hermann Burmeister, *Descripción de Tucumán* (Tucumán: UNT, 1916), p. 45.

11. Paul Groussac, Alfredo Bousquet, Inocencio Liberani, Dr. Juan M. Terán, and Dr. Javier Frías, *Memoria histórica y descriptiva de la provincia de Tucumán* (Buenos Aires: M. Biedma, 1882), pp. 542-543. Tucumán Province, *Registro estadístico correspondiente al año 1882* (Buenos Aires: Coni, 1884), p. 63.

12. José Gómez to Minister of Government, June 17, 1882, AH, Sección Administrativa, T. 153, f. 336.

13. Groussac, *et al., Memoria descriptiva de la provincia de Tucumán,* pp. 529-533.

14. Ibid., pp. 547-548.

15. Until 1866 sugarcane cultivators who produced alcohol paid a land tax of 10B$ per hectare as their *contribución directa,* and they were not taxed for any sugar they produced. After 1866 sugar industrialists paid a 1/2 percent tax on their sugar inventory. Since the tax was calculated in January, when few sugar or alcohol stocks remained, such a tax was negligible. For later sugar license taxes, see Chapter IV.

16. José M. Cullen to Federico Helguera, September 10, 1867, AFH I, Letter 143.

17. José M. Cullen to Federico Helguera, June 14, 1868, AFH, I, Letter 144.

18. Law No. 291 establishing the Banco de Tucumán, September 19, 1868, Ramón Cordeiro, Carlos Dalmiro Viale, Horacio Sánchez Loria, and Ernesto del Moral, eds., *Compilación ordenada de leyes, decretos y mensajes del período constitucional de la provincia de Tucumán que comienza en el año 1852.* 33 vols. (Tucumán: Prebisch y Violeta, 1915-1919), IV:28; Atilio Saksonoff Velarde, "Historia de las instituciones bancarias de la provincia de Tucumán," *Primer Congreso de Historia de los pueblos de la Provincia de Tucumán* (Tucumán: Ministerio de Gobierno, Subsecretaría de Cultura, 1953), p. 262.

19. Law No. 354 of June 12, 1872, *Compilación,* IV:155.

20. *La razón* (Tucumán), advertisement, January 6, 1875, p. 3.

21. Ibid., April 23, 1876, p. 1.

22. Law No. 425, March 23, 1878, ibid., pp. 104-107.

23. Attorney-General's opinion, October 23, 1878, ibid., VII:207-209; Petition denied, October 24, 1878, ibid., pp. 209-210.

24. *La razón,* September 11, 1874, p. 2.

25. Ibid., editorial, September 20, 1874, p. 1.

26. Julio C. Bosonetto, "Distribución de los ingenios azucareros tucumanos," *Geographia una et varia: homenaje al doctor Federico Machatschek con motivo de sus bodas de oro con el doctorado 1899-- 5 de noviembre de 1949.* Instituto de Estudios Geográficos, Publicaciones Especiales II (Tucumán: UNT, 1951), pp. 43-55; Teodoro Ricardo Ricci, *Algunas consideraciones sobre la economía de Tucumán.* Facultad de Filosofía y Letras, Departamento de Geografía, Serie Monográfica 19 (Tucumán: UNT, 1971), p. 41.

27. Emilio J. Schleh, *La industria azucarera argentina; pasado y presente* (Buenos Aires: n.p., 1910), pp. 9-16.

28. Ibid., pp. 18-63; Emilio J. Schleh, *Noticias históricas sobre el azúcar en la Argentina* (Buenos Aires: Centro Azucarero Argentino, 1945), pp. 89-100. In these and Schleh's other works on the sugar industry Bishop Colombres appears as the savior of Tucumán.

29. Donna J. Guy, *Politics and the Sugar Industry in Tucumán, Argentina, 1870-1900.* Unpublished dissertation, Indiana University, 1973, Appendix A, pp. 316-325.

30. Burmeister, *Tucumán*, p. 46.

31. Copy of March 2, 1858 contract between Urquiza and Aguirre in Schleh, *Noticias*, pp. 159-160.

32. Ibid., p. 165.

33. Aguirre to Urquiza, April 22, 1858, ibid., pp. 163-164.

34. Aguirre to Urquiza, November 20, 1859, ibid., pp. 165-166.

35. Ibid., pp. 176-191.

36. Wenceslao Posse to Rudecindo Ybaceta of Córdoba, February 27, 1865, AWP, Copybook I.

37. Posse to J. Uriburu y Cía., December 21 and December 28, 1866, AWP, Copybook II.

38. Posse to Rudecindo Ybaceta, January 28, 1867, AWP, Copybook II.

39. Francis Ignacio Rickard, *The Mineral and Other Resources of the Argentine Republic in 1869* (London: Longmans, Green and Co., 1870), p. 231.

40. Ibid., p. 232.

41. Granillo, *Provincia de Tucumán, 1872*, p. 110.

42. Ibid.

43. Adapted from Ricci, San Miguel, pp. 84-85n; and M.G. and E.T. Mulhall, *Handbook of the River Plate. Comprising Buenos Ayres and the Provinces of the Argentine Republic and the Republics of Uruguay and Paraguay* (London and Buenos Ayres: Edward Sanford and M.G. and E.T. Mulhall, 1875), p. 263.

44. Mulhall, *Handbook of the River Plate*, 1885, p. 518.

45. *El orden* (Tucumán), August 8, 1884, p. 1.

46. Granillo, *Provincia de Tucumán, 1872*, p. 110.

47. Two such estimates are found in Report of November 1880, *Compilacion*, VII: 532-533; and Mulhall, *Handbook of the River Plate*, 1885, pp. 518-519.

48. Schleh, *La industria azucarera argentina; pasado y presente*, p. 77. See Appendix, Table 9.2 for official exchange rates. Real exchange rates in Tucumán are impossible to calculate.

49. Mulhall, *Handbook of the River Plate*, 1885, p. 521.

50. San Pablo Inventory of December 31, 1884, ASP, Inventario I:137-138. Earlier imports of machinery listed 54 percent added charges; 1882 Inventory, ASP, Inventario I:107; 1883 Inventory, ASP, Inventario I:122.

51. Eichner, *The Emergence of Oligopoly*, pp. 31-32.

52. Schleh, *Noticias históricas sobre el azúcar en la Argentina*, p. 205.

53. San Pablo Inventory of December 31, 1875, ASP Inventario I:1-10.

54. Urbano Lardière to Ambrosio Nougués, February 7, 1876, ASP, Lardière Correspondence.

55. Lardière to Ambrosio Nougués, April 1, 1876, ASP, Lardière Correspondence.

56. Lardière to Ambrosio Nougués, July 6, 1876, and July 20, 1876, ASP, Lardière Correspondence.

57. Lardière to Ambrosio Nougués, October 6, 1876, ASP, Lardière Correspondence.

58. San Pablo 1876 Inventory, ASP, Inventario I:11-28.

59. *La nación*, May 5, 1876, p. 1; *La prensa*, November 7, 1876, p. 1.

60. May 1881 Message, Museo Roca, *Documentos*, II:3. Later on page 14 the president noted that even Santiago del Estero had freed itself from its *caudillos* through construction of irrigation canals that stimulated nascent sugar and wine industries.

61. Heraclio Mabragaña, *Los mensajes: historia del desenvolvimiento de la Nación Argentina: redactada cronólogicamente por sus gobernantes, 1810-1910*. 6 vols. (Buenos Aires: Compañía General de Fósforos, 1910), III:455-457.

CHAPTER II
Family, Friends and Politics

I always urge my brother Eudoro to see you, but I don't know if he will do it. It is an American custom to desert you once you get into office. They seek the first opportunity to resent you and then they go on nourishing the baseless discontent.

Nicolás Avellaneda to Federico Helguera, 1878

From 1874 to 1890 three *provinciano* presidents, two from Tucumán and one from Córdoba, urged Congress to approve programs all agreed were necessary to create the new Argentina. Similarly local groups pressured their representatives to help their own special interests. At times presidential plans and local aspirations conflicted and crises arose. In many ways the success of the Generation of Eighty can be measured by the ability of the various presidents to satisfy demands of local groups without disrupting the fragile coalition that kept the nation together. The interaction of the two Tucumán presidents with their friends and relatives in Tucumán, especially those who became governor, offers a useful way to see how these presidents coped with local politicians and where sugar fit into the politics of that time.

Nicolás Avellaneda of Tucumán first directed the new political group and provided the blueprint for the 1880s. His shrewd planning opened new channels of political action at a time of great economic and political stress. He won new allies for national unification by encouraging industry in the interior as well as in urban coastal areas, buttressing foreign investment to develop these industries and offering patronage to provincial elites often neglected in earlier governments.

When Avellaneda first commanded national attention in 1868 at the age of thirty-one, few Argentines imagined that the short, bearded, frail young lawyer, often derisively called "Taquito" by his enemies, would lead the country into a new period of prosperity and glory. At that moment President Sarmiento had named Avellaneda Minister of Education, a relatively unimportant position. From this position, Avellaneda began to plan his presidential campaign early in 1872 at the first industrial exposition at Córdoba. While surveying the rather sorry state of local industry, Avellaneda organized provincial governors into the *Liga de Gobernadores* (Governors' League) to support his candidacy in 1874. Avellaneda spoke at the close of this important exposition on the political and economic significance of the exposition:

> We had to bring a festival of work and progress
> to the center of our interior regions in order to
> call attention to a new way to revive its activities
> and its dreams for the future. We had to show
> foreigners that one might easily and advanta-
> geously reach the interior, and finally we had to
> show these same regions that they are not alone
> and isolated despite their distant location. [1]

He encouraged the inhabitants of the interior to unite and seek their fortunes in new industrial pursuits.

When the formal campaign began later that same year, Avellaneda
chose Córdoba rather than Buenos Aires as his headquarters because in
Córdoba he could use his friends and family connections. Certain that
his provincial friends would support him, he wrote Roca in November:

> In the interior at this moment there is no other
> candidate except me. I believe that general opin-
> ion favors it, and local officials support my candi-
> dacy. Still there are even deeper roots that do
> not depend upon the changing political climate.
> They come from my family, which is spread out in
> three provinces, Catamarca, Tucumán, and Cór-
> doba, from my school years with the youths of
> these provinces and from the numerous relation-
> ships that I have been cultivating for the past
> four years. [2]

The political aspirant needed all the friends he could muster to offset the influence of General Mitre and his attempt to recapture the presidency. As the 1874 campaign unfolded, electoral plots distorted the
substantive differences between the presidential candidates, but the results favored Avellaneda. His landslide vote then triggered an angry
Porteño revolt led by Mitre, and the nation found itself temporarily at
war. The insurrection, quickly quelled, emphasized the persistent need
to buttress the interior against the powerful coastal area and its partisan
politics.

Unfortunately Avellaneda not only faced the aftermath of revolutionary activity, but also inherited a financial depression, the direct result of the 1873 panic. Nevertheless railroad mileage doubled during
those difficult years despite public disapproval of its costs. To compensate for increased expenditures and in response to a strong congressional
lobby sympathetic to infant industries, Avellaneda's administration authored the first general protective tariffs. Though the politicians justified
the tariffs on fiscal rather than on protectionist grounds, the results still
stimulated domestic industry.

Tucumán was profoundly affected by Avellaneda's political plans.
Voters there initially supported him for a variety of reasons. First of
all, like many other interior provinces, Tucumán was swept up in the
growing "autonomist" movement that demanded greater independence from
Buenos Aires. Second, to many Avellaneda rather than Mitre or Alsina
"personified truly national interests." [3] Finally, the fact that Avellaneda
came from Tucumán was as important as any other specific qualification.

On a different level Avellaneda held other advantages. Many Tucumán citizens remembered that during the Rosas tyranny his father died
a martyr with his head on a pike. Others knew and respected Avellaneda's
two brothers, Marco and Eudoro. Marco, who first served as national
deputy for Tucumán during Sarmiento's administration, already had a long
record of community service. During the late sixties and early seventies
he had acted as the province's commercial intermediary and banker in

Buenos Aires. After 1884 Marco resided permanently in the national capital, often representing Tucumán in the Chamber of Deputies (1870-1874; 1876-1884; 1894-1902) and serving as president of both the Guaranteed Banks (1885-1900) and the Banco de la Provincia de Buenos Aires.[4] At the same time he maintained his absentee co-ownership with brother Eudoro and Brígido Terán in the Los Ralos sugar factory from 1876 to 1886.[5]

Eudoro, the other brother, preferred to reside in Tucumán, where he watched over the family's business and political interests. He managed Los Ralos, was named Minister of Government to Federico Helguera (1871-1873) and to Benjamín Paz (1883) and served as provincial deputy and senator for several terms. He managed to leave his business in Tucumán long enough to replace Marco in the national Chamber of Deputies from 1886 to 1890.[6] As a provincial politician Eudoro initiated and supported local legislation designed to help develop the sugar industry and change the nature of labor relations in the province.

The Avellaneda brothers represented a new breed of Tucumán politicians who gained power in the late seventies: sugar politicians. When Tucumán's *La razón* published Avellaneda's electoral committee lists in 1873, the list included many proto-sugar industrialists who modernized their rudimentary operations into powerful factories during the next decade.[7] The people already experimenting in sugar cultivation and those considering it were among the first to support a politician who understood their needs.

PRESIDENTS AND GOVERNORS

Letter writing became the primary means of communication between the interior and Buenos Aires. Correspondence between the Avellaneda clan and other influential Tucumán citizens shows how rhetoric combined with patronage helped Avellaneda keep Tucumán under control. Most of the extant correspondence comes from the papers of Federico Helguera, twice governor of Tucumán (1871-1873; 1877-1878) and cattle merchant.

Avellaneda made sure that Helguera remained loyal to him through a combination of praise and patronage. Perhaps Helguera had taken Avellaneda's advice proffered in a November 1871 letter and encouraged the governor to choose his ministers wisely and not to expect the impossible from his subordinates.[8] Patronage came in a more direct fashion than advice. Helguera made two major requests to the national government, one for funds to construct a bridge over the Río Salí (of great importance to keep parts of the province from being isolated during the heavy summer rains) and the other for funds to construct a normal school in Tucumán. Both petitions received close attention from Avellaneda. In June 1872 Avellaneda wrote: "I have, as a good Tucumano should, dispatched a decree from the Ministry of the Interior to release another thousand pesos fuertes for the Municipality canal works. . . ."[9] Nicolás also promised to submit a bill to authorize the normal school: "In that way our Tucumán will have another great educational establishment." Three months later Nicolás reported that the Chamber of Deputies, at his request, had appropriated 21,000 pesos fuertes for the school.[10]

Both Nicolás and Marco tried to help Tucumán whenever possible. In return Avellaneda supporters delivered Tucumán votes to their candidate. This was no easy task, and it appears that the electoral battles of 1874 placed great strains on local politics, despite claims to the contrary from Paul Groussac, who lived in Tucumán at the time. Groussac claimed that any violence that occurred from 1872 to 1874 had been minimal, as were efforts to influence election results.[11]

In contrast to Groussac's recollections, other sources reported great difficulties for the Avellaneda campaign. During the 1872 deputy elections a definite split took place among the ruling Liberal faction. They divided into Alsinistas and Avellanedistas, the former supporting Delfín Gallo for deputy, the latter Uladislao Frías. The split, like the issue, was personal in nature and disruptive to the Liberal party.

When Marco found out about the split from Helguera, he became bitter and cynical about the likelihood of useful elections in Tucumán:

> You know that electoral battles are a long way from accomplishing anything good there, because you neither educate the public in the ways of democcracy, nor let anyone else teach them anything unless it demoralizes and perverts them. After all, political parties don't use the press to proclaim their platform . . . . They just leave everything up to fraudulent elections, falsifying the voting tables and tempting vices and passions. I have always believed that it is unrealistic to think that completely free elections can take place in Tucumán. Free elections imply a knowledgeable group of voters, which among us simply doesn't exist. [12]

The eventual winner of the deputy election, Delfín Gallo, had not been backed by Avellaneda. The Liberal split would become even more evident in the 1874 election. And if Groussac thought that politics in those years proceeded smoothly, perhaps he was dazzled by the social whirl of local society, the life of *fiesta y siesta*, as he put it. [13]

Despite the party split, which carried over to the 1874 presidential election, Helguera succeeded in naming a successor loyal to the Avellanedas, Belisario López. When Avellaneda heard that López had won the 1873 nomination for governor, he wrote Helguera:

> Your administration has been useful and will now be even more important because you have managed to name our friend as your successor. He will govern as you have--that is to say well, with patriotism and with an ability to rise above the petty quarrels that have enveloped Tucumán. [14]

Those petty quarrels to which Avellaneda referred did not disappear during López's administration, but continued afterwards. López tried to keep order, although the repercussions of the 1874 Mitre rebellion led the governor to order the confiscation of all unlicensed firearms on October 7 and to declare a state of seige on October 10. [15] Economic depression and charges of mismanagement of provincial funds ultimately led to López's resignation a year later. [16] His successor and Avellaneda ally, Tiburcio Padilla, found that a new governor could not solve Tucumán's problems. By October 1876 economic conditions and political recriminations were so bad that Padilla felt it necessary to travel to Buenos Aires to plead with his old friends to do something for Tucumán.

The legislature granted Padilla permission to present his case to the president. The Tucumán governor had two main goals: to convince the federal government to release at least part of the funds already allocated to the Tucumán school system and to request that the Córdoba-Tucumán railroad segment be opened for public service before the scheduled date. President Avellaneda not only granted the Tucumán governor's requests; he also traveled to Tucumán after an absence of nineteen years to inaugurate personally the new railroad on October 31, 1876. [17] At that time Avellaneda acknowledged that the railroad opened at a very opportune moment:

New industries have been waiting [for the railroad]
so that they can compete in new markets. Tucumán sugar will be available for consumption in
Córdoba within the next twenty days and then
will also be for sale throughout the littoral. The
opening of this line is a national event and will
soon be felt throughout the country. [18]

President Avellaneda's plans for the Córdoba-Tucumán line and for
the sugar industry became a reality, and Tucumán turned into one of the
nation's most powerful and prosperous areas.   Tucumán did not, however, blindly follow Avellaneda during his years as president.   The
president's native province was as vulnerable to political dissension as
any other place in the Republic, and often the president himself provided
enough controversy to feed existing passions.
A case in point was Avellaneda's dream of political conciliation with
Mitristas and bipartisan politics.   In an effort to unite divergent groups
throughout the nation, Avellaneda had tried to impose conciliation from
the top by announcing an amnesty for the participants of the 1874 rebellion.   In his 1877 Annual Message to Congress the President stated his
belief in the need for strong opposition:

A party can not exclusively dominate public life
without its leaders resorting to despotism or to
the treachery of usurping oligarchs. . . . It
cannot remain alone and govern with institutions
that guarantee liberty for all [without a loyal op-
position].   There is always a need for a counter-
weight. And similarly, without an opposition party,
the dominant party finds that it will divide within
its own ranks.   Without loyal opposition there are
no political parties, only rebellions and conspiracies. [19]

To lend credence to his plan the President later that year appointed
prominent Mitristas to key cabinet posts.   Unfortunately Avellaneda's
actions antagonized both Mitristas and Avellanedistas and conciliatory
politics dismayed Avellaneda's allies and enemies alike.
Tucumán proved to be a good example of these problems.   The
governor in 1878 was Domingo Martínez Muñecas, a man loyal to Avellaneda but wary of local Mitristas. Because of this fear Governor Martínez
Muñecas in 1879 refused to allow elected Mitrista legislators to be sworn
in and thereby control the provincial legislature. If this had occurred,
future gubernatorial and national senate elections would have been affected, since the provincial legislature functioned both as an electoral
college and a legislative body. [20]
The Mitrista campaign had also angered Martínez Muñecas by ac-
cusing his administration of trying to ruin artisans with heavy taxes and
of acting as puppets for the powerful Posse family--both charges designed
to infuriate voters. [21]   Regardless of the motivating circumstances, the
local constitution prevented Martínez Muñecas from acting because he
could not judge the validity of legislative elections. After the governor's
illegal actions outraged legislators petitioned Congress and the President
to intervene in the province.
President Avellaneda wanted to prevent violence in Tucumán, resolve the political dilemma and revive the conciliatory spirit there.   He
first telegrammed the governor and urged him to abandon his political
stance but not resign. [22]   Then the President sent two Tucumán politicians, Tiburcio Padilla and Benjamín Paz, to act as his personal emissaries
in this matter. [23]   In this case Avellaneda managed to resolve the conflict

without force. The governor withdrew his objections to the elections and did not resign as he had earlier threatened. To save face, though, Governor Martínez Muñecas made his Minister of Government Silvano Bores a scapegoat and forced him to resign.

The confrontation ended peacefully, although it neither eliminated the desire to control elections nor discouraged politicians from creating violent electoral crises. Instead, presidential candidates in 1880 willingly conducted partisan campaigns.

JULIO ROCA

What qualities did General Julio Roca have that prepared him to be the next president of the Republic, a president who completed the unfinished process of national unification? How did he ultimately command such power that he could dominate Argentine politics until his death in 1914? First of all, like Avellaneda, Roca's provincial background made his leadership acceptable to interior politicians. Second, Roca's impressive military career provided him with ample opportunities to develop leadership qualities and to increase his group of acquaintances. Finally, Roca was as ambitious as he was politically adept.

Born in Tucumán in 1843, Julio Argentino Roca found himself related to Marcos Paz, Mitre's vice-president and to the Posse clan.[24] Thus Roca's immediate family provided him with key contacts in the north.

Roca's school years further expanded the group of acquaintances who would later help him win the presidency. At first Roca attended a local school in Tucumán. When he was thirteen he was sent off to study at the Colegio de Concepción in Entre Ríos. At these schools Julio made lasting friendships that later proved useful in his political career. A prime example of such an acquaintance was Lucas Córdoba. Córdoba, twice governor of Tucumán (1895-1898; 1901-1905) and national senator from 1898 to 1901, began his friendship with Roca as a student.[25] They They became especially close during their respective military careers and continued their friendship long after both had entered politics. Other classmates of Roca included Victorino de la Plaza, Ventura Ruiz de los Llanos, José E. Uriburu and Isaac M. Chavarría, all of whom found their friendship rewarded during Roca's political career.[26]

Marriage ties provided additional bonds between Roca and important traditional families of the interior. When Roca married Clara Funes in 1874, their union linked Roca to important Cordobese families, including that of politician Miguel Juárez Celman, Roca's *concuñado* and presidential successor.

Roca's military career also prepared him as a politician. After eighteen years of military service Roca knew the country as few others, and he used this knowledge during and after his presidential campaign. Many men who served with Roca later became political contacts. Eliseo Cantón, for example, was a noted Tucumán doctor who had met Roca while serving in the army. Later Cantón won elections as national deputy for Tucumán and for the Federal District (Tucumán: 1888-1892; 1894-1902; Capital: 1904-1912).[27]

Through friends and relatives Roca developed a network of political alliances comprised of provincial oligarchs and supported by electoral manipulation of a limited and mostly uneducated electorate.[28] Political realities in the eighties had not changed much since Marco Avellaneda's 1872 observations, and Roca took full advantage of the situation.

Roca began helping Tucumán long before he officially declared his candidacy for president in 1879. Tucumán could thank Roca for keeping the Taboadas in line during Sarmiento's administration. Even more important, Roca helped local politicians later defend their government by supplying local army posts with additional guns and munitions.

The arming of Tucumán came about in 1878, when Governor Federico Helguera requested two hundred rifles to protect Tucumán during the next presidential election. At first Roca responded that he expected no widespread violence in 1880.[29] In June 1878, however, Roca informed Helguera that Córdoba's Minister of Government, Juárez Celman, would send fifty Remington rifles to Tucumán. If Helguera needed more, Roca promised to do what he could. He only asked that Helguera not disclose the source of the rifles "so that there would be no way to misconstrue my actions."[30] Roca's compliance indicated the difference between Roca, who believed in force, and Avellaneda, who believed in conciliation.

Roca attracted further support in the interior by promising that, should he win the presidency, Buenos Aires city would finally be designated as the national capital. By selecting this question as his major issue, Roca guaranteed the exclusion of Porteño and Mitrista support, since they opposed the federalization of Buenos Aires. Nevertheless the young general agreed with his friend Eduardo Wilde that: "A nation without a capital. . .is not a nation. . . . And here the national government is only the guest of those who merely tolerate it and treat it badly."[31]

In May, 1879 Roca proclaimed his candidacy in the Avellaneda strongholds, Córdoba and Tucumán. With the help of Miguel Nougués, a Tucumán politician and sugar industrialist, Roca organized a political campaign strengthened by the continued shipments of arms to several interior provinces.[32] As in 1874, the Liga de Gobernadores won the electoral battle for a provinciano candidate whose victory precipitated another unsuccessful Mitrista insurrection, the so-called Revolution of 1880.

It soon became evident that Roca agreed with his predecessor that the commercial strength of the coastal cattle economy had to be offset by expanding activities in the interior regions. Echoing Avellaneda, Roca felt railroad expansion provided the key to any program to stimulate the interior. When he took the presidential oath he specifically noted that:

> As far as I am concerned, it would be my administration's greatest glory if, within three years from this date, we could find the locomotives greeting San Juan and Mendoza, region of vineyards and olives; Salta and Jujuy, region of sugar, coffee and other tropical products, and little by little opening the doors to Bolivian commerce, which would bring us the metals from its rich and inexhaustible mines.[33]

Although the president could not boast of all these specific accomplishments within three years, he could take credit for vast advancements.

Railroad and industrial expansion formed only one facet of Roca's program. To protect and encourage commercial and industrial growth, Argentina needed a sound currency. Eventually a series of monetary reforms culminated in the creation of the Guaranteed Bank System in January 1885.[34] For the first time the Argentine government controlled circulating currency and after 1883 even the interior no longer dealt in foreign coins and notes.

Equally important, President Roca assured regional industrialists access to loans. In his 1884 Annual Message Roca showed that the Banco Nacional had helped the interior:

> The Banco Nacional . . . is one of the most powerful influences in the surprising industrial and commercial growth in the interior. Perhaps in this Chamber there are vintners and sugar industrialists of Mendoza, Santiago, Salta and Tucumán,

> cattlemen of Córdoba and farmers of Santa Fe and
> Entre Ríos, and they can testify whether this
> establishment . . . has responded to the ends
> envisioned by its founders. [35]

Near the end of his first term in September 1886 Roca also created a new
national bank, the Banco Hipotecario Nacional (National Land Mortgage
Bank). Like the Banco Nacional the Banco Hipotecario Nacional had
branches in major cities of the interior as well as in Buenos Aires, but it
specialized in mortgages rather than currency emission. Thus Roca's
administration played an active part in creating a new environment for
nascent regional industries.

SUGAR, POLITICS AND LABOR

During the momentous years that Avellaneda and Roca ruled Argentina, the province of Tucumán quickly responded to new economic and
political conditions. Encouraged by the railroad and new markets during
the Avellaneda presidency, Tucumán sugar production rose from 1,200
metric tons in 1872 to 9,000 metric tons in 1880; 4,700 more hectares of
land became sugar plantations in those six years. [36] In 1878 Governor
Martínez Muñecas announced a general reduction in the sugar license tax
and observed that "since it is the most important industry and promises
a great future for the province, we should not think about taxing it. On
the contrary, it deserves public protection until it reaches maturity." [37]
At only one moment did the unusually low taxes provoke an unfavorable reaction by a Tucumán governor, but he did not hold office long
enough to change the law. José María Astigueta was named governor
delegate for several weeks in 1880. During his brief term he presented
a New Year's Day annual message to the provincial legislature in which
he lashed out at excessive protection of the sugar industry:

> There is injustice when the cattleman, the tanner
> and other industrialists are taxed more than the
> plantation owner, whose industry receives more
> state protection than any other . . ., to the point
> where special legislation, like the Police Code,
> which guarantees the services of day laborers is
> passed for the sake of sugar factory owners . . .
> and it would not be daring to say that one-quarter
> of all police service is used to protect the sugar
> industrialists. [38]

Astigueta found few sympathetic listeners. Santiago del Estero,
Tucumán's main competitor in sugarcane production, had several relatively successful sugar plantations that enjoyed complete exoneration
from provincial and municipal taxes. [39] These plantations also had the
advantage of being near relatively large labor populations. If Tucumán
could not grant its sugar industrialists some tax advantages and help
them secure a stable labor supply, Santiago might become a more important sugar area. [40] Tucumán's sugar industry was attracting regional
labor, creating local fortunes, and Tucumán had no choice but to protect
the sugar industry with low taxes, while building up a stable labor force.
The labor shortage in Tucumán was so great that sugar industrialists began to use their influence in the legislature to pass new legislation to replace the 1856 Police Code. This code required all day laborers
to be registered with the police and included specific rules for both employers and employees. The revised code of 1877 included new provisions

for forced labor of vagrants, domestic servants and minors whose parents or guardians had been unable to control them.

Once the 1877 police code became operative sugar industrialists requested the services of vagrants and unemployed workers discovered by the police. Industrialists also supplemented local labor pools by sending recruiting agents to nearby Santiago del Estero and Catamarca, where they procured Indian families. Eventually such practices angered nearby provinces, whose legislatures taxed Tucumán labor recruiters and whose governors sent notes of complaint.[42] Tucumán governors, at the request of local industrialists, also complained to neighboring governors that border patrols prevented the voluntary exit of workers.[43]

While Tucumán legislators tried to create a stable labor pool, federal officials tried to help Tucumán find new labor sources. On November 4, 1878, General Roca sent Governor Martínez Muñecas a letter proposing the shipment of captured pampas Indians to the sugar factories in Tucumán if suitable contracts could be made.[44] Roca concluded his offer by observing that:

> Your Province has resorted many times to hiring the Matacos of the Chaco to help find suitable labor to meet your expanding industrial needs. I think you will find obvious advantages in substituting these stupid, good for nothing Indians with those from the Pampas and Ranqueles, who, even though they are morally and culturally inferior to the Gaucho, are not lacking in strength and intelligence.[45]

Governor Martínez Muñecas placed an order with Roca for 500 Indians after consulting with leading industrialists. In the same letter requesting the Indians the governor claimed that a suitable contract should take into consideration that the Indians would be ignorant in agricultural matters, so they would do little actual work the first year. Consequently, their salaries should be low. Low salaries would also keep them from buying alcohol, a constant problem in Tucumán among the lower classes. The Tucumán governor admitted that such provisions were unusual but necessary.[46] The final contract offered a two-year contract at B$4 pesos per month for men and half that amount for women and children.[47] The employer would have to feed and clothe the Indians, although he could deduct the cost of all garments from the Indian's salary. The Indians would be under the jurisdiction of the Defender of the Children and the Poor.[48]

The first pampa Indians arrived in January 1879, when provincial officials distributed them among the prominent sugar industrialists. These shipments continued at least until 1885. The pampas Indians proved to be more of a problem than an asset. They were reluctant to work in the sugar fields like slaves. Instead of receiving the treatment promised them by the contract, Indians were poorly fed and maltreated by plantation owners. By 1886 most of the Indians sent to Tucumán had died of malnutrition or disease or had escaped.[49] Though Roca's plan to resettle the Indians and help sugar industrialists failed, it opened new channels of communication between sugar industrialists and national politicians.

With all the help from national and local government, sugar industrialists still complained of the inadequate labor supply in the province. Finally in 1888 the *Ley de Conchabos* (Servants' Law) made labor contracts more specific and broadened the applicability of legally forced labor. It applied to all day workers who earned less than fifty pesos per month, a category that included many skilled as well as unskilled laborers. The main reason the bill succeeded that year was that Santiago del Estero had already passed such a law, and thus the sugar industry was confronted with a labor shortage unless Tucumán passed similar provisions.[50]

The Ley de Conchabos was not only more explicit; in some senses it was much harsher than the previous police codes in its treatment of workers. For example, striking workers could be arrested as vagrants. Peons who refused to work could be locked up by their employer as long as the employer informed the police within twenty-four hours. The police force had much more specific duties, as it was bound legally to capture and return runaway peons. In addition the police had to keep three sets of books: one that listed all names and registration numbers of indentured workers; a second, which listed all runaway workers; and a third, which listed all peons granted temporary leaves of absence. Two aspects of the law that benefited the workers were the prohibition of corporal punishment and new contractual provisions that included the obligatory presence of peons to witness their own contracts.[51] These safeguards ideally eliminated some of the more obvious mechanisms used to exploit workers, but the worker could still be easily cheated under the new law. Life as a sugarcane cutter in Tucumán did not improve much with the promulgation of the new work laws. Men, women and children still had to work twelve to fourteen hours a day, seven days a week during the one-hundred-day harvest season from June to mid-September. The expanding sugar industry offered more work, but the quality of work did not improve. In many ways the modernization of the sugar industry had made working conditions worse.[52]

Indications that the new labor laws were as onerous as the earlier ones came from the police statistics of the time. From 1869 to 1895 the population of Tucumán doubled, most of the influx due to the migration of male laborers.[53] Despite their need for work, peons often fled their plantation jobs. The Ley de Conchabos did not diminish this tendency. Indeed, the largest number of runaways was reported after the passage of the law, a fact that might have indicated great dissatisfaction on the part of the worker to the implementation of the laws or greater efforts on the part of employers and police to identify and return runaways. In either case, the laborer immediately felt the consequences of this law.[54]

During this intense migration into Tucumán the number of arrests soared from 2,000 to 17,000. Here, too, the 1888 law had its impact because such laws encouraged the detention of unruly workers as a form of social control. Curiously, the relative frequency of specific charges remained constant throughout this period except for the categories of runaways and disorderly conduct.[55] Thus the legislators accomplished one of their goals--to attract and keep a sizable labor force in Tucumán--but failed to legislate successfully to keep that larger labor force from drinking and fighting. What remains unclear is why Tucumán never became subject to organized discontent, often experienced in other sugarcane growing areas, until the twentieth century.

IRRIGATION AND TRANSPORT LAWS

Controlling the labor supply formed only one part of the general legislative efforts of the eighties designed to reinforce the sugar industry. Controversies such as water rights and the construction of local transport systems became part of sugar politics. The question of irrigation had plagued the province for years, as Tucumán's abundant rivers were often diverted for the use of large landowners. Individual questions concerning water rights were decided by local judges or committees, but these decisions did not resolve completely the question of whether or not the province should further subsidize the sugar industry by constructing public canals or installing running water. As early as 1872 Governor Helguera had named a commission consisting of several distinguished

Tucumán citizens to draw up a set of irrigation statutes, a task that remained unfinished until the nineties.[56]   The decision to finance publicly the construction of canals, however, came in the early eighties.

On March 15, 1881 Governor Miguel Nougués sent a message to the legislature to support an irrigation loan of 1,000 pesos fuertes to draw up plans for canals along the eastern bank of the Salí River.[57] For the Lules River, another major water source for sugar plantations, Nougués named a committee consisting of Emidio Posse, Clodomiro Hileret, Juan L. Nougués and Isaías Padilla, all sugar industrialists, to draw up rules for water distribution.   Their decision, reported during the height of the zafra, granted all sugar factories using water-driven motors the right to fill their canals and keep their motors operating.   They also provided water supplies for distilleries and tanning establishments.[58]   By naming committees sympathetic to sugar industrialists and by authorizing irrigation canals, Governor Nougués and his successors turned the control of water resources over to the large factories and plantations.

The improvement of local transport systems also helped the sugar industry.   The North Central railroad revived Tucumán interprovincial commerce after 1876 and within the province the ox carts previously used for long-distance travel by the mid-eighties had been integrated into the sugar industry to haul cane to the factory.

The railroad and ox-cart system, however, could only serve certain communities, and the lack of alternatives prompted private investors to seek new transport arrangements.   Two such proposals consisted of a network of carriages run on tracks by horses or oxen to provide basic passenger and light cargo service from the railroad stations to the city and nearby plantations. These enterprises augmented passenger service but could never replace a railroad and its ability to handle sugarcane, bagged sugar, firewood and other bulk items.[59]   Consequently, other entrepreneurs made plans for a provincially owned and operated railroad.

The provincial railroad, later known as the Ferrocarril Noroeste Argentino (Northwest Argentine), began as a concession granted in 1885 to Samuel Kelton in order to connect La Madrid, located in southernmost Graneros district, with the city of San Miguel.[60] The line eventually connected many sugar plantations and urban areas with the capital, as well as with the North Central line.   By 1888 the Northwest line consisted of small trunk lines added to the La Madrid line and linked eight major sugar factories to San Miguel.[61]   The trunk lines comprised both private and public lines, and utilized small French locomotives purchased to give industrialists greater control over transport schedules. To assess fully the importance of transports to the sugar industry, an inventory conducted by the head of the provincial Statistics Office, Paulino Rodríguez Marquina, clearly demonstrated how factories invested in private feeder lines and carts by 1889. (See Table 2.1)

All of this would have been impossible prior to the advent of the North Central railroad.   It would have also been difficult to pass the necessary labor, water rights and tramway legislation had local sugar elites not been in control of the governor's office and the legislature. The governors of the time, especially after 1880, were either sugar elites (Miguel Nougués, Santiago Gallo, Juan Posse, Ambrosio Nougués, Lídoro J. Quinteros) or close friends or relatives of sugar elites (Silvano Bores, Próspero García, Lucas A. Córdoba).   They appointed their friends to the proper commissions and served as a broker between local industrialists and national authorities, as in the case of Martínez Muñecas and Roca.

THE LIMITS OF FAMILY AND FRIENDS

The continued growth of the sugar industry and the social and economic infrastructures that supported it would ultimately depend on help from national politicians.   There were cases, however, when inter-

TABLE 2.1

FACTORY-OWNED
RAILROAD TRACKS AND CARTING EQUIPMENT, 1889

Factory	Rails (meters)	Wagons	Carts	Animals
Manantial	50	1	16	80
Amalia	500	3	24	200
San Felipe	2,000	6	40	320
Unión	50	2	15	60
Colmenar	500	4	12	80
Perseverancia	500	2	4	24
Los Ralos	200	5	20	150
San Miguel	400	10	45	400
Paraíso	2,000	12	40	350
Concepción	1,250	162	20	250
Cruz Alta	200	3	30	450
Esperanza	1,200	18	45	376
San Vicente	240	4	45	450
Bella Vista	2,100	20	10	50
Reducción	7,500	25	27	220
San José	60	2	8	100
Providencia	6,000	50	26	300
Trinidad	500	12	49	280
Santa Bárbara	300	5	30	200
Lastenia			45	370
Luján			33	200
Industria Argentina			20	120
San Juan			22	200
San Andrés			30	150
Lules*			40	200
San Pablo			80	300
Mercedes			50	400
Nueva Baviera			27	150
Santa Rosa			30	180
Azucarera Argentina			65	480
San Felipe de las Vegas*			20	150
La Invernada			20	150
Santa Lucía	3,000	12	20	150
Totals	28,550	358	1,008	7,540

*calculated

vention by national politicians could be detrimental to the sugar industry as well as to Tucumán, and an examination of several such incidents indicated the limits local elites would place on honoring the demands of their national counterparts.

Two important confrontations involved President Roca and Governor Miguel Nougués. It was logical that Nougués might find himself in agonizing situations, as he backed Roca but realized that the president could exert undue influence when necessary. The first incident, which involved the Banco Hipotecario de la Provincia de Buenos Aires, was resolved to Roca's satisfaction, but the second one, which involved the proposed candidacy of José "Pepe" Posse, left the president displeased.

In the first case the Banco Hipotecario de la Provincia de Buenos Aires wanted to open a Tucumán branch. If the Porteño bank had succeeded, it would have increased the domination of Buenos Aires over the interior and provided a direct challenge to President Roca. When Paulino Llambi Campbell approached Governor Nougués and proposed the Tucumán branch, Nougués at first reacted favorably and sent a letter to the legislature encouraging the approval of the Banco Hipotecario's petition. [63] Nougués was forced, however, to reconsider his approval once he became aware of the possible dangers of the Porteño bank in Tucumán. Consequently, Nougués called upon the bank's president, Llambi Campbell, and presented his objections. As Llambi Campbell explained:

> [Nougués] was against the establishment of the bank because he feared that it would interfere with the present political situation. I had a long meeting with him and in the evening he came to visit me at the hotel, and he told me that acceptable bank statutes had to include assurances that the bank would not interfere in political matters. I protested his insinuation, but I did not openly refuse his conditions. [64]

When Nougués finally realized there was no way to guarantee political impartiality, he refused to sanction the project.

A further explanation of the political implications Nougués envisioned came in a letter to the Tucumán legislature from Llambi Campbell, who decided to explain the circumstances behind Governor Nougués's change of mind:

> During the meeting of March 26 . . . the details of the contract were all worked out with a few details . . .; and it was resolved that the contract would be notarized on the 27th.

> On that day I went to the Governor's office, and instead of notarizing the contract the Governor told me that he had received a communiqué from Buenos Aires assuring him that enemies of this government had already been selected to fill the positions of manager and other employees of this Branch. Consequently the Governor refused to sign the contract and left all negotiations pending the outcome of the gubernatorial elections. [65]

Though the Banco Hipotecario de la Provincia de Buenos Aires could have relieved Tucumán's commercial and financial problems, Roca's political coalition aided by a loyal Tucumán government prevented the Porteños from penetrating the northwest.

Governor Nougués allowed his loyalty to Roca to stop a bank contract, but he drew the line at accepting orders that might endanger local alliances. The one issue that could infuriate people most quickly would be the reentry of the Posse family into politics. Don Pepe Posse wanted to become national deputy for Tucumán, and he knew Roca could use his influence there. In January 1881 the President began to make inquiries of Governor Nougués and of Governor Juárez Celman of Córdoba to see what they could do for Posse.

Nougués, who rose to prominence after the anti-Posse factions took control of the province in the sixties, refused to consider any request to help Posse. Nougués told Juárez Celman in his letter of March 17 that his friends would accept Don Pepe's candidacy only if "the candidate were imposed by force. If it were done by official means, it would signify a rupture of relations with my friends."[66] Undaunted, the President pursued this matter throughout 1881, but the results were still negative. Nougués remained convinced that various factions in his party would break away if he were to agree to Posse's candidacy. It was not that Nougués wished to defy the president. As he wrote to Juárez Celman in July:

> If Roca or you had a desire or wanted to suggest
> something, you know that no one would be better
> disposed to please you than I. However, I think
> that you should not pursue the matter any more,
> due to the inevitable damage it would cause and
> that I think wise to avoid.[67]

Roca accepted Nougués's adamancy and Pepe Posse failed to become the official candidate for national deputy, a blow that embittered Posse deeply.[68] The President understood that certain local alliances and prejudices could not be changed without destroying the relationship between the President and provincial governors.

Along the lines of Avellaneda's working relationship with the governors, Roca insisted that his allies impose his gubernatorial candidate, and the outgoing governor would be rewarded with a senatorial post. Nougués turned Tucumán over to Roquista Benjamín Paz in 1882 and Nougués, along with Roca's cousin Emidio Posse, were sent to the national senate. Nougués managed to remain in the senate until 1892, constantly defending Roca. Governor Paz, however, found that Tucumán would not remain uncritical about Roca.

The Paz administration faced deep opposition to Roca in Tucumán. Hostility led to armed conflict each time Paz tried to deliver elections to Roquistas.[69] By the time thoughts turned toward the next presidential election, Roca's critics had won substantial adherence in Tucumán. Thus by 1884 Governor Paz had few hopes of imposing a Roquista as governor. So instead of trying to fix the legislative elections as Martínez Muñecas had done, Paz decided to rewrite the election laws. He convoked a long-overdue provincial constitutional assembly. Originally the stated goal of the assembly was to eliminate the role of the legislature as an electoral college and to guarantee honest elections.[70] The new constitution only partly achieved these goals.

The 1884 constitution finally separated the legislature from the electoral assembly; but did not eliminate the electoral college. Rather it became a separate entity that, like the legislature, was elected directly and had a semipermanent character since it only renewed one-third of its members each year. The electoral college's only function consisted in the election of the governor.

Other aspects of the 1884 constitution tended to further diffuse power formerly concentrated in the unicameral legislature, by creating a bicameral legislature. The number of deputies and senators elected depended upon the population of a particular district, although senators represented larger proportions of the population. The creation of two chambers and the separation of the legislature from the electoral college both weakened the legislative branch relative to the executive. The only advantage of these changes was increased representation of heavily populated districts in both the legislature and the electoral college. Ultimately this would strengthen the political power of sugar elites that controlled populous plantations. [71]

The passage of the 1884 constitution occurred too late to help Governor Paz name his successor. Instead, Santiago Gallo, an open critic of Roca, won the election and managed to have a number of relatives and friends placed in positions of power. He then used the increased powers of the governor's office to keep Roca's candidates for president and governor from winning votes in 1886. Thus the attempt to change laws that might have helped Roca and his allies eventually served their opponents equally well.

Family and friends made Tucumán a stronghold for Avellaneda and Roca in the late seventies and early eighties. Once entrenched in local government, these people used their positions to help the local sugar industry. The 1884 constitution strengthened the position of the governor and of the sugar industry, and all this was also supposed to ensure Tucumán's loyalty to the new ruling group. But like family and friends, the 1884 constitution had its limitations and no one could guarantee family, friends and governors would be loyal forever. Despite this insecurity, most Tucumanos were pleased that the political evolution of Tucumán at that time created a golden age of sugar.

ENDNOTES TO CHAPTER II

1. Speech of January 20, 1872, in Nicolás Avellaneda, *Discursos de Nicolás Avellaneda, I. Oraciones cívicas*. Biblioteca Argentina, No. 27 (Buenos Aires: La Facultad, 1928), p. 68.

2. Avellaneda to Roca, November 8, 1872, Museo Roca, *Documentos*, V: 53.

3. *La razón*, June 15, 1873, p. 1.

4. Argentine Republic, Congreso Nacional, Cámara de Diputados, *El Parlamento argentino, 1854-1947* (Buenos Aires: Imprenta del Congreso, 1948), p. 350; Vicente Osvaldo Cutolo, *Nuevo diccionario biográfico argentino*. Vols. 1-3 (Buenos Aires: Elche, 1968-)- I:270.

5. Although the bill of sale was dated 1886, a marginal note signed by Marco indicated that he did not receive his 100,000-peso share until 1891. Escritura, April 27, 1886, AAT.

6. Argentine Republic, *El Parlamento argentino*, p. 350; Cutolo, *Nuevo diccionario*, I:270.

7. The membership list included Tiburcio Padilla, Juan M. Terán, César Mur, Lídoro Quinteros, Pedro Alurralde, Pedro Alurralde (h), Domingo Martínez Muñecas, José Padilla, Belisario López, Justiniano Frías, Manuel Posse, Ezequiel Molina, Bernardo Colombres, Juan L. Nougués, Vicente Gallo and Isaías Padilla. *La razón*, July 2, 1873, p. 1.

8. Avellaneda to Helguera, November 1, 1871, AFH, I, Letter 44.

9. Avellaneda to Helguera, June 30, 1872, AFH, I, Letter 49.

10. Ibid.; Avellaneda to Helguera, September 31, 1872, AFH, I, Letter 50. The school opened in May 1875. The bridge, after many delays, was finally constructed in the mid-seventies. The plan was so faulty, however, that the finished bridge did not straddle the river. This defect was not remedied until 1881. Groussac, *et al.*, *Memoria descriptiva*, pp. 342-343.

11. Paul Groussac, *Los que pasaban: José Manuel Estrada, Pedro Goyena, Nicolás Avellaneda, Carlos Pellegrini, Roque Sáenz Peña*; 2nd ed. (Buenos Aires: Editorial Sudamericana, 1919, 1939), pp. 175-177.

12. Marco Avellaneda to Helguera, January 20, 1872, AFH, I, Letter 20.

13. Groussac, *Los que pasaban*, p. 190.

14. N. Avellaneda to Helguera, October 9, 1873, AFH, I, Letter 55.

15. Decree, October 7, 1874, *Compilación*, V:424; Declaration of State of Siege, October 10, 1874, ibid., p. 427.

16. Resignation speech, October 6, 1875, ibid., VI:144.

17. Report of Governor Padilla to the Legislature concerning his journey, ibid., p. 144.

18. Nicolás Avellaneda, *Escritos y discursos*. 12 vols. (Buenos Aires: Compañía Sudamericana de Billetes de Banco, 1910), IV:239. See also Avellaneda to Governor Padilla, November 11, 1876, ibid., p. 242.

19. Annual Message, May 1877, Mabragaña, *Los mensajes*, III:443.

20. According to the 1856 Tucumán Constitution the legislature consisted of deputies and electors during elections, thereby doubling its size for voting purposes. The legislature then voted for governor, and the winner needed a majority plus one. The legislature also nominated national senators until 1884. Ismael A. Sosa, *Historia constitucional de Tucumán (período 1820-1884)*. Facultad de Derecho y Ciencias Sociales, Publicación no. 379 (Tucumán: UNT, 1945), pp. 111, 211-212. See also *Compilación*, I:382-395 for 1856 Constitution.

21. Domingo Martínez Muñecas to Helguera, January 14, 1879, AFH, II, Letter 784.

22. *La prensa*, March 14, 1879, p. 1; Avellaneda, *Escritos y discursos* XI:292-293.

23. Telegram, President Avellaneda to Senators Benjamín Paz and Tiburcio Padilla, March 8, 1879, ibid., p. 294; Telegram, Avellaneda to Paz, ibid., p. 295.

24. Augusto Marcó del Pont, *Roca y su tiempo; cincuenta años de historia argentina* (Buenos Aires: L. J. Rosso, 1931), pp. 14-16, Carlos Páez de la Torre (h), "Personajes en el olvido," *La gaceta* [Tucumán], May 4, 1970.

25. Orlando Lázaro, "Tres aspectos del gobierno de Lucas A. Córdoba," *Revista de la Junta de Estudios Históricos de Tucumán*, 1:1 (marzo 1968): 9.

26. Marcó del Pont, *Roca*, pp. 24, 74-76.

27. Argentine Republic, *El Parlamento argentino*, pp. 364-366.

28. Germán O. E. Tjarks, Olga G. d'Agostino, Hebe G. de Bargero, Laura B. Jany, Ana E. Magnavacca, María Haydée Martín, Elena Rebok, María Susana Stein, "Aspectos cuantativos del estado económico y social de la ciudadanía argentina potencialmente votante (1860-1890)," *Boletín del Instituto de Historia Argentina "Dr. Emilio Ravignani,"* 11:18-19 (1969), passim.

29. Roca to Helguera, May 25, 1878, AFH, I, Letter 376.

30. Roca to Helguera, June 21, 1878, AFH, I, Letter 377.

31. Eduardo Wilde to Roca, March 1, 1880, Museo Roca, *Documentos*, I:19.

32. Lía E. M. Sanucci, *La renovación presidencial de 1880*. Departamento de Historia, Colección de Monografías y Tesis (Buenos Aires: Universidad Nacional de la Plata, 1959), pp. 57-58; *La prensa*, May 25, 1879, p. 1; Bartolomé Galíndez, *Historia política argentina: la revolución del 80* (Buenos Aires: Coni, 1945), p. 139n.

33. Roca, Presidential Message, October 12, 1880, Museo Roca, *Documentos*, VI:48.

34. John Henry Williams, *Argentine International Trade Under Inconvertible Paper Money, 1880-1900* (Cambridge: Harvard University Press, 1920), pp. 33-36.

35. Roca, Presidential Message, May 1884, Museo Roca, *Documentos*, VI:101.

36. Guy, *Politics and the Sugar Industry in Tucumán, Argentina, 1870-1900*. Appendix B-2, p. 327.

37. Governor Helguera, Message accompanying License Law, August 17, 1878, *Compilación*, VII: 234.

38. Interim Governor José María Astigueta, Message, ibid., pp. 375-376.

39. Santiago del Estero first exonerated the Contreras sugar factory from provincial and municipal taxes and by November 11, 1880 all sugar factories and plantations had been exonerated. Santiago del Estero Province, *Recopilación de leyes, decretos y resoluciones de la provincia de Santiago del Estero*. 6 vols. (Buenos Aires: Peuser 1897-1910), III:223, 432, 478, 643.

40. Donna J. Guy, "The Rural Working Class in Nineteenth-Century Argentina: Forced Plantation Labor in Tucumán," *Latin American Research Review*, 13:1 (Spring 1978): 135-145.

41. 1877 Police Code, Section V, ibid., VI:368-374; Manuel García Soriano, "La condición social del trabajador en Tucumán durante el siglo XIX," *Revisión histórica*, I:1 (mayo 1960): 24.

42. Ibid., p. 28; Alejandro Gancedo, *Memoria descriptiva de la provincia de Santiago del Estero* (Buenos Aires: Stiller and Laass, 1885), pp. 127-128; Santiago del Estero Province, *Recopilación de leyes*, IV:90, 390.

43. Tucumán Governor Benjamín Paz to Governor of Catamarca, April 14, 1884, *Compilación*, X:335.

44. Roca to Governor Martínez Muñecas, November 4, 1878, *Compilación*, VII:248.

45. Ibid.

46. Governor Martínez Muñecas to War Minister Roca, November 18, 1878, ibid., p. 249.

47. Contract of December 8, 1878, ibid., p. 252. According to Eduardo Quintero, peons received 10-11 Bolivian pesos per month in 1877. Eduardo Quintero, *Ocho días en Tucumán* (Buenos Aires: M. Biedma, 1877), p. 26.

48. Contract, *Compilación*, VII:252-253.

49. Manuel García Soriano, "El trabajo de los indios en los ingenios azucareros de Tucumán," *Revista de la Junta de Estudios Históricos de Tucumán*, 2:2 (julio 1969); 120-124 covers the newspaper reports; Report of the Defender of the Poor and Minors, February 10, 1879, examines the treatment of Indians at Clementino Colombres's sugar plantation, *Compilación*, VII:255-256.

50. Governor Quinteros's message and provincial debates, *Compilación*, XIII:295-325.

51. Ley de Conchabos, Articles 16, 20, 37, 40, 61, ibid., pp. 326-375. The prohibition of corporal punishment had been included in earlier Police Codes, but evidently not practiced. Article II should also be considered in this argument as it condoned debt labor, although other articles such as number 9 attempted to limit the amount of indebtedness a peon could incur. One more point is that even though all work laws specified payment in specie at the end of each day if the worker desired, all accounts of labor practices indicate that workers were paid at the end of the year or harvest season or else given coins or promissory notes to be used in a company store.

52. Guy, "The Rural Working Class in Nineteenth-Century Argentina," p. 139.

53. The 1895 census listed 35,821 residents of Tucumán out of a total population of 215,742 who claimed nearby provinces as their birthplace. Since the census was taken before the harvest season, it did not include those who migrated for seasonal employment. The census also did not distinguish how many of the 164,196 native Tucumán residents had parents who had migrated to Tucumán. Argentine Republic, *Segundo Censo Nacional*, II:540-541.

54. Guy, "The Rural Working Class in Nineteenth-Century Argentina," p. 140.

55. Ibid., p. 142.

56. Decree that created an irrigation committee consisting of Uladislao Frías, Juan Manuel Terán and Wenceslao Posse, January 23, 1872, *Compilación*, IV:322.

57. Governor Miguel Nougués, Message, *Compilación*, VIII:81; This particular project was ultimately suspended in 1885, AHL, Diputados, 1883-1885, p. 172.

58. A previous committee consisting of Vicente Márquez, Leoncio Herrera and Serapio Gomez, none known as industrialists, was deposed by the new committee. Decree naming committee, August 31, 1881, *Compilación*, VIII: 152-153; Committee report, October 4, 1882, ibid., pp. 378-379.

59. *El orden*, December 15, 1884, p. 1; Law approving commercial statutes of Sociedad Anónima Tramways Ciudad de Tucumán, February 25, 1880, *Compilación*, VII:390.

60. Sugar industrialists like Ambrosio Nougués took part in the Kelton concession debates and the final contract guaranteed that contractors would consult sugar industrialists about sidetracks. AHL, Diputados, 1883-1885, April 8, 1885, pp. 163-164. Resumé of legislative history of this line can be found in *Compilación*, XI:122-123, and in Vicente Padilla, *El norte argentino. Historia política, administrativa, social, comercial de las provincias de Tucumán, Salta, Jujuy, Santiago y Catamarca* (Buenos Aires: Ferrari, 1922), pp. 160-161.

61. List of sidetracks of Northwest Argentine Railroad, *Compilación*, XIII:394.

62. Paulino Rodríguez Marquina, "Memoria descriptiva de Tucumán. Su industria, su presente, pasado y porvenir estadística." 3 vols. Unpublished manuscript, II:182-184.

63. Governor Miguel Nougués to the Legislature, March 23, 1882, *Boletín oficial*, 12 (1882): 79-80.

64. Paulino Llambi Campbell to Dardo Rocha, May 23, 1882, AGN/ADR, 1882 política. A letter from Carlos Bouquet Roldán, a Cordobese living in Tucumán, to Juárez Celman dated April 6, 1882, showed that Tucumán politicians feared the consequences of the Porteño branch bank in Tucumán, AGN/AJC, 1882 correspondencia A-L.

65. Llambi Campbell to Governor Miguel Nougués, May 29, 1882, AH, Sección administrativa, T. 153, ff. 190-191; reprinted in *Compilación*, VIII:311.

66. Nougués to Juárez Celman, March 17, 1881, AGN/AJC, 1881 correspondencia, T. 1.

67. Nougués to Juárez Celman, July 25, 1881, AGN/AJC, 1881 correspondencia, T. 1.

68. José Posse to Domingo F. Sarmiento, August 18, 1881, Antonio P. Castro, *Epistolario entre Sarmiento y Posse, 1845-1888;* [Aclaraciones y biografía por Antonio P. Castro]; Archivo Histórico Sarmiento, 1946), II:490.

69. Posse to Sarmiento, May 27, 1882, ibid., p. 499. Governor Paz's message to the Legislature, January 1, 1883, *Compilación*, IX:5-6; Lizondo Borda, *Historia de Tucumán Siglo XIX*, p. 116.

70. Sosa, *Historia constitucional de Tucumán*, p. 132.

71. Ibid., pp. 157-158; 1884 Constitution, ibid., pp. 227-273, and *Compilación* X:267-299.

CHAPTER III
The Maturing of the Sugar Industry:
The Introduction of Conflict

Tucumán families involved in sugar during the sixties and seventies could not, by themselves, complete the modernization of the industry. New investors and entrepreneurs were needed to infuse the sugar business with additional capital and management skills and help local producers fight for national protective legislation. Some of these entrepreneurs went directly to Tucumán, purchased plantations, and constructed processing factories capable of producing white unrefined sugar and alcohol. Others, usually individuals associated with import-export businesses, lent money to sugar industrialists, went into the wholesale sugar business, bought shares in the first domestic refinery, the Refinería Argentina, and later participated in the formation of a sugar syndicate to maintain the retail price of sugar during periods of overproduction. Together, old guard sugar producers and their new business associates completed the task of modernizing the Argentine sugar industry.

This evolutionary process did not encourage industrial unity. Whereas prior to 1888 and the opening of the Refinería Argentina the sugar business proceeded harmoniously, after 1888 the agricultural and processing sector became separated from the refining and commercial sector and this produced infighting among the different groups. Thus the maturation of the sugar industry also signaled the beginning of industrial dissension.

NON-BRITISH INVESTORS AND THE SUGAR INDUSTRY

One of the most striking features of the new investors and entrepreneurs who became associated with the Tucumán sugar industry was their Argentine and French nationality. Of the many bankers, investors and businessmen who became involved in Argentina during this period, the British were the most prominent. By the 1880s the British had invested heavily in most of the railroads, public utilities and government bond issues in Argentina, and soon they would be deeply involved in the meatpacking industry. Because so many British ventures were located in the national capital and because British investments were crucial to the development of imports and exports, it appeared that the British had great influence throughout the Argentine economy.[1]

That impression diminished if one looked at who invested in domestic industry in the littoral, as well as in regional industry in the interior. British bankers and entrepreneurs for the most part did not invest in non-import-export-related activities. Instead, another group of foreign and native investors backed by French, Belgian, German, Swiss and Argentine capital filled the gap left by the British and provided the needed capital, technology and industrial experience.

Unlike their British or British-backed counterparts, non-British investors did not concern themselves solely with foreign markets and service-oriented ventures. Although some made their initial fortunes in import-export activities, by the eighties they had turned to industries whose future market would be the expanding coastal population. Besides owning or controlling domestic industries, non-British investors also lent money to local entrepreneurs who wished to purchase foreign machinery and to provincial governments that needed new public facilities and local banks. It thus appears that British and non-British investors performed complementary functions in the development of the Argentine economy.

Tucumán and its sugar industry offered an excellent investment opportunity for those interested in domestic industry. The non-British investors who became involved in sugar can be placed in three categories: outsiders, new members of the Tucumán elite, and local traditional elite. Once a typical entrepreneur decided to invest in sugar, he discovered that the cultural milieu and flexible social structure that existed in Tucumán welcomed outsiders as well as local families into the sugar business. A brief biographical sketch of some entrepreneurs who were not part of the traditional Tucumán aristocracy suggests various ways one could enter the sugar industry and how outsiders discovered Tucumán.

THE OUTSIDERS

Among the first group, the outsiders, three men stood out because of their extensive involvement in Tucumán sugar: Ernesto Tornquist, Otto Bemberg and Barón Portalis. These men helped revolutionize the sugar business in Argentina.

Ernesto Tornquist was a second generation Porteño merchant who began his career as an importer of Belgian and German machinery and an exporter of leather, meat and grains. With the experience he gained in this line of business, Tornquist then branched out and helped found new industries throughout Argentina.[2]

He became interested in the sugar industry in 1885, when he announced his intention to build Argentina's first domestic refinery. The following year he purchased the Nueva Baviera sugar factory in Tucumán. Then from 1890 to 1900 he formed the Compañía Azucarera Tucumana, a complex of five Tucumán factories with extensive company plantations. Finally, he encouraged other sugar producers to unite and form a political lobby and a marketing syndicate to advance the interests of the domestic sugar trade. By the time these organizations began to function, Tornquist was indispensable to the Argentine sugar industry.[3]

Otto Bemberg, like Tornquist, was a businessman who started in commerce and eventually wound up in the sugar business. Otto's father had been a wheat exporter and financier. By the 1880s Otto began to diversify further his father's empire. In 1887 both father and son founded the Brasserie Argentine Quilmes, one of Argentina's most successful local breweries. A year later Otto set out on his own and became an intermediary between French capitalists and Argentine provinces that sought foreign loans. Within a short period of time Otto had negotiated a series of loans for Tucumán, Catamarca, Corrientes, San Luis, San Juan and the municipality of Buenos Aires.[4]

By the time Otto Bemberg died in 1932 he had amassed an incredible fortune based upon extensive industrial enterprises in Argentina.[5] For Tucumán Bemberg's most significant businesses consisted of his alcohol distillery, the Distilería Franco Argentina, and his San Juan sugar factory in Misiones. It was Bemberg who brought the alcohol cartel to

Tucumán and through his membership in the sugar lobby, the Centro Azucarero, helped unite alcohol and sugar groups.

Barón Federico Portalis, though not so well known as Tornquist or Bemberg, had an equally important impact on the development of the sugar industry. Originally involved in the creation of the Banco Francés del Río de la Plata and railroad construction in Santa Fe, Portalis later became an importer of farm equipment, sugar and alcohol.[7] For many years he served as a representative of the Decauville Company, whose lightweight railroad engines and tracks made it possible for sugar factory owners to get their cane to the factory and the processed sugar to main railroad lines. In the late eighties the Barón was also a salesman for the Fives-Lille Company of Paris, the main supplier of sugar processing equipment. Through this job Portalis became the principal private lender to sugar industrialists, since he often advanced them money to purchase his company's machinery.[8] By the 1890s the adventurous Frenchman also made a successful entry into the wholesale domestic alcohol trade and thereby further involved himself in the sugar industry.

NEW MEMBERS OF THE TUCUMÁN ELITE

Although the first group of new industrialists never permanently moved to Tucumán, most newcomers to the Tucumán sugar industry chose to take up residence on their company plantations or in the city of San Miguel. This second group consisted mainly of French immigrants. As early as the independence period French immigrants settled in Tucumán and often sent for relatives and friends back home. Together these newcomers, often political refugees, brought with them the experience necessary to engage in the most profitable pursuits of mid-nineteenth-century Tucumán: commerce, tanning, lumber and flour mills. By the early 1870s Frenchmen also cultivated sugarcane and, as commercial conditions deteriorated, tanners, lumbermen and merchants became full time sugar industrialists. In this way the sugar oligarchy was expanded by entrepreneurs of French heritage.

Among the most important nineteenth-century sugar industrialists of French extraction were Juan Nougués, León Rougés and the Etchecopar brothers, Evaristo and Máximo. All originally emigrated from southern France. The Nougués arrived in the 1820s and their cousins, the Rougés, eventually joined them. First they worked for the Nougués; later León Rougés founded his own sugar factory, the Santa Rosa. Evaristo Etchecopar arrived in Argentina in 1836, went to Tucumán and set up the primitive La Banda sugar factory in 1847. By 1870 the enterprise had been improved by his younger brother, Máximo, and renamed Lastenia in honor of Máximo's wife. These three families made up the core of early French immigrants.

Clodomiro Hileret did not find his way to Tucumán until the seventies. He originally emigrated to Argentina at the beginning of the decade to work on the Córdoba-Tucumán railway. His engineer's salary, along with the capital of his partner, a French tanner named Juan Dermit, enabled Hileret to start a tanning business in Tucumán. By 1889 he owned two sugar factories, Lules and Santa Ana, and acquired a new associate, Barón Portalis. Hileret eventually became one of the richest men in the province.

There were but a few of the Frenchmen who built up the Tucumán sugar business. Others who owned sugar factories in Tucumán included Juan Recalt, Julio Dubourg, Francisco Duport, the Garnaud brothers and Jorge Vergnes.[9] Together the French community formed a powerful enclave that exerted strong economic influence within the province. By the mid-eighties a cultural impact could also be observed among the upper class as it adopted French culture to set itself off from the lower classes.[10]

Local politics formed additional bonds between the French enclave and local elites, since the newcomers supported more traditional elites in their industrial and social policies.

Because entrepreneurs of French origin made such an impact on the elites of Tucumán, the province continued its tradition of pursuing a way of life distinct from that of its neighbors. Even those provinces engaged in limited sugarcane cultivation like Salta, Santiago del Estero, Jujuy, Misiones, Chaco and Formosa failed to attract many Frenchmen.[11] And with the presence of these industrialists in Tucumán it was not surprising that they bought most of their machinery from French and German firms rather than from British companies.

CORDOBESE ENTREPRENEURS

Tucumán's opportunities for outsiders, and the fact that until 1885 and the opening of the Buenos Aires-Rosario line all products sent from Tucumán by rail had to pass through Córdoba, spurred yet another group of outsiders to invest in the Tucumán sugar industry. Cordobese merchants and politicians, some of whom actually moved to Tucumán, became deeply involved in Tucumán business and political intrigue.

The railroad links between Tucumán and Córdoba stimulated other activities besides shipments of sugar between the two provinces. First of all, Cordobese merchants became so involved in Tucumán commerce that several actually bought sugar factories there in order to ensure an exclusive source of sugar and alcohol for their clients. In 1882 a group of prominent Cordobese merchants formed the Sociedad Córdoba del Tucumán to run the Providencia factory. A few years later José Federico Moreno, a native of Mendoza, bought the Santa Lucía factory with funds borrowed from Cordobese investors. Along with these two enterprises, other Cordobese merchants and investors found their way to Tucumán.[12]

Second, Tucumán's increased cultivation of sugarcane and rapid rail service between Córdoba and Tucumán resulted in new consumer markets for Cordobese products. With a decreased supply of locally produced food in Tucumán, grains and meat had to be shipped in by rail or cart. The North Central route thus became even more crucial to Cordobese traders. As governor and later senator from Córdoba, Miguel Juárez Celman was often asked to make sure that the railroad manager provided sufficient rolling stock to send cattle to Tucumán. The lively cattle trade there particularly favored those Cordobese ranchers who could not compete with the export market dominated by Buenos Aires.[13]

Third, the strategic role of the railroad and the geopolitical importance of Córdoba further cemented the trade interests between Córdoba and Tucumán through politics. Juárez Celman interceded on behalf of private Tucumán requests even though he refused to speak publicly in their favor. Another Tucumán friend throughout his long stay in Congress--as deputy from 1880 to 1889 and senator from 1889 to 1898--was Cordobese politician Carlos Tagle. He often appeared in the forefront of the group that favored the protection of domestic sugar, since Córdoba profited from good business conditions in Tucumán.[14]

The combined strength of all these groups associated with the sugar business augured a great future for Tucumán if they could persuade the federal government to help the sugar industry. These requests began first as petitions for lower railroad tariffs and higher sugar duties. Once these were enacted, a number of proposals were made that would commit government, either national or provincial, to guarantee profits on a sugar refinery. The era of national sugar politics had arrived.

RAILROAD AND SUGAR TARIFFS

Political intervention for sugar began on a personal level and then spread to an open confrontation at the institutional level. Requests by Tucumán politicians and industrialists for low freight rates and high tariffs began in 1880 and by 1884 national authorities granted the lower freight rates, an indication of the increased importance of Tucumán sugar. Other measures pushed through Congress confirmed the new political thrust. Though general tariff revisions of 1883 had already changed the sugar tariff from twenty-five percent *ad valorem* to a specific duty of five centavos per kilo of sugar--a substantial increase--it was raised once more to seven centavos per kilo effective in 1885.[15] Although these changes were presented as a purely fiscal measure, no one could overlook the beneficial effect they had on the domestic sugar industry.

Whether or not a politician responded to these early demands ultimately had other political repercussions in Tucumán. Miguel Juárez Celman responded to the 1884 Tucumán petitions in a flippant manner that almost endangered the sugar tariff increase for that year.[16] Though he was willing to help friends, he balked at any public identification with protectionism. In contrast, Bernardo de Irigoyen, Juárez Celman's campaign opponent in the 1886 presidential elections, willingly authorized lower railroad rates in 1884 and publicly expressed his wish to help Tucumán sugar.[17] Possibly Juárez Celman's neglect of Tucumán's sugar industry and Irigoyen's cooperation as minister of the interior influenced the outcome of the 1886 presidential elections when Irigoyen captured the Tucumán vote.[18]

PUBLIC AND PRIVATE CREDIT

Once sugar industrialists secured reduced freight rates and higher sugar duties, they were in a position to capture the national market by planting more cane and buying the latest processing equipment. Initial financial help came from the short-lived Banco de San Juan and the Banco Muñoz Rodríguez y Cía., as well as from the Tucumán branch of the Banco Nacional. The opening of the Banco Hipotecario Nacional branch in 1887 was even more helpful to industrialists. Within a year the bank shifted its early emphasis from urban to rural credit. Not only did the bank lend money to expand plantations, it also granted gold peso loans to purchase foreign machinery.

TABLE 3.1

MORTGAGES HELD IN TUCUMÁN BY THE
BANCO HIPOTECARIO NACIONAL[19]

Year	Urban Loans	Total	Rural Loans	Total	Total Loans	Total Pesos
1887	52	1,038,000	22	343,000	74	1,381,000 m/n
1888	17	252,000	10	1,149,000	27	721,000 m/n
						680,000 gold
1889	5	98,000	25	1,274,000	30	1,052,000 m/n
						320,000 gold
1891	52	466,000	58	2,583,000	110	3,049,000 m/n
	4	90,000	8	910,000	12	1,000,000 gold

In addition to formal bank loans, men like Barón Portalis offered financial credit. Portalis, for example, made arrangements with Camilio Bouvier, another Fives-Lille salesman, to let the Nougués brothers purchase new machinery on credit without any interest charges if the Nougués paid their bill within one year.[20] Portalis also personally advanced industrialists large sums of money on favorable terms. Such arrangements, especially during the early years, allowed some entrepreneurs to renovate totally their sugar factories.

For smaller loans industrialists depended upon personal favors. Sometimes sugar industrialists made loans to each other. In other cases, if an industrialist had friends among the board of directors of a bank in Buenos Aires, Rosario or Córdoba, he wrote and asked for loans there. Letters preserved in the Juárez Celman archives from Silvano Bores, Eudoro Robles, Miguel M. Nougués and José Padilla of Tucumán and Luis G. Pinto of Santiago all asked Juárez Celman to take care of bank matters related to sugar. Juárez Celman apparently granted most of these favors. The archives of the Nougués San Pablo factory also show that regular loans were contracted in a number of banks outside Tucumán.[21]

If an industrialist could not depend upon his own resources or those of his friends and allies, his chances of success in the sugar business diminished. Of thirteen sugar factories constructed in the eighties, only six remained in the possession of the original owners in 1895. The period of consolidation might have been discouraging to some industrialists, but for other entrepreneurs it allowed them to buy out bankrupt industrialists.

The factories founded during Tucumán's "Golden Age" of sugar brought wealth and power to those who succeeded. At the same time increased sugar production brightened the prospects of eliminating competition from imported sugar. In a few years Argentina would produce enough sugar to meet domestic demands.

THE REFINERÍA ARGENTINA

The desire to dominate the national sugar market led Tucumán and other sugar producing areas to consider plans for an Argentine sugar refinery. Despite good fortunes reaped by Tucumán's preeminence in local sugar markets, no domestic sugar could hope to dislodge refined sugar used in the littoral. A refinery, along with the new high tariff barriers, would finally eliminate foreign sugar.

Until Argentina entrepreneurs constructed their first refinery, all refined sugar came from France and Germany. The cultivation of sugar beets there, along with technological improvements in the refining of both cane and beet sugar, had revolutionized nineteenth-century sugar markets. Year by year the price of beet sugar lowered, thereby forcing cane sugar producers either to lower their prices or to limit themselves to local protected markets. To compete successfully in the world market, sugarcane growers had to refine their own sugar or sell less expensive unrefined sugar to a foreign refinery.[22] Even though Argentines had no immediate hopes of selling their sugar abroad, they realized that the technological advances in Europe affected the local market in Argentina.

Projects for an Argentine refinery appeared as early as 1880, but financial backing was not forthcoming until increased sugar production and high tariffs encouraged serious consideration.[23] By 1885 Ernesto Tornquist had announced that he would construct a refinery along the Paraná River in Rosario if the national government would guarantee limited profits for the company.[24] He took his plan to his old friend, President Julio Roca, who in turn presented Tornquist's petition to Congress. In his letter to Congress urging a favorable decision for the Tornquist venture, Roca emphatically stated that Argentina could never be self-sufficient in sugar without a refinery.[25]

Congress did not take up the matter until September 1886, just prior to the presidential election. By November the Chamber of Deputies began to discuss the petition. Advocates for the refinery knew that many coastal deputies traditionally opposed protective tariffs. Consequently they planned a crafty strategy to make the Tornquist concession more palatable to those opposed to protecting national industry. Before the refinery bill was discussed, they presented a petition from several Tucumán industrialists that demanded a two-centavo increase on the sugar tariff from seven to nine centavos per kilo. The sugar industrialists anticipated opposition to their petition, but the request served its purpose as an undesirable alternative to the Tornquist project. [26]

After legislators objected strongly to the Tucumán tariff petition, Minister of Finance Wenceslao Pacheco announced his disapproval of increased sugar duties by pointing out the advantages of a refinery:

> The problem with this industry is that one-third of its production is unsuitable for consumption because people prefer refined sugar for certain purposes . . . . If we raised the tariff two centavos . . . would this solve the problem? Of course not. Therefore I believe that Sr. Tornquist's proposal to guarantee a refinery is an adequate way to resolve the difficulties. [27]

Pacheco wanted to show the legislators how safe Tornquist's project was, compared to the proposed tariff increases. A refinery, unlike duties, would not provoke the feared tariff war often threatened by Brazilians against Argentine beef. Pacheco's persuasive argument helped end the Tucumán tariff petition, but at the same time deputies accepted the idea of a refinery. [28]

Once legislators worked out details of the government concession, such as how much profits should be guaranteed and whether or not the factory should be exempt from local taxes, both the Chamber of Deputies and the Senate quickly approved the petition in late 1886. [29]

The success of the refinery venture revealed the growing importance of Tornquist to the Generation of Eighty and the value of protecting certain local industries. As Emilio Civit, deputy from Mendoza and member of the Chamber of Deputies' budget committee, noted:

> It is true that a few years ago some people in Tucumán tried to establish a similar kind of establishment. It is also well known that they could not do it despite all the refinery proponents' time, effort and expense. They failed precisely because they lacked a guarantee by public officials and because they could not find the necessary capital in Argentina. [30]

This argument was further supported by the contention that only a man like Tornquist, who had the necessary European connections to build the refinery, could assure legislators that the factory would be constructed within a reasonable length of time. [31] Such arguments permitted the Tornquist proposal to demand provisions such as a seven-percent guarantee, which was usually reserved for public utilities.

Rather than finance the project solely by foreign subscription as anticipated, Tornquist invited sugar producers and investors to buy shares in the Refinería Argentina. The first board of directors reflected the merger of various sugar groups. Representing the local sugar producers were Manuel Ocampo Samanés, owner of the Mercedes sugar factory of Santa Fe, and David Methven, an Englishman who owned the

Azucarera Argentina factory of Tucumán. Representing Tucumán politicians were Delfín Gallo and Marco Avellaneda. Representing coastal financiers were Ernesto Tornquist and his associates, Teodoro de Bary, Carlos Carranza and Francisco Mallman. Of the 200,000 gold pesos preferred shares first issued, Tornquist bought 95,000, which gave him control of the corporation. Nevertheless, Tucumán industrialists and politicians on the board of directors held one-quarter of the shares.[32] The presence of Tucumán investors as principal stockholders and board members indicated Tornquist succeeded in his campaign to encourage the local participation. He needed to maintain harmonious relations with sugar producers. Tornquist retained firm control of the refinery by supplying all the technicians and management, mostly German nationals. The refinery's general manager, Máximo Hageman, was Tornquist's personal protégé.

Few complained during this pioneer period. The refinery stimulated more cane cultivation needing more workers, which in turn expanded the local food markets. For the immigrants who made their way to Santa Fe, the refinery promised a new source of work, since the immigrants comprised the basic labor force for the refinery as well as the technical task force.[33] Sugar promised many things to many people.

The creation of the Refinería Argentina signaled a great watershed not only in the technological progression of the Argentine sugar industry but also in its politics. After it began operating, industrial squabbles appeared. These disputes continued to occur, as the refining and commercial sectors grabbed an ever-increasing share of profits as well as a dominant voice in the sugar business.

In political terms the increased complexity of the sugar industry was translated into requests for government aid and protection that often served only the needs of the more powerful sugar sectors. Ernesto Tornquist and his associates in the Refinería began to lobby for the refinery long before it began operations by backing the move to increase the tariff on refined sugar. Such a request attracted attention to the sugar industry without actually harming it. Later moves by the refinery, however, exposed the entire industry to public scrutiny and often threatened the agricultural sector. By then Tucumán sugar producers would have to learn how to defend themselves in this new situation.

REFINERY POLITICS

The Refinería Argentina's first political test came in 1887, two years before the refinery began processing sugar. When President Juárez Celman delivered his May 30, 1887, budget message, he openly criticized the sugar industry and its desire for protection and specifically cautioned Congress against proposing any additional protection as it "would accentuate the protection which the industry now enjoys."[34] Yet when the Chamber of Deputies' budget committee reported on the presidential tariff bill in November, it recommended, among other measures, that tariffs be raised for refined sugars.

The budget committee based its proposal upon the proposition that unrefined sugars such as *quebrado* (broken sugar) should not be charged the same duty as refined since *quebrado* sugar contained less sugar and more impurities than the same quantity of refined sugar. When an incredulous deputy suggested that the same ends could be achieved by simply lowering the tariff on *quebrado* sugar, Deputy Carlos Tagle responded obliquely: "That is true, but we cannot do everything at once. We must take our national industry into account."[35]

When curious legislators questioned the committee's motives for altering the content and intent of the presidential bill, Minister of the Interior Eduardo Wilde defended the committee by claiming that the president had changed his mind about the sugar tariff because of some radical changes proposed in other clauses of the customs bill. [36]   The final version of the sugar tariff listed refined sugars with a duty of nine centavos and unrefined with seven centavos.   The revisions applied to all sugars imported after January 1888.

The 1887 tariff revisions offered the Refinería Argentina's sugar a safer market to work in than had existed before 1888. Unrefined sugar was not affected by the change. The increased protection of both refined and unrefined sugar after 1888 came more from the falling price of imported sugar than from increased fiscal protection. This can be seen by comparing the sugar duty to the price of imported sugar: [37]

TABLE 3.2

Year	Duty		Amount of Protection		
	Refined	Unrefined	Refined	Unrefined	Quebrado
1880-1882	25% ad valorem		25%	25%	25%
1883-1884	.05	.05	26.3	35.7	43.4
1885-1887	.07	.07	36.8	58.8	58.8
1888-1893	.09	.07	47.3	53.8	53.8
1894-1899	.09	.07	90.0	87.5	87.5

The new tariff aroused a lot of hostility towards the domestic sugar industry, and Tucumán sugar producers were blamed for high prices for refined sugar.   Nevertheless, no domestic sugar producer criticized the new tariffs.

The second major political campaign sponsored by Tornquist and the Refinería did draw considerable criticism when domestic sugar producers realized that refinery politics could destroy them.   As the refinery first began to process sugar late in 1889, the company did not have enough crude sugar to keep the refinery operating full time and at maximum efficiency.   Consequently, Tornquist approached Finance Minister Wenceslao Pacheco in October 1889 to obtain permission to refine imported crude sugar when there were insufficient supplies of domestic sugar. [38]

After Tornquist received permission to refine imported sugar, he ordered at least two shiploads and received 4,500 metric tons of *muscovado* sugar from Pernambuco. *Muscovado* sugar is coarse brown sugar whose extremely low price and high quantity of by-products in comparison to the more highly processed Tucumán sugars made it ideal for refining. Even more important, muscovado sugar did not specifically appear on the 1889 duty list, which merely distinguished between refined and unrefined.   Claiming that "unrefined" referred to unrefined white or *quebrado* sugars, Tornquist petitioned the government to let his *muscovado* sugar enter as an unclassified product.   As such, it would only be subject to a low twenty-five percent *ad valorem* general duty. When Minister Pacheco granted this new request on November 9, critics throughout Argentina demanded an explanation. [39]

Publicly, Tucumán industrialists protested the Tornquist petition but not too loudly.   They knew that Tornquist could sell refined Brazilian sugar for less than their refined, but they wondered whether he would and whether they could stop him if he did.   Privately, industrialists asked other questions.   Could sugar industrialists fight Tornquist without souring advocates of the refinery or political allies?   Would a scandal end with the removal of guarantee privileges?   In a letter to President Juárez Celman dated November 18, 1889, Ambrosio Nougués pointed out that, despite selfish actions by refinery officials, punishing them would serve no purpose:

> The question comes down to this: is it advanta-
> geous to the National Interests to destroy the
> approximately 40 million pesos investment repre-
> sented by this [Tucumán] industry . . ., which
> never requested any guarantee, to protect another
> less important industry that does have a guarantee
> . . . . On the other hand, the Nation will also lose
> out if it removes the guarantee. . . .[40]

As an alternative Ambrosio counseled the president to consider mediations between Tucumán industrialists and officials of the Refinería Argentina.

Tucumán officials sent Silvano Bores, once again provincial Minister of Government, to Buenos Aires so that he could work out a compromise with the Refinería. After Minister Pacheco, Tornquist and Bores met several times, they announced their decision. They all agreed that the Tornquist muscovado imports violated the customs law as well as the re- finery guarantee. Accordingly, the federal government nullified the November 9 decision but allowed already purchased sugar to enter the country exempt from the seven-centavo duty.[41]

Until the refinery became more of a threat, Tucumán industrialists felt that the early clashes with the Refinería had resulted in a *modus vivendi* between the two groups. Sugarcane growers and processors would help defend the refinery so long as the refinery recognized its dependence on domestic sugar. With the two groups in close alliance, Tucumán turned to pressing local problems that hindered the continued expansion of the sugar industry.

Prior to 1886 a number of long-term public projects had been dis- cussed but never carried out for lack of funds. Now that the prospects for the sugar industry seemed so good, provincial irrigation projects and a provincial bank seemed more important than ever. Two major issues of the late eighties--the negotiation for a foreign loan that would finance public works and a local bank, along with a dispute over who should pay for these new services--directly affected the sugar industry and its poli- tics. These issues also led to a political revolt in Tucumán.

Such consequences, however, were unforeseen as the sugar indus- try blossomed and expanded with the help of diverse groups. Protected by national laws, the Tucumán sugar industry, along with the Refinería Argentina, became one of the most highly successful and valuable indus- tries in Argentina. Tucumán became a new kind of garden in the Repub- lic. The glory may have been momentary but it was nonetheless real.

ENDNOTES TO CHAPTER III

1. For the classic studies of British investment in Argentina in the nineteenth century see Henry Ferns, *Britain and Argentina in the Nineteenth Century* (Oxford: Oxford University Press, 1960); J. Fred Rippy, *British Investments in Latin America, 1822-1949; A Case Study in the Operations of Private Enterprise in Retarded Regions* (Minneapolis: University of Minnesota Press, 1959); and Desmond C. M. Platt, *Latin America and British Trade, 1806-1914* (New York: Barnes and Noble, 1973).

2. *Ernesto Tornquist, 1842-1942; estudio biográfico de su vida publicado con motivo del centenario de su natalicio* (Buenos Aires : Compañía Impresora Argentina, 1942), pp. 17-33; Guillermo Heins [Capitán Nemo], *América industrial y comercial* (Buenos Aires: Pan América, 1936), pp. 201-210; Ricardo Pillado, *Anuario Pillado de la deuda pública y sociedades anónimas establecidas en la República Argentina para 1899* (Buenos Aires: La Nación, 1899), passim; Jules Tilmant, "Ernesto Tornquist et le commerce anversois," reprinted in *In Memoriam: Ernesto Tornquist* (Buenos Aires: privately published, 1908), pp. 251-299.

3. Guy, *Politics and the Sugar Industry in Tucumán, Argentina, 1870-1900*, Appendix A, pp. 318-319; Centro Azucarero Argentino, *Cincuentenario del Centro Azucarero Argentino, desarrollo de la industria en medio siglo 1880-1944* [Emilio J. Schleh] (Buenos Aires: Centro Azucarero, 1944), pp. 5-6.

4. Cutolo, *Nuevo diccionario*, I:403-404; Pillado, *Anuario Pillado, 1899*, pp. 30, 35, 39, 57-58, 61, 212.

5. José Luis Torres, *Los "Perduellis"* (Buenos Aires: Editorial Freeland, 1973), pp. 79, 183-186.

6. Schleh, *Noticias históricas sobre el azúcar en la Argentina*, p. 363.

7. Alejandro Dussaut, *La oolonia francesa en el Río de la Plata, conferencia pronunciada con motivo del Centenario el 13 de mayo de 1966* (Buenos Aires: privately printed, n.d.), p. 24; Centro Azucarero Argentino, *Cincuentenario*, p. 172; Jules Huret, *En Argentine: de Buenos Aires au Gran Chaco* (Paris: E. Fasquelle, 1911), p. 308.

8. Centro Azucarero Argentino, *Cincuentenario*, p. 172; Mulhall, *Handbook of the River Plate*, 1885, p. 61, Advertisement Section.

9. Guillermo Furlong Cardiff, *Ernesto Padilla, su vida, su obra*. 2 vols. (Tucumán: UNT, Facultad de Filosofía y Letras, 1959), I:36, 331-332.

10. Emile Daireaux, *La Vie et les moeurs á la Plata*. 2 vols. (Paris: Hachette, 1888), pp. 434-435; *South American Journal and Brazil and the River Plate Mail*, 26:26 (December 24, 1892):713; Huret, pp. 308-309.

11. List of Argentine Sugar Factories in 1894, Centro Azucarero Argentino, *Cincuentenario*, p. 14.

12. *El orden*, May 24, 1884, p. 2; Vicente Padilla, *El norte argentino;* pp. 348-352; "José Federico Moreno," anonymous speech given at the Círculo de Magisterio, August 5, 1933, in San Miguel de Tucumán; typed manuscript, AAT.

13. A. M. Funes to Juárez Celman, September 14 and 29, 1884, AGN/AJC, 1884 correspondencia. According to Funes's descendent, Javier Frías, Funes's plan to sell cattle in Tucumán never reached fruition.

14. Argentine Republic, *El Parlamento argentino*, pp. 452, 498.

15. Diputados, September 11, 1884, pp. 978-979.

16. Argentine Republic, Cámara de Senadores, *Diario de Sesiones, 1854-* (Buenos Aires: Imprenta del Congreso de la Nación), October 2, 1884, p. 668.

17. Message of Bernardo de Irigoyen to Governor of Tucumán, October 10, 1884, *Compilación*, X:306.

18. See Chapter IV.

19. Argentine Republic, Banco Hipotecario de la Nación, *Memoria y balance, 1887-1891* (Buenos Aires, 1888-1892), 1887, p. 54; 1888, p. 68; 1889, p. 84; 1891, pp. 79-81.

20. Undated telegram, Ambrosio Nougués to Miguel Nougués, 1884; Telegram, Portalis Frères to Nougués Hermanos, October 2, 1884, ASP, Miscellaneous Letters.

21. Miguel Nougués to Juárez Celman, June 22, 1880, AGN/AJC, 1880 correspondencia, T. 6; José Padilla to Juárez Celman, April 12, 1883, AGN/AJC, 1883 correspondencia, T. 1; Luis G. Pinto to Juárez Celman, December 9, 1884 correspondencia. The letters from Bores and Robles were written in 1889, AGN/AJC, 1889 correspondencia. Banks noted in yearly inventories for San Pablo include the Buenos Aires branch of the Banco Nacional, the Banco de la Provincia de Buenos Aires, and the Banco de Italia. ASP, Inventarios I and II, passim. These financial statements also indicate that the Nougués Brothers either lent or borrowed money from Pablo San Germés (Santiago del Estero), Pedro G. Méndez and Clodomiro Hileret, all sugar industrialists.

22. For a general survey of sugar history in the nineteenth century see Deerr, *The History of Sugar.* Sugar refining and its impact in the United States is analyzed by Alfred S. Eichner, *The Emergence of Oligopoly.* The European sugar market in the nineteenth century has been studied by Yves Guyot, *The Sugar Question in 1901* (London: H. Rees, Ltd., 1901), and Prinsen Geerligs, *The World's Cane Sugar Industry.*

23. For the 1880 proposal see Ing. Samson, "Proyecto para una sociedad anónima para la elaboración y refinación de azúcar en la provincia de Tucumán," *Boletín del Departamento Nacional de Agricultura*, 4 (1880):311-315.

24. Donna J. Guy, "Tucumán Sugar Politics and the Generation of Eighty," *The Americas*, 32:4 (April 1976):575-576.

25. Diputados, September 10, 1886, pp. 838-839.

26. José Padilla to Juárez Celman, August 18, 1866, AGN/AJC, 1886 correspondencia.

27. Diputados, November 10, 1886, p. 671.

28. Ibid., p. 675.

29. Guy, "Tucumán Sugar Politics," pp. 577-578.

30. Diputados, November 17, 1886, p. 810. The Refinería Argentina by 1893 cost 1,071,685.15 gold pesos, equivalent to almost 3,000,000 pesos m/n. As a point of comparison, the 1895 value of individual Tucumán factories, including company plantation land, ranged from 89,000 to 2,500,000 m/n. Gabriel Carrasco, *La producción y el consumo del azúcar en la República Argentina* (Buenos Aires, 1894), p. 51; *Compilación*, XX, "Datos generales sobre la zafra de 1895-1896."

31. Ibid., November 17, 1886, p. 811.

32. Carrasco, *La producción y el consumo del azúcar en la República Argentina*, pp. 45-46; Refinería Argentina, "Libro de Actas," p. 1, ACT. The rest of the 200,000 shares were bought by Tornquist associates and other investors. This capital stock was finally expanded to the 500,000 pesos stipulated by the national concession.

33. Juan Bialet Massé, *El estado de las clases obreras argentinas a comienzos del siglo*; 2nd ed. (Córdoba: Universidad Nacional de Córdoba, 1968 [orig. 1904]), p. 241.

34. Diputados, May 30, 1887, p. 45.

35. Ibid., pp. 843-844.

36. Ibid., November 7, 1887, pp. 852-853.

37. Chart adapted from Tubal C. García, *La industria azucarera argentina y las consecuencias de su protección.* Tesis presentada para optar al grado de Doctor en Ciencias Económicas (Buenos Aires: Universidad Nacional de Buenos Aires, Facultad de Ciencias Económicas, 1920), pp. 142-143. The calculations include the *aforo*, another customs tax. For calculations that differ somewhat from these, see Emilio Lahitte, *Informes y estudios de la Dirección de Economía y Estadística;* 2nd ed. 2 vols. (Buenos Aires: Ministerio de Agricultura, 1916), I:128-130.

38. *El orden*, October 21, 1889, p. 1.

39. Refinería, Argentina, *Memoria* (Buenos Aires: Peuser, 1890), p. 4; *La prensa*, November 10, 1889, p. 7; *El orden*, November 18, 1889, p. 1.

40.   Ambrosio Nougués to Juárez Celman, November 18, 1889, AGN/AJC 1889 correspondencia.

41.   *Boletín de la Unión Industrial Argentina,* No. 140 (December 5, 1889):2; No. 144 (January 2, 1890):2.

CHAPTER IV
The Tucumán Rebellion of 1887

I would like to inform your Excellency that at 10 o'clock this morning the revolution [in Tucumán] ended with the surrender of the Cabildo and the imprisonment of the governor and his ministers...

Throughout the twenty-four hour conflict there has been no movement in the city to defend the government and the revolutionaries had ample support from the countryside as well as the obvious approval of the masses.

I have seen this with my own eye, and this is how I explain the triumph of the revolution. [1]

> *Telegram of Salustiano Zavalía, special presidential emissary to Juárez Celman, June 13, 1887.*

The overthrow of the Tucumán government was inevitable from the day that Dr. Juárez Celman won the presidency. The government there was guilty of not believing that Dr. Juárez Celman was the most suitable man to head the government. [2]

> *Tucumán Deputy Delfín Gallo, Chamber of Deputies, June 18, 1887.*

One of the principal goals of the Generation of Eighty was the cessation of political conflict. Ironically, the progress that followed the termination of armed insurrection brought with it new opportunities for wealth and power, opportunities that encouraged new political disputes. By 1886 and the election of Miguel Juárez Celman as president, it became increasingly difficult for political leaders to contain the greed of their allies as well as their own desires.

Within the province of Tucumán the rapid growth of the sugar industry had brought a Golden Age of progress. Since sugar had become so important to the province, sugar industrialists sought to ally themselves with those political groups interested in the advancement of the sugar industry. In this way sugar became intimately involved in the resurgence of armed conflict in Tucumán.

The Tucumán rebellion of 1887 was not an isolated incident. President Juárez Celman inaugurated the era of the *unicato* (one-party rule) when he allowed federal troops to intervene in Tucumán and legitimize a Juarista revolution. After this first experience with provincial conflict, Juárez Celman frequently used the precedent to justify federal intervention in other provinces. Yet the situation in Tucumán, as in other provinces, had been the outcome of intrigues both local and national in origin, involving more than the whims of the president. Armed conflict had little to do with the imposition of monolithic party rule. Indeed, the basic source of rebellion in the late eighties sprang from power struggles among rivals of Julio Roca who refused to relinquish party control to others, from ambitious provincial elites who learned to take advantage of such rivalries and from the political and economic needs of individual provinces. The ultimate costs of the Tucumán revolution—a provincial loan contracted abroad by Roca, the increased strength of the sugar industry and the precedent for national intervention--demonstrated how much local politicians could profit from strong central government.

Trouble had been brewing in Tucumán ever since preparations for the April 1886 presidential elections had split ruling families into three main factions: the Juaristas, Rochistas and Irigoyenistas, who supported their respective candidates: Miguel Juárez Celman, Dardo Rocha and Bernardo de Irigoyen. From the outset the group most likely to win Tucumán elections were the Irigoyenistas, whose closest friends in Tucumán, the Gallo family, maintained firm control of the province with the help of the Colombres clan and two Posses. Santiago Gallo was governor and therefore in control of the police. His brother Delfín was national deputy for Tucumán. Another Gallo brother, Vicente, provided the campaign financial backing through his sugar factory and business. [3]

The Colombres had two politicians to serve the Irigoyen campaign, as did the Posses. Ernesto Colombres first published the Irigoyenista newspaper, *El orden*, which was set up in 1883 specifically to oppose Roca's *El deber*. Ernesto then became Deputy for Tucumán in 1886 and turned the paper over to León Rosenvald. Ignacio Colombres became Minister of Government under Juan Posse. Like the Colombres, two Posses joined the Irigoyen bandwagon: Emidio, then deputy for Tucumán, and Juan Posse who became governor in 1886. [4]

These three families had captured complete control of provincial posts. Not even Juárez Celman could break through and win elections there, despite the fact that he too had important families like the Nougués and Padillas to advance his candidacy. The Rochistas, led by Eudoro Avellaneda, Pepe Posse and Próspero García, had similar difficulties. [5]

Even though Juárez Celman's campaign manager, José Padilla, saw growing opposition, both official and popular, he refused to consider some of the illegal tactics suggested by other Tucumán Juaristas. As early as November 1885 they had plotted to discredit the incumbent government by forcing it to commit acts of violence during impending congressional elections. [6] Carlos Bouquet Roldan then suggested to Juárez Celman that the Juaristas falsify the February 1886 elections by forming duplicate voting tables. [7]

Governor Gallo used the police to prevent the Juaristas from implementing their plan and Juarista candidates, Lídoro Quinteros, Dr. Vicente Padilla and Carlos Bouquet Roldan, had no hopes of winning the February 1886 elections. In desperation the Juaristas sent President Roca a telegram requesting federal election surveillance. To their dismay, Roca named Governor Gallo as supervisor and thus the Irigoyenistas won. Ernesto Colombres, Eudoro Avellaneda and Pedro Huidobro joined other anti-Juarists in the Chamber of Deputies. [8]

Obviously, Juárez Celman had been unable to provide votes for his Tucumán allies because Roca had not supported him. Indeed, both Roca and Carlos Pellegrini, Juárez Celman's running mate for vice-president, had been doing their best to undermine the Tucumán Juaristas.

The February 1886 congressional elections were not the first signs of Roca's machinations in Tucumán. It started back in 1885 when Roca filled the head Tucumán posts of the Banco Nacional, the post office, the public schools and the North Central Railroad without consulting Juárez Celman. This left the future president with no possibility of rewarding his loyal friends. [9] Thus Lídoro Quinteros's appointment as manager of the railroad, Silvano Bores's job as headmaster of the Escuela Normal and Eudoro Vázquez's position as head of the post office all came from Roca, and Juárez Celman was left with no real hold over his reputed henchmen.

Pellegrini further hindered the Juárez Celman campaign with his promises to respect the existing political situation in Tucumán. In January 1886 Pellegrini circulated a letter to that effect in Tucumán and caused Silvano Bores to grumble in a letter to Juárez Celman:

> He has done us more harm than all our enemies put together. This Dr. Pellegrini believes that he has the right to walk wherever he pleases in the north, and because of this he writes such encouraging letters against his political friends. [10]

Pellegrini's willingness to compromise and work with the opposition probably won him the Tucumán electoral votes for vice-president, while the presidential votes went to Bernardo de Irigoyen. The Rochistas also realized that Pellegrini's spirit of compromise had helped them get some candidates in office. [11]

The February 1886 congressional election disaster finally forced Juárez Celman to confront Roca and Pellegrini with the complaints made by Tucumán Juaristas. Roca's response is unknown, but in a letter dated February 8 Pellegrini denied writing the letters circulated in Tucumán. [12] Later that month he advised Juárez Celman to act prudently and not listen to disenchanted Juaristas like Bores, who had private as well as political reasons to contest the elections. [13]

At first Juárez Celman accepted the cautious advice. No evidence appears to indicate that he ever planned to intervene there after the April presidential election. The crisis arose not in response to Juárez Celman's own campaign failure, but rather to the September 1886 election of Juan Posse as governor. His election stirred up old anti-Posse grievances as well as current partisan feelings. The conflicts that ensued also prevented Posse's government from directing its attention to the needs of the sugar industry. These combined factors prompted local Juaristas to plan a rebellion.

PRELUDE TO REBELLION

Before the 1886 gubernatorial elections could be held, two important questions had to be resolved: when Santiago Gallo would step down, and who would replace him. The election date had become an issue since the 1884 Tucumán constitution changed the governor's tenure from two to three years. Although Gallo had been elected before the new constitution was passed, he could have challenged the applicability of the new provisions. To avoid such a conflict a June meeting took place in Buenos Aires between Santiago Gallo, Delfín Gallo and General Roca, at which time Santiago agreed to resign. [14]

In testimony offered to the Chamber of Deputies on June 18, 1887 Delfín disclosed other compromises worked out by General Roca. Delfín claimed that Roca had come to the meeting prepared to accept Santiago's resignation and support Juan Posse's candidacy, even though no Juaristas

had been consulted.[15]   When Tucumán Juaristas were finally apprised of
the arrangement, they refused the imposition of Posse unless they could
have two provincial ministries, half of the legislature, half of the electoral
college and their man as Chief of Police or, as Delfín put it, "the keys to
the castle."[16]   Since the opposition refused to concede these terms, the
Juaristas plotted revenge.

Hints of rebellion appeared in the Tucumán press in June 1886, but
nothing happened until May and June 1887. In the meantime many people
tried to avoid conflict by encouraging Juárez Celman to have Lídoro
Quinteros elected governor instead of Posse. Silvano Bores not only requested Quinteros's selection; he questioned why the president was treat-
ing his Tucumán allies so shabbily as to allow the opposition to win.[17]
Martín Posse, another Juarista conspirator, openly warned that Juan Posse
might be overthrown if he were elected.[18]   Yet despite all the admonitions
from his friends, Juárez Celman did not challenge the Roca compromise.

Santiago Gallo resigned as expected on September 3. Two weeks
later the Tucumán electoral college met and elected Juan Posse, who in
turn appointed Irigoyenistas and Rochistas to fill provincial posts. Quinteros and his friends, joined by other disgruntled office seekers, openly
denounced the elections as a fraud. Even the Rochistas publicly expressed their dissatisfaction over their share of patronage, and El orden claimed that revolutions were in the making.[19]

Governor Posse's administration seemed doomed from the outset.
He had become governor through a compromise rejected by Juaristas. To
add to his problems Posse received the blame for all problems in the province, while any attempts he made to correct the situation were met with
disapproval.   One example of this was his plan for a provincial bank,
which many industrialists strongly supported. Because of other urgent
issues and the refusal of the national government to facilitate a loan,
Governor Posse had to wait almost a year before he sent a bill to the provincial legislature that authorized the negotiation of a three million gold
peso loan. The loan could be contracted either inside or outside the Republic, and its proceeds would be divided equally between public works
projects and a provincial bank.[20]   The bill did not pass the legislature
until April 27, 1887, shortly before the revolution began.

Two other events occurred that crystallized the rebellion. The
first took place during local elections of November 1886, when Posse used
the police to keep the Juaristas from voting, thus causing bloody riots to
break out in Lules and Monteros.[21] Then the second disaster, a serious
cholera outbreak, occurred just two weeks later.[22]

From November 28 until February 1887 all business and industry in
Tucumán was halted by the increasing number of cholera cases. Aided
by the hot, damp summer weather and by the fact that laundresses
washed contaminated clothing in rivers also used for drinking water,
several thousand cases of the disease were reported with at least 828
deaths in the city of San Miguel in 1886 along.[23] Confronted with such
devastation, both human and economic, Governor Posse halted his plans
for a bank and spent his money relieving the sick and poor. His actions,
despite their nobility, gave further proof to sugar industrialists that the
Posse government was incapable of helping them.

Throughout the summer and fall of 1887 Posse was blamed for the
epidemic, as well as for anything else that upset Tucumán residents.
Finally the situation became serious enough in May 1887 for Quinteros and
Bores to move.   First a libelous pamphlet printed by El deber, whose
editor was Silvano Bores, began to circulate in Tucumán. The publication, called La porra, was sent out through the public mails and mocked
Governor Posse. Asserting his legal rights, Posse demanded the confiscation of the broadside and prohibited its circulation. Yet post office
officials ignored the order and more issues were delivered.

Posse soon found out who had organized the plot. Paulino Rodrí-guez Marquina, a Spanish immigrant currently serving the army, authored the pamphlet. Silvano Bores was responsible for *La porra*, since it had been printed on his presses. Eudoro Vázquez, head of the post office, had distributed it. And behind it all stood Lídoro Quinteros, the princi-pal plotter. Yet Posse could not stop the organizers. He managed to arrest Bores, but when he tried to imprison the others they took refuge with the army recruiting officer, who granted them asylum.

At this point the Tucumán conspiracy became a national issue, since federal appointees had defied the governor. To redress this griev-ance Governor Posse began on May 29 to send a series of telegrams to the Minister of the Interior, Eduardo Wilde.[24] Wilde then sent the telegrams to the Chamber of Deputies on June 1. From the first moment Tucumán became a topic of discussion, Deputy Delfín Gallo put the blame for the incident squarely on the President:

> There is a political group in Tucumán that, be-
> cause it is part of the group that brought Dr.
> Juárez Celman to the presidency, believes that
> they have the right to call themselves the regen-
> erators, the liberators, the only governors of Tu-
> cumán.
>
> The President of the Republic . . . has placed in
> their hands the Banco Nacional, the Banco Hipo-
> tecario, the manager of the railroad, the post
> office, the Normal School and almost all the pro-
> fessional posts there.[25]

Gallo went on to say that, with all this opposition, the chances of the Posse government remaining in power were slight. Others who spoke out on the Tucumán issue wanted to wait for further reports from Tucumán that would clarify the situation. In the meantime, President Juárez Cel-man sent Dr. Salustiano Zavalía as a special personal emissary to Tucu-mán, ostensibly to find out what had happened but really to bargain with so-called Juaristas. Yet the principal result of the scandal sheet incident was the imprisonment of Silvano Bores in a latrine that had been con-verted into a makeshift jail cell, a situation which more than anything else tarnished Juan Posse's reputation.[26]

The Tucumán Juaristas soon realized that more action was needed to make the federal government topple the Posse regime. Consequently on the morning of June 12 a special train filled with troops and police arrived from Córdoba. They were greeted by Tucumán revolutionaries accompanied by peons from the Hileret and Nougués sugar plantations. At that moment the Tucumán police force was conveniently seated in the San Miguel cathedral celebrating a *Te Deum*. By the time they heard shots, the police found the revolutionaries had already attacked the near-by cabildo and seized those officials who tried to defend the building. By June 13 the revolution had ended with forty dead or wounded and almost all the leading government officials imprisoned. *El orden* had been ransacked and its publisher imprisoned. Governor Posse first managed to elude the revolutionaries and proceeded to presidential emissary Dr. Zavalía's house to seek asylum. There Posse discovered that Zavalía would not grant him asylum, and soon after the rebels entered and seized the governor.[27]

Once reports of the June 12 attack began to filter into Buenos Aires, the Chamber of Deputies began to consider federal intervention. Various versions of the revolution came in from Zavalía and from an eye-witness, thirteen-year-old Vicente C. Gallo, nephew of Deputy Delfín and ex-governor Santiago Gallo. Dr. Zavalía presented the image of a

totally popular revolution devoid of violence and destruction. Vicente
C. Gallo's version contrasted strongly with Zavalía's in its graphic de-
scription of a bloody revolution filled with political persecution. [28]
    In between the two eyewitness accounts of the Tucumán revolution
presented in the Chamber of Deputies on June 18, Delfín Gallo explained
and defended the earlier political compromises he had worked out with
Roca and his brother Santiago. Delfín honestly believed that Juan Posse's
candidacy would have been accepted by the Juaristas, and he had been
surprised by their request for so many political posts. Later that day
Deputy Gallo dismissed the election compromises as factors that contributed to the revolution. As far as he was concerned, the revolution had
been planned by the president. To prove his point, Gallo noted that
Cordobese troops had been used to attack the only province that had not
voted for Cordobese president Juárez Celman. Gallo's statement was the
strongest he had yet made against the president, and it placed the incident outside the realm of local issues and into the category of political
vengeance. [29] This speech, more than any other uttered that day, in-
dicted the President.
    Throughout the investigation the President refused to comment on
Deputy Gallo's accusations. He neither defended himself nor chose to
separate his personal involvement from that of his associates in Tucumán.
The only statement reflecting the President's views came from Minister
Wilde on June 13 and 18. On June 13 Wilde agreed with the critics of the
revolution that national officials had exceeded their authority in Tucumán, but after all:

> The President is not the tutor of his employees;
> he cannot, certainly, be correcting them at every
> moment for deeds related to their private life. The
> only thing he has the right to say is this: You
> must carry out your duties.

> I am sure . . . that if there are federal employ-
> ees who, because they make revolutions, have
> forgotten to fulfill their duties, the President will
> punish them immediately. [30]

Four days later President Juárez Celman fired Eudoro Vázquez from his
job in the post office. [31]

FEDERAL INTERVENTION

    By June 18 the Chamber of Deputies resolved to have federal troops
sent to Tucumán to restore order. This, in fact, meant that the revolution had succeeded. Following Dr. Zavalía's recommendations, new elections took place for the entire legislature as well as for the governor.
    The decision to depose the legislature exceeded the revolutionaries'
most optimistic hopes, and it remains unclear exactly why Zavalía chose
to remove those elected officials. Many politicians close to Juárez Celman
opposed the idea. In a letter to Roca, Pellegrini reported:

> As for the legislature, they also intend to annul
> its authority, and the situation there is much more
> difficult . . . . I don't know how they will do it.
> The precedent is a horrible one. . . . I am posi-
> tive that the President did not know that the rev-
> olution was about to break out in the moment it
> did. His friends calculated that once they began
> they would not be abandoned. [32]

Evidently the President agreed with Zavalía that a new Tucumán legislature would best serve the new governor. In a letter written sometime later to Roca, Juárez Celman called the incident a piece of "luck" for the nation and for the party. [33]

The Porteño press greeted the Tucumán incident with heavy criticism of the President's decision to send a personal emissary, despite the precedent for such maneuvers. Prior to June 12 the popular press expressed the belief that events in Tucumán should be resolved by local authorities. [34] After the invasion of Tucumán the tone of the Porteño press commentaries became more bitter. [35] No newspaper remained in Tucumán to record the local reactions to national policy. The editor of *El orden* had been jailed, and *El deber* had not operated since Posse first imprisoned Bores.

When Congress decided to authorize intervention in Tucumán, the Porteño press criticized the legislators for not investigating the situation themselves. No legislator had voted against intervention, yet all the evidence presented had been clearly biased. As *La prensa* put it: "In all, we believe that the Congress, in having voted for the overthrow of the Governor of Tucumán without placing any sanctions, without paying respect to the legitimacy of his title, . . . has renounced its right to oversee the presidential power to examine the constitutionality of Sr. Posse's election." [36] Mitre's *La nación* merely blamed Juárez Celman for his desire to revenge the loss of the Tucumán presidential votes. The only Porteño paper that justified Congress's actions was *Sud América*, though it gave no reasons for its position. [37] None of the journalists sought to uncover the important role played by the provincial revolutionaries themselves.

After the August 10 elections that resulted in Lídoro Quinteros's election as governor and a Juarista legislature, Tucumán began to return to normal. Dr. Zavalía departed Tucumán shortly thereafter, and Juárez Celman eventually rewarded him by naming him to the Supreme Court. Thus the unicato had officially begun by turning out one group of Tucumán elites for another while doling out rewards to those who cooperated with presidential desires.

But what role did President Juárez Celman play in the Tucumán affair? Did he order the revolution? More likely he stood by while his friends in Tucumán planned it. If anyone had conspired in Córdoba with the Tucumán revolutionaries, most likely it was Juárez Celman's brother, Marco Juárez, the assistant chief of police. Certainly the president got little cooperation from the revolutionaries once the new government had been elected.

SUGAR POLITICS AND THE AFTERMATH OF REVOLUTION

Local Tucumán politicians rejoiced over their victory. To them it not only meant a Juarista victory; it actually signified a greater independence of action for them, despite their apparent allegiance to the PAN and to the President. Thus the Juaristas proceeded to map out a course totally unacceptable to the President: protecting and expanding the sugar industry.

During the fighting and the following period of national intervention, few rebels stopped to comment on their future plans. Their goals, however, became obvious when Quinteros became governor. He wanted the new local government to pay full attention to the sugar industry. Frustrated by Juárez Celman's sugar politics, especially his May 1887 message to Congress, in which he specially warned legislators about catering to the sugar interests by raising tariffs, Governor Quinteros planned to make the sugar industry too important to ignore. In a September message to the provincial legislature he stated his plan:

> When I became Governor I took the opportunity to
> say to you that I was a firm believer in the use of
> credit, in progress and in the continued economic
> transformation of the province; and I can tell you
> that this promise will be fulfilled immediately upon
> the passage of the legislation that I have author-
> ized. And we must hurry to regain lost time. The
> rest of the provinces with the help of loans have
> made surprising progress that enriches them as
> centers of production, while Tucumán, despite its
> valuable industries and feracious land, can not
> develop itself with the same ease because it lacks
> the capital to dedicate to industry and produc-
> tion.[38]

Like his predecessor Quinteros proposed a provincial bank. Similarly, he knew that an outside loan would be the only way to buy the
gold reserves required by national law. This time Quinteros asked the
legislature to sanction a six million peso loan, seventy percent of which
would be used to underwrite the Banco Provincial. The other thirty percent would be set aside for "other necessities related to hygiene and our
social progress."[39] The province could wait for running water, but not
for money. By May 4, 1888 the Tucumán legislature provided immediate
funds for the Banco Provincial from a Banco Nacional loan. Though the
initial funding was meager, at least it provided a start.

Simultaneously General Roca did his best in Europe to help Tucumán. The province named him its official representative and he thereupon
contracted a 3,024,000 gold peso loan for them through a syndicate headed
by Otto Bemberg and Company. Roca and Bemberg transacted this loan
on May 5, and the Tucumán government immediately ratified the agreement. The foreign loan assured the Banco Provincial a firm footing as
well as a new source of industrial financing.[40]

Sugar industrialists had no qualms about the new bank, since Governor Quinteros appointed the most powerful industrialists to direct its
future. Clodomiro Hileret was named president of the new bank and Juan
Nougués became a bank director, along with fellow industrialist Vicente
García. With good friends doling out credit and a fresh supply of currency that ultimately far exceeded its legal limitations, many Tucumán
industrialists began to commit themselves to a plan of extensive land and
machinery purchases.

The Banco Provincial was merely the first of a number of ambitious
schemes planned by the governor and his allies. After the Banco Provincial had been set up, they proceeded to plan a Banco Hipotecario
Agrícola. This new provincial land mortgage bank, similar to the Banco
Hipotecario de la Provincia de Buenos Aires, would specialize in short-
term loans for planters. The sponsors of the new bank, the Portalis
Carbonnier y Frères Company, had good reason to back such a venture.
As the principal private money lender to sugar industrialists, the Portalis
company needed assurance that its burden could be shared and protected.[41] The proposed Banco Hipotecario Agrícola could have helped Tucumán during the panic years of 1890-1891 by reducing the need to seek
loans at often usurious rates, especially after the Banco Nacional closed
its doors there. But the bank, like other dreams at the end of the
eighties, never came true.

Efforts to help the sugar industry by revising the tax laws were
more successful than the ill-fated bank. Since 1874 sugar license taxes,
the principal local sugar tax had been periodically revised to take into
consideration technological sophistication and increased division of labor
within the sugar industry. As machines became more complex, so did the
tax laws.

TABLE 4.1

SUGAR LICENSES TAXES (*PATENTES*)

Year	Class	Tax
1872	Any *ingenio* or distillery	5 Bolivian pesos/ cuadra^2 of 200 surcos
1874	1st - iron *trapiche*	8 ps./cuadra^2 of 200 surcos
	2nd - wooden trapiche	6
	3rd - land without ingenio or distillery	5
1879	1st - water or steam driven iron trapiches, centrifuge, vacuum pans	4.50 ps. fts./cuadra^2 of 168 surcos[a]
	2nd - same without vacuum pans	4.00
	3rd - same as 2 without centrifuge	3.75
	4th - animal-driven iron trapiche and centrifuge.	3.50
	5th - same as 4 without centrifuge	3.25
	6th - wooden trapiche	2.75
	Non-industrial plantations	2.00
1881	1st - iron trapiches, steam engine, cent. and "triple effect"	4.00 ps./hectare of .61 cuadras
	2nd - water or steam driven iron trapiches, centrifuges and vacuum pans	3.25
	3rd - same as 2 without vacuum pans	2.75
	4th - same as 3 without centrifuge	2.50
	5th - animal-driven iron trapiches, centrifuge.	2.00/hectare
	6th - no centrifuge	1.75
	7th - wooden trapiche	1.25
	Non-industrial plantations and cane sold to industrialists	1.25
1882	1st - 7th same	
	Cane purchased by 1st class ingenios	2.75/hectare
	Cane purchased by 2nd class ingenios	2.00
1884	1st - same as in 1881	3.50/hectare (m/n)
	2nd - same as in 1881	2.80
	3rd - same as in 1881	2.40
	4th - same as in 1881	2.20
	5th - same as in 1881	1.75
	6th - same as in 1881	1.50
	7th - same as in 1881	1.10
	Cane purchased by 1st class ingenio	2.40
	Cane purchased by 2nd class ingenio	1.75
1888	1st - same as in 1881	3.50/hectare = 50,000 kilos cane
	2nd - same as in 1881	2.80
	3rd - same as in 1881	2.40
	4th - have centrifuges	2.20
	5th - wooden trapiches	1.10

(continued)

TABLE 4.1 (continued)

Year	Class	Tax
1888	Cane purchased by 1st class ingenio	2.40
	Cane purchased by 2nd class ingenio	1.75
	Non-industrial plantation	1.10
1889	1st - capable of producing at least 100,000 arrobas of sugar	1500. pesos
	2nd - capable of producing 80-10,000 arrobas	1000.
	3rd - capable of producing less than 80,000 arrobas	500.
	Non-industrial plantations	1.10/hectare

[a]peso fuerte of 1875 = 1.033 peso of 1881
1 Bolivian peso = .578 peso of 1881

The tax revisions of 1888 and 1889 attempted to do several things. First of all, the 1888 revisions simplified tax categories and spread the tax burden among a larger group of plantation owners by reintroducing a separate tax for the non-industrial plantation. Second, instead of taxing land by its measurement, the 1888 law redefined the hectare as the amount of land needed to produce 50,000 kilos of cane. The 1889 revisions produced even greater changes. For the first time since 1874 sugar factories would not be taxed by the kind of equipment, but by how well the equipment operated.

The new tax structure particularly aided the most powerful sugar factories. Those who could produce at the lowest per unit cost now paid no taxes on any sugar they produced above 100,000 arrobas. Their land no longer formed the tax base, so they could grind larger amounts of company cane without suffering an increased tax. The large factories were also freed from reporting how much cane they purchased from independent growers, while the independent growers could no longer depend on having their tax paid by the industrialists who purchased their crop. When this bill was discussed in the provincial legislature, its defenders justified the new tax as easier to collect and less prone to tax evasion.[43] No one claimed it would encourage the construction of factories with larger production capabilities or the growth of large landed estates, but such developments soon followed the passage of the 1889 license law. The Padilla family's large land purchases in 1890 and the giant factories conceived at this time (Santa Ana, La Florida, renovation of Nueva Baviera) proved that provincial tax laws encouraged the growth of the sugar industry in Tucumán.[44]

Everyone connected with the sugar industry, as well as those who contemplated entering the sugar business, seemed caught up with the euphoric years of the Quinteros administration. Aided by official policies, liberal credit, favorable tax laws and the passage of the Ley de Conchabo to ensure a stable work force, farmers and industrialists alike turned to sugar. Some of the business deals contracted in the eighties turned into financial nightmares after 1895, but at the time few thought about the dangers inherent in the sugar industry.

Even the governor himself became more personally involved in the sugar industry. As early as 1884 Quinteros had set up a sugar plantation with Martín Posse.[45] After 1888 the governor bought more land in southern Tucumán. Eventually Clodomiro Hileret bought the property in the south to supply cane to his new Santa Ana factory. Quinteros remained in the sugar business, however, as he had purchased part of the ownership rights to the giant Concepción factory in 1887, and he remained co-owner until 1896. Thereafter, the ex-governor continued to defend the sugar industry as a lobbyist in Buenos Aires.

The Quinteros administration (1887-1890) coincided with the congressional campaign to raise the tariff on imported sugar by charging different duties for refined and unrefined sugar. Thus sugar politics emerged as a dominant theme in national as well as local-level politics in the Juárez Celman presidency. Yet the president himself opposed such politics and could do nothing to prevent his party members from advocating protective policies. Juaristas had proclaimed their allegiance to the man but not to his economic theories.

Governor Quinteros and his associates exemplified the sophisticated provincial caudillos who learned to survive national unification during the eighties. The revolution in Tucumán proved that old-time federalism had learned new tactics during the unicato. No longer did caudillos need their gaucho clothes. Now they could call out the local police or, if necessary, force federal intervention. Congress became the arena from which the new caudillo could protect his home province and advance his personal ambitions. For this reason the Chamber of Deputies consistently voted for intervention; no one dared to deny the desires they all shared for power and glory. These feelings were not restricted to the PAN party. Even members of the opposition, as seen by the Gallo and Colombres families, would resort to the same tactics as the unicato. Rather than a party, the unicato became a state of mind that encouraged self-indulgence and quick solutions.

ENDNOTES TO CHAPTER IV

1. Telegram read by Minister of the Interior Eduardo Wilde, Diputados, June 13, 1887, p. 143.

2. Ibid., June 18, 1887, p. 197.

3. Vicente C. Gallo, "Recuerdos de juventud. Mi primera actuación pública en la política. [Tucumán hace 55 años]," *Sustancia*, 1:3 (diciembre 1939):343-344.

4. Ibid., pp. 344-345; David Peña, *Viaje político del Dr. Bernardo de Irigoyen al interior de la República, (julio, agosto y septiembre de 1885)* (Buenos Aires: A. Moën, 1885).

5. Enrique Achaval to Dardo Rocha, April 20, 1886, AGN/ADR, 1886 política; Juan B. La Croix to Dardo Rocha, January 22, 1886, AGN/ADR, 1886 política.

6. José Padilla to Juárez Celman, October 11, 1884, AGN/AJC, 1884 correspondencia; José Padilla to Juárez Celman, November 15, 1885, AGN/AJC, 1885 correspondencia; Silvano Bores to Juárez Celman, November 15, 1885, AGN/AJC, 1885 correspondencia.

7. Carlos Bouquet Roldan to Juárez Celman, December 14, 1885, AGN/AJC, 1885 correspondencia.

8. Argentine Republic, *El Parlamento argentino*, pp. 350, 368, 398.

9. José Padilla to Juárez Celman, December 9, 1885; December 13, 1885, AGN/AJC, 1885 correspondencia; Roca to Juárez Celman, March 4, 1886, AGN/AJC, 1886 telegramas.

10. Bores to Juárez Celman, January 26, 1886, AGN/AJC, 1886 correspondencia.

11. Argentines voted separately for President and Vice-President. Pellegrini to Juárez Celman, April 2, 1886, AGN/AJC, 1886 telegramas.

12. Silvano Bores to Juárez Celman with postscript from Juárez Celman to Pellegrini, February 15, 1886, AGN/AJC, 1886 correspondencia; Pellegrini to Juárez Celman, February 8, 1886, February 23, 1886, AGN/AJC, 1886 correspondencia.

13. Pellegrini to Juárez Celman, February 17, 1886, AGN/AJC, 1886 correspondencia.

14. Gallo, "Recuerdos de Juventud," pp. 345-346, José Posse to D. Sarmiento, September 6, 1886, Castro, *Epistolario entre Sarmiento y Posse*, II:565-566.

15. Diputados, June 18, 1887, p. 197.

16. Ibid., p. 197.

17. Bores to Juárez Celman, August 26, 1886, AGN/AJC, 1886 correspondencia.

18. Martín Posse to Juárez Celman, August 14, 1886, AGN/AJC, 1886 correspondencia. José Posse expressed similar beliefs in an impending Tucumán revolution that would be made with the consent of both the President and General Roca. José Posse to D. Sarmiento, October 19, 1886, Castro, *Epistolario entre Sarmiento y Posse,* II:570.

19. Raquel Lanzetti, Norma Pavoni and Norma D. Riquelme de Lobo, "Aportes para el estudio de tres intervenciones a la provincia de Tucumán (1887-1893-1905)," *Cuaderno de la Cátedra de Historia Argentina,* Serie I, No. 2 (Córdoba: Universidad Nacional de Córdoba, 1968), pp. 3-4; *El orden,* October 16, 1886, p. 1.

20. *El orden,* April 28, 1887, p. 1; April 4, 1887, p. 1.

21. *La tribuna nacional,* November 11, 1886, p. 1; ibid., November 13, 1886, p. 1.

22. Irene García de Saltor, Ana María Musso Coloma de Risco, Mirta Elena Oliva, Nilda Esther Hernández and Felicidad María Carreras, "Crónica de la epidemia del cólera en Tucumán," *Cuadernos de Humanidades; aportes para la historia de Tucumán,* Facultad de Humanidades, 1:2 (Tucumán: Universidad del Norte "Santo Tomas de Aquino," n.d.):7-23.

23. Ibid., pp. 26-27.

24. Diputados, June 1, 1887, pp. 69-71.

25. Ibid., p. 74.

26. See Deputy Mansilla's speech, ibid., pp. 76-78.

27. Dr. Zavalía's account of his incident can be found in ibid., June 18, 1887, p. 189.

28. Ibid., p. 201. This account was given anonymously.

29. Ibid., pp. 196-198.

30. Ibid., June 13, 1887, p. 152.

31. Argentine Republic, *Registro Nacional de la República de Argentina, 1887* (Buenos Aires: Ministerio de Justicia e Instrucción Pública, 1887), p. 395; Lanzetti, *et al.,* "Aportes," p. 9.

32. Pellegrini to Roca, June 30, 1887, Museo Roca, *Documentos,* VII:12.

33. Undated letter from Juárez Celman to Roca written after July 8, 1887, Museo Roca, *Documentos,* VII:17.

34. *La prensa,* June 8, 1887, p. 3.

35. Ibid., June 19, 1887, p. 3.

36. Ibid., July 1, 1887, p. 3.

37.   *La nación*, July 16, 1887, p. 1; *Sud América*, July 16, 1887, p. 2.

38.   Governor Quinteros, Message to the Legislature, September 3, 1887, *Compilación*, XII:277-278.

39.   Ibid., p. 305.

40.   Ibid., XII:266-267.

41.   Quinteros, Message to the Legislature, February 1889, ibid., XIV: 462-463.

42.   1872 License Law, Alfredo Bousquet, *Estudio sobre el sistema rentístico de la provincia de Tucumán de 1820 a 1876* (Tucumán: La Razón, 1878), pp. 87-88; 1874 law, *Compilación*, V:347; 1879 law, ibid., VII:235; 1881 law, ibid., pp. 480-481; 1882 law, *Boletín oficial*, 13 (1882), pp. 86-87; 1884 law, *Compilación*, X:41-42; 1888 law, ibid., XII:534-535; 1889 law, ibid., XIV:102.   1 arroba = 25 pounds.

43.   Stated by Martín Posse, February 8, 1889, AHL, Senado, I:363.

44.   Guy, *Politics and the Sugar Industry in Tucumán, Argentina, 1878-1900*, Appendix A, pp. 316-325.

45.   Roberto Hat, *Almanaque, guía de Tucumán para 1884* (Buenos Aires: Guillermo Kraft, 1885), p. 152.

CHAPTER V
1890: National Revolution and Depression

The political and economic excesses of the Generation of Eighty rapidly took their toll in Argentina. Politically, the numerous federal interventions in provincial governments marked the unicato as a regime that brooked no opposition. Continued electoral fraud further reinforced opponents' allegations of the inherent corruption of the group in power. Economically, inflation and grandiose public projects heightened the speculative mood of the eighties. To raise money for its various ventures, the Juárez Celman government sold off national railroads and added more Argentine bonds and land certificates to already overburdened European stock markets. At home, confronted with spiraling inflation and increased financial obligations, the national government resorted to printing more money. Indicative of the rapidly deteriorating situation, the gold premium on paper pesos rose from 55 in February 1889 to 106 in September of the same year. By April it had reached 209 percent, just six years after the gold and paper peso had stood at par.[1] The high cost of gold and the decreased value of the paper peso led many banks to bankruptcy.

The Juaristas' failure to control their greed and political ambitions led to the formation of a new political coalition intent upon destroying the old political order. In mid-1889 a new group called the Unión Cívica called for the end of corruption and financial recklessness. Supported by such distinguished elites as Bartolomé Mitre and Bernardo de Irigoyen, the group first appeared in Buenos Aires and then found adherents throughout the Republic. Threatened by the growing ranks of the Unión Cívica and subjected to a constant barrage of criticism from the press, President Juárez Celman responded with a series of new cabinet appointments, but he failed to rally support. Even his party refused to help its leader. Aware of the need to place the blame somewhere, the PAN willingly sacrificed the president as a scapegoat rather than lose control of the government.[2]

After months of rumor about armed rebellion, the Unión Cívica launched its long-anticipated revolution on July 26, 1890. Aided by disgruntled members of the army, police and firemen stationed in Buenos Aires, the revolutionaries tried to seize power. Unfortunately the plotters planned the revolution poorly and executed it in worse fashion. PAN leaders succeeded in persuading Juárez Celman to resign and insisted that Vice-President Pellegrini assume the presidency. With government forces in firm control, Pellegrini set out to form a new government with Julio Roca as Minister of the Interior.[3]

The 1890 rebellion had culminated in the overthrow of the president without imposing political reforms. The new president directed all of his energies into staving off an impending financial crisis and maintaining social order. He had little interest in political reform. Consequently members of the Unión Cívica continued to plan revolutions.

The Revolution of 1890 and the ascension of Carlos Pellegrini to the presidency had drastic repercussions in Tucumán. At first the Juarista government there became caught up in the resignations that followed the revolution. The subsequent search for a new Tucumán governor, as well as for a suitable candidate to succeed Pellegrini, added new tensions to local politics. The province's reputation as a Roquista stronghold, along with the notoriety produced by its powerful sugar industry, got Tucumán involved in subtle PAN party battles. Besides the political events, economic programs also undermined Tucumán's earlier sense of well-being. When President Pellegrini disclosed how he would help the nation recover financially, it became clear that the Tucumán economy would be particularly hard hit by fiscal reforms. New national production taxes (impuestos internos) on alcohol, tobacco and eventually on wine and sugar helped pay the costs of national recovery. Tucumán thus figured so prominently in the post-1890 period that it was impossible for the province to cushion itself from these events.

During these confusing times from 1890 to 1893, sugar played a pivotal role. National and local leaders all wanted sugar taxes to solve grave financial problems. Unfortunately, sugar revenues failed to satisfy them and attempts to increase taxes heightened political tensions. Sugar politics helped solidify discontent in Tucumán and made it an ideal place to foment rebellion. Thus it seemed logical that disgruntled Tucumán elites should join with the group that called itself the Unión Cívica Radical, which advocated revolution as the only way to bring about a new era in Argentine politics.

TUCUMÁN AND THE REVOLUTION OF 1890

Even before hostilities broke out in Buenos Aires in July 1890, evidence of growing political discontent could be sensed in Tucumán. For several months Governor Quinteros had been dividing his time between Tucumán and Buenos Aires. His commuting allowed him to keep up with the rapidly changing events in the national capital but also provoked bitter criticism back at home, especially from the local Unión Cívica. The Tucumán branch had been formed by many politicians displaced by the 1887 revolution, and they were quite willing to see Quinteros overthrown along with Juárez Celman. José Posse, Santiago Gallo, Juan M. Terán, Juan Posse and Eudoro Avellaneda all served as officers for this new party.[4] Cognizant of an impending revolution in Buenos Aires and afraid of its possible repercussions in Tucumán, Quinteros resigned on June 12.

Quinteros did not leave so abruptly that he could not name a loyal successor. Silvano Bores, his Minister of Government, replaced him. The July rebellion in Buenos Aires, however, along with concerted pressure from the Tucumán Unión Cívica, forced Bores to resign. His mid-September farewell speech claimed that his sacrifice would save Tucumán the embarrassment of a government associated with the recently fallen president.[5]

The election of a new Tucumán governor not directly associated with the Juárez Celman government provided a preview of how the PAN would respond to growing pressure to share power with its former enemies. It also showed the strains such compromises could place on elected officials. Since there was no incumbent governor to dictate the outcome of elections, new groups could win elections provided they offered the best preelectoral bargains. The PAN tried to prevent this by cajoling its opponents to back an acceptable PAN candidate. Miguel Nougués became the PAN's choice for governor. To appeal to the more conservative elements of the Unión Cívica, Nougués promised to appoint old Liberales to his cabinet, including enemy Pepe Posse.[6] In a similar maneuver, the Unión Cívica nominated an equally respectable and conservative member of the community, Próspero García. García, a sixty-four-year-old former national deputy for Tucumán (1860-1866; 1878-1880), was an old-time Mitrista and respected Tucumán elite.[7] He won over Nougués by promising to share patronage with the PAN and the Unión Cívica. Once he became governor on October 15, García proceeded to appoint men from both groups to his administration.

Governor García soon became the victim of circumstances similar to those suffered by Juan Posse in 1886. Both lost the support of the groups whose compromise had led to their respective elections. Both found themselves caught in a combination of provincial intrigue and official disinterest in the fate of the Tucumán governor. In contrast to the 1887 revolt, however, those who plotted to overthrow Governor García in 1893 were not rewarded by the federal government. A long and severe military intervention was followed by the election of a man not associated with the rebels. The 1893 revolution in Tucumán thus marked the limits of federalism, as the caudillos of Tucumán discovered the costs of rebelling in post-1890 Argentina.

One of the first blows to the García government was caused by his own party's desertion. The new governor lost the support of the Unión Cívica just three months after the election, in a fight over how much patronage that party would receive.[8] This left the García administration without firm allies and beset by the lingering after-effects of Juarista regimes and the 1890 panic. When he tried to repair the damages of earlier administrations, Governor García discovered that even his best intentions displeased everyone.

The borrowing spree of the Quinteros administration had left the provincial treasury in shambles. The new government inherited many debts and few resources. Its principal obligation was the foreign loan. Tucumán had to repay the gold debt, but this commitment became untenable as national banks closed and the price of gold continued to rise.[9] Governor García met the first scheduled payment by literally emptying the treasury, but he had few hopes of finding income or credit to meet the next payment in June 1891. Consequently, he sent his Finance Minister, Benjamín Aráoz, to Buenos Aires. There he spoke with Marco Avellaneda, Julio Roca and President Pellegrini in the hope that federal officials would lend Tucumán 100,000 pesos. Everyone seemed sympathetic but no one had any money.[10]

Governor García then decided to renegotiate the terms of the loan. Provincial officials contacted Otto Bemberg and Company, and in June 1891 the two parties had worked out an agreement whereby the lenders agreed to suspend amortization of the provincial debt for ten years. In the meantime Tucumán proposed to pay the service charges by turning over the dividends on national bonds owned by the Banco Provincial de Tucumán and deposited in the newly formed Caja de Conversión. The agreement was confirmed by President Pellegrini.[11]

Despite presidential sanction and its conformation to some laws, the 1891 contract violated other national banking legislation. Consequently, the head of the Caja de Conversión refused to deliver the interest payments to Tucumán. Ricardo Pillado, the Caja's chief officer, justified his refusal in a series of letters written to Victorino de la Plaza.[12] Pillado stubbornly refused to give Tucumán its money and the debt remained unpaid until Pillado resigned and subsequent negotiations with both the federal government and foreign money lenders led to a new contract in March 1893.[13]

Tucumán was but one of several provinces that had contracted loans abroad during the eighties. All of them had to be renegotiated and the federal government in the form of the President, Congress and the head

of the Caja de Conversión became intimately involved in the negotiations.
Some of the loans should never have been solicited, for a number of provinces even in the best of circumstances could not have afforded them. Yet
even foreign observers noted that Tucumán stood out from the others:

> The condemnation which has been righteously be-
> stowed upon the recklessness of the River Plate
> borrowing scarcely applies to this particular prov-
> ince, which has "gone by the wall," not so much
> from any dishonest or wanton extravagance of its
> own, as from the calamity which has befallen the
> Republic of which it forms a part. . . . The hold-
> ers of its bonds were supposed to be guaranteed
> by the investment of a certain proportion of the
> loan in national funds. When the national collapse
> took place, Tucumán found itself unable to fulfill
> its engagements for the very simple reason that it
> could not pay what it did not receive. It fell prey
> to the high price of gold, and to the whole fabric
> of Argentine finance.[14]

Though such analysis might have calmed holders of Tucumán bonds, it
scarcely helped Governor García. Final arrangements to pay the foreign
debt were concluded only a few months before the governor's overthrow.

While the governor sought to rearrange Tucumán's external obligations, he also set out to stabilize internal affairs. He began by again
sending his Finance Minister to Buenos Aires, this time to plead for the
reopening of the Banco Nacional. Both provincial and private funds had
been frozen when the bank closed in Tucumán and the impending sugar
zafra required great amounts of money and credit. One industrialist re-
portedly had over one million pesos deposited in the Banco Nacional at the
time it closed. The situation was so bad that Ernesto Tornquist publicly
requested that the bank free those funds so that the crisis would not ad-
versely affect his business interests in Tucumán.[15] But not even Tornquist could revive the Banco Nacional. The bank remained closed and
eventually began to liquidate its assets. Meanwhile, Tucumán had to face
the harvest with little money and with prospects that extensive debts contracted by sugar industrialists would be liquidated.

Governor García's first message to the legislature in September 1891
noted that, although the sugar harvest had been a good one, Tucumán
needed more than bumper crops to solve its problems. The provincial
treasury had been the last to benefit from the harvest. Provincial salaries
that totaled more than 70,000 m/n had not been paid because tax collection
receipts had been poor. Teachers had not been paid at all; the more qualified had abandoned Tucumán to seek work elsewhere. Confronted with
over 1,800,000 m/n in local debts, the administration had been forced to
resort to private loans to meet daily expenses.[16] To raise more money the
governor reported that new and more efficient tax measures would have to
be adopted.

The new tax program announced in the September message would be
based upon the retrieval of back taxes and new ways to collect forthcoming
taxes. To begin with, the governor created three new committees to re-
assess property in the capital and newly created Cruz Alta district, the
heart of the sugar industry.[17] He left the tax rates established in 1889,
but decreed that evaders would now face fines equal to the unpaid tax.[18]
Of course all taxpayers would be subject to the new regulations, but sugar
producers ranked as the principal contributors and debtors. With no
banks open and industrialists still burdened with machinery contracts,
they found themselves critically short of funds. The governor thus added

new enemies to the long list of critics when he began his campaign on tax evasion.

TUCUMÁN AND ACUERDO POLITICS:
THE RISE OF RADICALISM

The replacement of Juárez Celman by Pellegrini as President did little but forestall the question of political reform until the next presidential elections, scheduled for 1893. Campaign battles began as early as 1891, and Tucumán became caught up in the intrigues of the moment. In this way Governor García had to cope not only with local economic and political problems, but with presidential politics as well.

When it came time to consider who might be a presidential aspirant, both Generals Mitre and Roca were expected to push for their own nominations. Members of the Unión Cívica favored both Mitre and Bernardo de Irigoyen. A number of people backed President Pellegrini, but he refused to be considered as a candidate. Because the country seemed to be on the verge of chaos due to the activities of the Unión Cívica, both Mitre and Roca struck upon an agreement made with Pellegrini's consent. The two generals presented an *acuerdo*, or patriotic agreement, to support only one list of candidates for the next election and thereby avoid conflict. Soon after the March 1891 acuerdo became public, a group within the Porteño Unión Cívica, previously allied with Mitre, disavowed the pact. They renamed themselves the Unión Cívica Radical and vowed to oppose any official candidate. [19]

Many in the Radical movement distrusted acuerdo politics. Soon after the agreement became public, newspapers like *Sud América* began to speculate about the true meaning of the acuerdo. In August 1891 this paper claimed that Roca would become the next governor of Tucumán as part of the acuerdo:

> Roca gives Mitre . . . the situation in 14 provinces . . . . Mitre gives Roca Tucumán so that Roca's party can share in the government. Roca in Tucumán would dominate the center and the north of the Republic, and the stability of the new government headed by Mitre would be assured. [20]

The newspaper continued to foment hostilities within Tucumán in order to force Roca and Mitre to make public their true intentions. The paper also tried to push federal intervention in Tucumán by publicizing the hostilities that existed in the legislature due to the governor's unpopular tax campaign. [21] *Sud América*'s final proof of Tucumán's involvement in the presidential campaign came in the December 12 Tucumán election of Julio Roca to the national senate to replace Miguel Nougués. The vote of twenty-five to one in the Electoral College gave clear evidence of fixed elections. [22] Roca would work through the Tucumán seat in the Senate to retain his control in the government.

Eventually neither Roca nor Mitre ran for president. Both políticos realized that their respective candidacies would only serve to divide the nation. Their very alliance had promoted distrust and the rise of the Radicales. The Radicales had already asserted their defiance by trying to advance the candidacy of Roque Sáenz Peña, a young man from the elite with wide popularity, who favored political reform. To counter this move, Roca and Mitre jointly supported Luis Sáenz Peña, Roque's father, in the hope that the son would remove himself from the campaign. Roque withdrew and Luis and his running mate, José E. Uriburu, won the presidency and vice-presidency. Luis's election prevented the Radicales from winning but failed to stop the revolutionaries from plotting new civil disturbances, one of which would take place in Tucumán.

PELLEGRINI'S ECONOMIC REFORMS: IMPUESTOS INTERNOS

Preoccupied by both local problems and the intrigues of presidential politics, Tucumán also had to summon all its energy to cope with President Pellegrini's solutions to the 1890 financial crack. The president wanted to renegotiate the foreign debt and had to convince foreign bankers that Argentina could meet her international obligations. He planned to reassure them by creating new taxes and improving the collection of existing ones. Hopefully the bankers would loan money to Argentina to enable her to pay her most urgent debts and also to refund the foreign debt on more favorable terms. Accordingly, Pellegrini sent a message to Congress on December 18, 1890, accompanied by six bills. Three bills augmented license, stamp and tariff laws. Two bills created new production taxes on domestic commodities consumed locally, as well as export taxes for those consumed abroad. The last bill established new procedures for collection designed to eliminate fraud. In his congressional message the president urged legislators to consider the six bills as a package. Unless all were passed in the near future, the tax scheme would be unbalanced and Argentina's negotiator, Victorino de la Plaza, would have little support for his negotiations. [23]

The most unique aspect of the Pellegrini plan was the *impuesto interno* (production tax). The national industries designated to bear the new tax had flourished while protected by high tariffs and included beer, alcohol, matches and playing cards. Previously their protective duties had generated income for the government; now domestic production taxes would replace revenues lost through import substitution. The proposed tax rates were intentionally moderate in order to discourage fraud and to make sure that national products still had an advantage over their foreign counterparts. Pellegrini also emphasized that the law would be a transitory one to comply with constitutional provisions that sanctioned federal production levies only on a temporary basis and only for the purposes of defense, security and well-being of the nation. [24]

Modified versions of Pellegrini's bills, excluding the one intended to eliminate tax fraud, all passed the extraordinary congressional sessions that lasted until January 26, 1891. Congress had supported the presidential request to increase national tax revenues as quickly as possible. With the prospects of new revenue sources available to the Argentine government, Victorino de la Plaza's refunding scheme, guaranteed by a lien on customs duties, was approved by foreign bankers in January 1891. The passage of the impuesto interno laws had thus been vital to the negotiations' success. Ultimately, however, the 1891 agreement was abandoned by the Argentine government and replaced in 1893 with another agreement. [25] When that occurred, the production tax was separated from Pellegrini's original refunding plan. By that time impuestos internos were too remunerative and too controversial to abolish. In fact the impuesto interno law was a kind of Pandora's box that, once opened, could never again contain the conflicting groups that used the yearly renewal of these taxes as part of narrow political campaigns.

SUGAR POLITICS AND IMPUESTOS INTERNOS

The sugar industry became one of the industries hardest hit by annual tax battles. At first indirectly taxed through alcoholic by-products and then later directly taxed, sugar received more than its share of attention. Tax revisions that affected sugar became an emotionally charged issue, its defenders and enemies each with his own rationale. In self-defense sugar producers had to devise some sort of strategy to protect themselves from new attempts to increase national taxes.

The need for a strong sugar lobby became evident when President Pellegrini sent his last budget message to Congress on July 18, 1892. This message differed greatly from those of the previous two years, especially in the part related to domestic production taxes for 1893. Through the addition of new items to the tax rolls, namely wine and sugar, as well as an increase of more than one-hundred percent in the alcohol tax, the national government could net twelve million pesos m/n each year. For these reasons Pellegrini suggested that domestic wine pay five centavos per liter, that alcohol taxes be increased to twenty centavos, and that domestic sugar pay five centavos per kilo.

When the presidential bill reached the Chamber of Deputies' floor on November 30, 1892, their budget committee, headed by Tucumán's Francisco L. García, accepted the higher alcohol taxes but suggested that the national interest would be better served if sugar and wine taxes were not passed. [26] The new finance minister, Juan J. Romero, a close Tornquist ally, agreed with sugar and wine producers that their products should remain tax free and disclosed to legislators that a bargain had been struck between the new president Luis Sáenz Peña and the budget committee. If Congress kept the twenty-centavo alcohol tax and suppressed the sugar and wine tax, Sáenz Peña would not object. If, however, Congress suppressed all three tax increases, the President would veto the bill. [27] Even though many distillers had not been apprised of the bargaining and many deputies opposed higher alcohol taxes, Congress honored the bargain.

The congressional tax battle of 1892 disclosed that sugar politicians and producers had worked out a strategy whereby sugar would be saved from direct taxation by accepting higher alcohol taxes. In this way high alcohol taxes satisfied the President, the treasury and the sugar and wine industrialists. All the arguments about liquor as a social vice, the common nineteenth-century strategy used to justify alcohol tax increases, masked the political compromise.

Once sugar politicians had worked out this compromise they also became quite successful at keeping the customs duties at nine and seven centavos. Congress rejected sugar tariff revisions introduced by Porteño legislators in 1891 and 1892. [28] It also undermined presidential efforts to lower the tariffs in 1894 and 1898. The sugar tariffs remained constant while the alcohol tax increased.

Pellegrini initiated the alcohol tax and sponsored its first increase. Thereafter his successors, especially José E. Uriburu (1895-1898), successfully proposed a series of alcohol tax increases. This did not mean, however, that the national coffers overflowed with alcohol taxes. Despite increased liquor consumption and attempts to make tax collection as efficient as possible alcohol taxes increased, while yearly collection figures usually proved disappointing to treasury officials. (See Table 5.1). Nevertheless, President Uriburu continued to increase the alcohol tax until incoming President Roca authorized the last tax increase late in 1898.

Alcohol taxes were not the only ones subject to the whims of presidents. Wine, sugar and tobacco taxes eventually became almost as remunerative as alcohol taxes, and together they formed a major source of revenue. While taxes upon these regional products increased, taxes on littoral products such as beef and hides remained constant and cereal crops remained tax free unless they were used in the distillation of alcohol or production of beer. In other words, products from the interior, and especially the northwest, bore a much larger national tax burden than other sectors of the economy. Industrialists from Tucumán, Santa Fe and Mendoza all had reason to believe that they had been singled out for punishment, since they paid more taxes than other industrialists and received fewer benefits than other industrial groups.

TABLE 5.1

ALCOHOL TAX COLLECTION, 1892-1900 (m/n) [29]

Year	Tax	Estimated Collection	Actual Collection	Surplus	Deficit
1892	.07-.10	3,000,000	2,832,543.75		167,456.25
1893	.20	5,000,000	5,042,101.39	42,101.39	
1894	.20	5,000,000	5,203,102.66	203,102.66	
1895	.20-.30	5,000,000	5,427,596.66	427,596.66	
1896	.30	9,000,000	6,605,764.22		2,394,235.78
1897	.35	9,000,000	10,627,951.90	1,627,951.90	
1898	.60	10,500,000	7,543,769.47		2,956,230.53
1899	1.00	20,000,000	13,625,599.22		6,374,400.78
1900	1.00	16,000,000	14,674,188.14		1,325,811.86

RADICAL REBELLION IN TUCUMÁN

The new national tax structure along with the tumultuous politics of the times did nothing to help Tucumán and helped bring about the overthrow of Governor García. Caught in the middle of Roca's ambitions as Senator for Tucumán, Pellegrini's production tax scheme and conspiracies of the local Unión Cívica Radical, Governor García longed to free himself from these intrigues. To appease the Radicales he discontinued his close relationship with PAN politicians shortly before the February 1892 congressional elections. [30] His decision to separate himself from Juaristas reverberated in Buenos Aires, where everyone knew that Tucumán occupied a principal spot in Roca's acuerdo politics. García's independent stance was soon met with veiled threats. Letters began to pour in from Buenos Aires to warn García of Roca's intrigues and Mitre's intentions. Some warned him of the dissident Radicales, others of an impending revolution to be led by Quinteros and Bores. [31]

President Sáenz Peña recognized the precarious state of Tucumán politics and tried to prevent the outbreak of hostilities by having the governor resign voluntarily. The president made indirect gestures to offer the governor the Ministry of Foreign Relations in return for his resignation. When the governor did not respond to these gestures, national officials demonstrated their displeasure with him in other ways. Throughout 1892 it appeared evident that someone would try to overthrow the governor. To protect his government, Governor García requested guns from the Minister of War, Carlos Pellegrini. Pellegrini, like the President, agreed that it was not worth defending Governor García. But after procrastinating for a while, Pellegrini finally sent a shipment of guns to Tucumán. [32]

Besides incurring the dissatisfaction of leaders in Buenos Aires, Governor García lost the support of sugar industrialists. Although he was well aware of the financial burdens on industrialists due to the national alcohol tax and the attempts of the Banco Nacional to call in loans, the governor also knew that only the sugar industry could provide funds for the provincial treasury. Accordingly, his government pushed through a new and controversial sugar tax. The new tax, proposed in December, 1892, doubled the 1889-1892 tax on the productive capacity of sugar factories, as well as the per-hectare tax on plantations. It also levied a specific tax of one-half centavo per kilo of sugar manufactured in Tucumán. This new one-half centavo tax would be used specifically to make up an estimated budget deficit of 1,247,375 pesos. [33]

Sugar industrialists were caught in a difficult situation. Although well represented in the legislature they could hardly deny the governor's request without offering other possible taxes. Yet a large part of the 1892 sugar harvest still remained unsold, as sugar prices had fallen since 1891. The new taxes struck the already financially troubled small factories, which could only provide promissory notes that went unredeemed. By February 1893 even the *South American Journal* was commenting on the dissension caused by the sugar tax:

> A strong agitation has arisen amongst the sugar planters of the province of Tucumán against a tax of 1/2 percent per kilo on manufactured sugar lately sanctioned by the Provincial Government. The object of this tax is to cover a deficit in the budget estimates of the province for the current year, amounting to $1,247,375 of which no less than $683,000 is destined for the support of a force of 450 vigilantes or local militia. The sugar planters point out that the National Government is doing its best to protect the sugar industry, whilst the Provincial Government is doing its best to kill it. [34]

After his refusal to resign and the passage of needed but unpopular legislation, Governor García forced an open confrontation with his enemies. His period of office would end with new gubernatorial elections on August 16. The existing Electoral College, however, contained many men openly hostile to the governor. Since he could not hope to impose a successor with the Electoral College filled with enemies, he wanted to postpone gubernatorial elections until September 1, the same day one-third of the Electoral College would be replaced by elections. Once new electors loyal to García had been sworn into office, gubernatorial elections could proceed. Otherwise the PAN-dominated Electoral College would vote for Pedro G. Méndez, a banker and sugar industrialist closely allied to the Tornquist group, rather than for García's choice, Wellington de la Rosa. [35]

El orden, defender of the Unión Cívica Radical in this dispute, forewarned the governor in April 1893 that efforts to impose a successor would only lead to federal investigation. Yet later that month Governor García was openly plotting to have his candidates win seats in the Electoral College. [36] He then waited for the proper moment to spring his plot. President Sáenz Peña provided just such an opportunity on August 14, when he declared a state of national siege in Buenos Aires, Santa Fe and San Luis. Governor García decided to extend the state of siege to Tucumán or, at least, to use the state of siege as an excuse to postpone the gubernatorial elections. When national officials informed the governor that the state of siege should not affect elections in Tucumán it was too late. García had already sent the police to keep the Electoral College from voting for governor until September 1. With an altered Electoral College, Tucumán elected Wellington de la Rosa. [37]

In response to the governor's actions, recently retired members of the Electoral College petitioned the Minister of the Interior and the Argentine Congress to intervene in Tucumán. They wanted the old Electoral College to select the next governor and thereby annul the recent elections. As the slow bureaucratic machinery of Congress impeded a rapid decision on the matter, the scene was set for revolution.

On September 7 Tucumán Radicales led by Dr. Martín Berho, Eugenio A. Méndez and Manuel Paz started a revolution by seizing buildings in San Miguel. By the 8th a number of small villages in strategic parts of the province had been occupied by rebel forces, while other forces concentrated on the defense of the capital. After four days of fighting but no authority to intervene in an official capacity, President Sáenz Peña sent in federal troops to defend federal buildings in San Miguel. The eleventh battalion arrived in San Miguel for that end, but one of its leaders then defected to the insurgents' side by supplying them with arms and munitions.[38] The new supplies gave the rebels enough strength to seize full control of Tucumán by September 20.

Even though Congress had received complaints from Tucumán officials back in mid-August, no official decree of intervention had been sanctioned. Yet something had to be done, or otherwise the Radicales could create a stronghold in the northwest. Consequently the president sent troops from Buenos Aires to Tucumán under the control of General Francisco Bosch and accompanied by Carlos Pellegrini. It took four days to reach San Miguel because rebellious Radical activity throughout the interior had disrupted transports by the destruction of bridges and threats of derailment.[39] Once the troops were in Tucumán, mediation talks led by Pellegrini, along with the overwhelming force of loyal federal troops, ended revolutionary activity in six hours.

The end of the rebellion was just the beginning of a serious problem for Tucumán and for federal officials. Congress still had not authorized intervention and no one knew how to proceed. Who should be governor? Próspero García tried to resume his post as governor, but Minister of Interior Quintana would not recognize him. Wellington de la Rosa met a similar fate on October 15.[40] Back in Buenos Aires legislators did not begin to discuss intervention in Tucumán until December 4 and then spent a week debating four separate projects, each of which differed on who should be reelected in Tucumán. In the meantime Tucumán remained under unofficial military rule. Radicales imprisoned by government forces had to wait until an order from the Supreme Court liberated them on December 12. On December 16, Congress finally voted for federal intervention that led to new elections in the Electoral College and the provincial legislature, as well as for a new governor. An official intervenor, Domingo T. Pérez, was sent to supervise Tucumán's return to constitutional rule.

Although the Tucumán revolution occurred at the same time the Radicales made a concerted attempt to overthrow provincial governments throughout Argentina, this did not mean that Radicales in every province fomented revolutions for the same reasons. Without denying that communications networks helped coordinate activities and allowed local groups to bring in help from the outside, Radicales managed to spark violence only in those provinces where local as well as national issues proved irritating enough to generate conflict. In the Tucumán case the dissolution of the coalition that brought Próspero García to power, along with special federal and provincial tax burdens imposed upon the sugar industry, angered all Tucumán citizens. The problems that beset the sugar industry thus solidified the discontent present in Tucumán since 1890 and helped precipitate conflict there.[41]

Why had Governor García run the risk of inciting the Radicales and possible military intervention? Was it purely a local affair or merely the consequence of coordinated Radical activities? Most likely the governor's intent will never be known. Perhaps he wanted to provoke intervention and thereby put down revolutionary ferment.[42] Or maybe he tried to prove that independent provincial politics was a dream of the past. More important than the governor's motive was the reaction it provoked. If the Radicales had not been organized, most likely another group would have led the revolt. The Radical revolution was not just a "popular expression of a new social force that exploded when confronted with a government... that disparaged republic and representative government."[43] It also did not fit the picture of an incipient socialist revolt.[44] And somehow, even though the revolution had tactical similarities with contemporary Radical-inspired revolts, that did not make it part of a unified national movement. The Tucumán revolution of 1893 broke out for essentially local and selfish reasons, and its perpetrators came from the same social group as the government in power. Yet, despite its local flavor, the revolution still had its roots in national issues of the moment.

Events in Tucumán had become inextricably linked to national politics and intrigues. Long before Governor García exercised his right to name a successor, he knew that his fate had been sealed by a series of events beyond his control. Called upon to contribute to national recovery, mistrusted as a center of Roquista support and selected as a Radical target, Tucumán could no longer pretend that what happened in Buenos Aires would not affect it. At the same time, Tucumán industrialists realized that critics of the present order would seek revenge by attacking the sugar industry.

By the time new elections were finally held in 1894 Tucumán had witnessed several months of severe political repression. All groups recognized the futility of the 1893 revolt. Under the careful supervision of the federal intervenor, Tucumán elected a government that responded to the Roca-Mitre acuerdo. Dr. Benjamín Aráoz, Governor García's former finance minister, became the next governor. He in turn named Lt. Colonel Lucas Córdoba and Sixto Terán Minister of Government and of Finance, respectively. Córdoba was the intimate friend of both Roca and Tornquist; Sixto Terán was a long-time Liberal and respected mathematician. The Radicales ended up with no government posts.

Even after the occupation troops left in 1894 Tucumán did not return to normalcy. Before the province could adjust to the revolution it faced another series of crises: recurring agricultural boom and bust cycles, political crises related to federal sugar and alcohol taxes and industrial conflicts. By 1900 the province of Tucumán, by then entirely dependent upon the sugar industry and its national political alliances, completed the evolution of a mature sugar industry.

ENDNOTES TO CHAPTER V

1. Williams, *Argentine International Trade Under Inconvertible Paper Money, 1880-1900*, pp. 114-115. See also Table 9.2.

2. Roberto Etchepareborda, *Tres revoluciones: 1890-1893-1905* (Buenos Aires: Pleamar, 1968), pp. 87-91; Juan Balestra, *El noventa; una evolución política argentina;* 4th ed. (Buenos Aires: Luis Fariña Editor, 1971), pp. 206-210.

3. Ibid.

4. *El orden*, June 7, 1890, p. 1. Other adherents to the Unión Cívica included Próspero García, Federico Helguera, Delfín Jijena, Brígido Terán, Juan Manuel Terán and Sixto Terán, all former Liberales.

5. Ibid., September 18, 1890, p. 1; Resignation speech of September 16, 1890, *Compilación*, XIV:415.

6. Telegraphic interview between Próspero García and Francisco López García, September 24-25, 1890, AGN/APG, s-7, c-20, a-3, No. 14, ff. 135-154.

7. Argentine Republic, *El Parlamento argentino*, p. 388; García family tree, AGN/APG, s-7, c-20, a-3, No. 12, ff. 302-309.

8. *El orden*, December 22, 1890, p. 1. Martín Berho, one of the leaders of the 1893 revolution, had been García's Finance Minister.

9. Explained in letter from Benjamín Aráoz to Otto Bemberg, June 30, 1891, *Compilación*, XVI:155-156.

10. Benjamín Aráoz to Próspero García, February 8, 1891, AGN/APG, s-7, c-20, a-3, No. 12, f. 20; Julio Roca to Próspero García, April 20, 1891, AGN/APG, s-7, c-20, a-3, No. 13, ff. 254-255.

11. The Caja de Conversión was set up to exchange paper money for gold and then burn the paper. Pellegrini authorization, August 8, 1891, *Compilación*, XVI:155-156.

12. Ricardo Pillado to Victorino de la Plaza, June 26, 1891, AGN/AVP, s-7, c-5, a-2, No. 3, f. 346; July 1, 1891, ff. 352-353; July 21, 1891, ff. 374-375; August 18, 1891, f. 406.

13. Governor Próspero García to the Legislature, March 27, 1893, *Compilación*, XVII:198-200.

14. *Financial News*, quoted in *South American Journal*, 31 (August 29, 1891):277. Williams, *Argentine Trade*, p. 135 and 135n.

15. *Sud América*, May 20, 1891, p. 1.

16. Message to the legislature in pamphlet form, 1891, AGN/APG, p. 5-21.

17. Ibid., pp. 22-23.

18. Copy of provincial decree, October 1891, AH, Comprobantes de Contaduría, T. 211, f. 000471.

19. Thomas Francis McGann, *Argentina, the United States and the Inter-American System, 1880-1914* (Cambridge: Harvard University Press, 1957), pp. 188-189; As Próspero García noted in a letter to General Mitre on July 8, 1891: "Tucumán is the only province that has radically modified its political situation and despite this agitation continues . . . . I have no doubt that something will happen here . . . since it has been pointed out as the center of the northern provinces." García to Mitre, July 8, 1891, in Pellegrini, *Obras*, II:393.

20. *Sud América*, August 20, 1891, p. 1.

21. Ibid., September 9, 1891, p. 1.

22. Ibid., December 14, 1891, p. 1; *Compilación*, XVI:167.

23. Diputados, December 18, 1890, pp. 799-804.

24. Ibid., pp. 800-801.

25. Williams, *Argentine International Trade Under Inconvertible Paper Money, 1880-1900*, pp. 127-128.

26. Diputados, November 30, 1892, p. 379.

27. Ibid., p. 385. Romero later became an official of the Refinería Argentina.

28. 1891 attempt, Diputados, November 4, 1891, pp. 432-439; 1892 attempt, Senado, December 6, 1892, pp. 450-451.

29. Adapted from Argentine Republic, Poder Ejecutivo de la Nación, Ministerio de Hacienda, *Memorias* (1892-1900) (Buenos Aires: 1893-1901), 1899, II:161; 1900, p. 33.

30. *El orden*, January 7, 1892, p. 1.

31. José Olmos to Próspero García, July 17, 1892, AGN/APG, s-7, c-20, a-3, No. 13, ff. 137-140; Pedro Argerick to Próspero García, April 22, 1892, AGN/APG, s-7, c-20, a-3, No. 12, ff. 37-38.

32. Col. R. Bravo to Próspero García, September 16, 1892, AGN/APG, s-7, c-20, a-3, No. 12, ff. 104-105.

33. Tax law, February 1, 1893, *Compilación*, XVII:66-73; *El orden*, December 15, 1892, p. 1.

34. *South American Journal*, 34:7 (February 18, 1893):170.

35. Sommariva, *Intervenciones*, II:228-229.

36. *El orden*, April 10, 1893, p. 1; April 27, 1893, p. 1.

37. *Compilación*, XVII:244; Diputados, September 4, 1893, p. 546.

38. Etchepareborda, *Tres revoluciones*, p. 213.

39. Pellegrini, *Obras*, II:409.

40. Ibid., pp. 421-422; Sommariva, *Intervenciones*, II:236.

41. Other aspects of the relationship between sugar problems and politics can be found in Chapter VIII.

42. Lizondo Borda, *Historia de Tucumán, Siglo XIX*, p. 127.

43. Ibid.

44. Manuel García Soriano, "La condición social del trabajador en Tucumán durante el siglo XIX," p. 37.

45. Etchepareborda, *Tres revoluciones*, pp. 211-216.

President Carlos Pellegrini

Lt. Coronel Lucas A. Córdoba,
governor of Tucumán

Pedro G. Méndez

Juan Posse, 1904

President Nicolas Avellaneda,
1874-1880

Teodoro De Bary, 1907

Otto Bemberg

Ernesto Tornquist

President Julio A. Roca,
1880-1886, 1898-1904

Marco Avellaneda

Clodomiro Hileret

Salón de Maquinara,
Lules Factory, 1882.
From *Memoria histórica y
descriptiva.*

Lules Factory photos courtesy of Harvard University
Library Photographic Department, Widener Library,
Cambridge, Massachusetts.
All other photos courtesy of the Archivo General
de la Nación, Buenos Aires, Argentina.

CHAPTER VI
Industrial Crisis and Confrontation

The first battles over internal taxes had taught domestic sugar producers an important lesson: they had to organize a strong defense or risk the possibility of arbitrary taxation. The pressures to organize a lobby increased when President Sáenz Peña established a special tariff commission on January 12, 1894 to study possible ways to lower the tariff. Industrialists, especially those involved in nonexport activities, feared this investigation and the main spokesman for national industry, the Unión Industrial Argentina, organized a campaign to retain existing tariffs.[1] Most of the industrialists, however, came from the city of Buenos Aires and perceived the tariff controversy differently from regional businessmen.

Although some sugar men were members of the Unión Industrial, they set out to form their own lobby. Ernesto Tornquist and Miguel Nougués invited several industrialists to an organizational meeting held on January 23 in Buenos Aires. Besides the two organizers, Benjamín Zorilla, Lídoro Quinteros, Juan Videla, Mauricio Mayer, Jorge Frías, Vicente García, Teodoro de Bary, a Sr. Segovia of the Bemberg Company and Federico Carlisle of the Azucarera Argentina Company attended the meeting. They represented factories in Tucumán, Chaco, Formosa and Misiones, as well as the Refinería Argentina and the major alcohol distributor, Otto Bemberg. The meeting transformed sugar politics with the formation of the Centro Azucarero.[2]

For the next meeting invitations were sent to all sugar industrialists in a letter that made a militant plea to defend protective tariffs and specifically criticized the President's intention to lower the sugar tariff just as the sugar industry was about to approach its goal of self-sufficiency.

In March an even larger group of industrialists met in Buenos Aires to discuss strategy. To finance the organization they decided to assess monthly dues for factory owners according to their factory's productive capacity. Then they nominated an executive commission that instituted several important policies:[3]

1. The hiring of a special secretary (José Ceppi) to handle public relations.

2. The drafting of a petition to exempt from municipal taxes all sugar that arrived in the Federal Capital but destined for other markets.

3. The publishing of a professional journal (*Revista azucarera- La industria azucarera*) for planters as

well as industrialists to inform them of the state of
the sugar industry inside and outside Argentina.

4. The establishing of a low monthly fee for planters
and an invitation to them to join, regardless of
their number.

5. The meeting of sugar lobbyists with the members
of the Tariff Review Commission.

Some of these decisions, such as the journal, the petition and the
meeting with the Tariff Review Commission, arose logically from the desire
to make the national lobby strong and effective. The decision to invite
planters reflected local considerations, especially in Tucumán, where numerous independent planters controlled a substantial portion of the provincial cane crop. The adhesion of these planters to the Centro was
imperative because the large Tucumán factories did not produce enough
company cane to keep their machine operating at maximum efficiency. The
Centro hoped to win the planters' loyalty by including them in the organization and by supplying them with technical information usually not available except to factory owners or specialists. The Centro would then not
only receive the planters' cooperation on important issues: it would also
encourage them to grow better sugarcane.[4]

The Centro's 1894 tariff campaign, however, destroyed these early
hopes for industrial unity. The Refinería and the sugar factories, even
though they needed cane from small plantations, found it convenient to
blame planters' avariciousness to explain recent high prices. The explanation won the sugar industry a temporary reprieve from additional taxation
but also created deep resentment in Tucumán.

THE TARIFF CAMPAIGN

On April 30, 1894 the executive commission of the Centro met with
Tariff Commission members Juan Videla and Ventura Martínez Campos, the
two most likely to be responsive to the lobbyists. Juan Videla, one of the
most important shoe manufacturers in the Republic, was the president of
the Unión Industrial. He was also a member of the Centro Azucarero because he owned the Manantial sugar factory in Tucumán. The other member of the commission, Ventura Martínez Campos, was scheduled to become
president of the Unión Industrial in 1898. During the course of their
conversations the two Tariff Commission members promised to defend the
sugar industry against the proposed reductions of the sugar tariff. The
promise was then quoted in the *Revista azucarera*.[5]

Once the Centro secured Videla's and Martínez Campos's support,
the sugar lobby launched another plan. In July sugar industrialists invited Minister of Finance José A. Terry to visit Tucumán to evaluate personally the development of the sugar industry. At the same time the
invitation was extended to several senators and deputies, the president of
the Banco Nacional, the directors of the Banco de la Nación, the Banco
Hipotecario Nacional, the Banco Alemán Transatlántico and to prominent
journalists. The Centro even reserved special trains to take the guests
to Tucumán.[6]

The honored guests arrived early in July. Tucumán industrialists
dazzled their visitors with a series of tours and gourmet dinners. During
banquets at plantation chalets Terry demonstrated his recently acquired
knowledge of the sugar industry. He lauded it as the "most national"
industry and agreed with his hosts that the industry deserved recogni-
tion. He left Tucumán with the impression that he wished to see the sugar
industry progress even more.[7]

The true purpose of the Minister's trip to Tucumán soon became evident. In August, shortly before the Tariff Review Commission began its formal sessions, Terry published a *Memoria* paid for by the Centro Azucarero and dedicated to President Sáenz Peña. Terry claimed in the *Memoria* that the president had sent him on a fact-finding mission to Tucumán, at which time new information about the sugar industry became available. Contrary to rumors of great wealth, the rapid transformation of the Tucumán sugar industry had left factory owners with combined debt of approximately ten million pesos. Further, recent high sugar prices had nothing to do with windfall profits. Indeed, sugar industrialists suffered in the midst of prosperity. High shipping charges, poor crops and exorbitant cane prices had robbed industrialists of profits. Terry especially criticized the independent plantation owners. They knew factory owners could not refuse the planters' prices, so they charged what they pleased. Until the railroads based their rates on a more realistic level and planters acted more charitably toward the industrialist, there would be high sugar prices. Thus no one could blame the industrialist. Indeed, the sugar manufacturer deserved sympathy for his unfortunate plight.

Terry concluded his analysis of the sugar industry by recommending no reduction of the sugar tariff. Instead, he wanted to increase the availability of loans to industrialists, expand sugar production and lower the price of sugarcane. With these measures, along with a readjustment of the railroad charges, the sugar industry would be ready for taxation.[8] Terry's report was just what the sugar industry needed. The Centro disseminated the minister's report throughout the Republic and the journalists who had accompanied Terry supported his contentions.

Sugar lobbyists were well armed when they met with the Tariff Commission. Lobbyist Lídoro Quinteros made it clear that the Centro would never condone a tariff reduction although it would agree to a production tax "when the time comes":

> The former would not be acceptable today, tomorrow or ever. We must become self-sufficient producers of sugar because a giant part of our territory--Salta, Tucumán, Jujuy and the Chaco--can only produce sugar. It we restrict this industry, we will condemn the territory to ruin and backwardness.[9]

That same day Quinteros also defended the fortunes that had been made in sugar:

> They talk about Hileret's fortune. To this I must respond that fortunes are made in every business, no matter how bad that business might be. And this is precisely what had happened with this man. He had the luck to situate his factory on a piece of Tucumán land . . . where coffee, bananas, and tobacco grow well and where sugarcane, at any time of the year, reaches ripe maturity. This explains his success while others working around him suffer considerable losses . . . .[10]

Confronted with such articulate sugar lobbyists those in favor of lower tariffs changed their tactics. Instead of overall reductions, members of the commission introduced a motion on September 14 to lower only the tariff on refined sugar. As Martín García Merou, the proponent of this new measure, explained, the major sugar price increase came not from Tucumán processed sugar but from sugar refined in Rosario. A lower refined sugar tariff would force the Refinería Argentina to drop its prices.[11]

This time Teodoro de Bary, a business associate of Tornquist, came to the defense of the Refinería Argentina. He informed the commission that the refinery had taken measures to protect itself from arbitrary taxation. Instead of refining and selling sugar purchased from others, the Refinería now refined sugar on consignment only. Thus sugar opponents could not intimidate the Refinería Argentina by threats to change the sugar tariff. The only group that would be hurt by such a measure would be regional sugar industrialists, who would have to absorb new taxes.[12] De Bary's disclosure convinced the Commission that a partial reduction of the sugar tariff would be disastrous and García Merou withdrew his motion on September 1. The final recommendations of the Tariff Commission mirrored Terry's *Memoria*: sugar should keep its protective tariffs, but domestic sugar should be added to the list of products subject to the impuesto interno and specifically charged two and one-half centavos per kilo.

By the time Congress finally debated the 1895 tariff bill, the Centro Azucarero and the Porteño press had made the general public well aware of the sugar industry's attitude toward projected tariff revisions. A series of articles in *La prensa,* the *Boletín* of the Unión Industrial and the *Revista azucarera* reinforced the Terry report. A pamphlet composed of all the articles written by José Ceppi (under the pseudonym of Aníbal Latino) was published as a supplement to the *Revista* and sent to the proper individuals.[13]

The Tariff Commission report did not end the sugar tariff controversy. However, President Sáenz Peña helped sugar lobbyists by accepting the findings of the Tariff Commission and incorporating them into the presidential tariff message of October 8. Though he noted that sugar customs receipts had fallen from 1,750,494 to 874,602 gold pesos, he was willing to make up the difference in a production tax.[14] Although the President now favored no change in the sugar tariff, certain deputies did.

In opposition to presidential wishes, Deputy Francisco Barroetaveña, a Radical politician from Buenos Aires, renewed the drive to reduce the sugar tariff. His defense rested upon two arguments: the populist claim that high tariffs taxed the poor consumer and the classic Porteño complaint that sugar tariffs created international reprisals against other Argentine products, namely cattle and wheat. Tariff debates continued to divide the Chamber of Deputies on a regional basis, and at one point several deputies from the coast tried to push for an immediate production tax on sugar. Finally, on November 22 Barroetaveña dropped the impuesto interno proposal and concentrated on having a one-centavo tariff reduction authorized for both refined and unrefined sugar. The proposal passed 30-14, but the Senate immediately rejected the revisions by refusing to consider them. The 1895 sugar tariff remained at nine and seven centavos.[15]

THE SUGAR CRISIS IN TUCUMÁN

While sugar industrialists poured their time and money into the Centro Azucarero's national campaign, the provincial administration in Tucumán returned to daily concerns following the 1893 revolution. Although Governor Aráoz had been elected through federal intervention and the auspices of the acuerdo, the official support gave him little assurance that he could resolve the financial and political problems that had plagued his predecessor. The tariff battle in Congress did not help him either, as the partisan campaign had alienated many Tucumán planters. They joined the ranks of those industrialists on the verge of bankruptcy. These two groups would later provide vocal opposition to any more partisan campaigns.

Many sugar industrialists had real fears that they might lose their establishments to creditors. The tax burden on small factory owners, as well as on some of the larger ones, had become formidable. By May 1884 Domingo García of the San Andrés factory owed 3,085.70 pesos for the provincial sugar tax dating back to November 1893.[16] The Padilla family had signed notes valued at 3,387.15 pesos. Méndez and Chavanne of Lastenia factory owed 16,000 pesos.[17] In April 1894 Alfredo Bousquet, head of the provincial tax office, estimated that certain uncollected back taxes (patente and *contribución directa*) from 1892 to 1894 amounted to 28,186.66 pesos and that the Capital district alone had unpaid taxes dating back to 1889 that amounted to 123,191.99 pesos most of it uncollectible.[18] These provincial debts were just the beginning. Many factory owners owed the federal government for unpaid alcohol taxes, and Abraham Medina of San Vicente factory already found himself under prosecution.[19] With all these mounting obligations factory owners turned to the province for help.

Contrary to their expectations, sugar industrialists discovered that Governor Aráoz had no intention of changing Próspero García's tax laws. The new governor not only kept the 1893 tax: he also hired additional tax collectors. Since most people had believed that the controversial one-half centavo sugar production tax had been a temporary measure, they were, as usual, enraged. *El orden* opposed the governor's decision to keep the production tax, and it noted that the existence of such a local tax might encourage the national government to add sugar to items taxed by the impuesto interno.[20] The governor resisted these admonitions. No other industry could withstand higher taxes, and local government needed money. However, the governor did help planters and industrialists by first extending the final date to pay taxes and then by suggesting the legislature restructure the tax system to make it more equitable.

On November 3, 1894, the governor presented his new tax scheme to the legislature. In order to "tax the contributors more equitably and proportionately, and therefore eliminate resistance or criticisms that have some legal basis," he offered the legislators four alternatives:

1. Increase the license tax 350 percent on sugar machinery, double the land tax and eliminate the one-half centavo production tax;

2. Raise the production tax to three-quarters centavo per kilo, keep the land tax the same and eliminate the license tax on machinery;

3. Keep the one-half centavo tax and double the land tax and eliminate the machinery tax; or

4. Raise the sugar plantation land tax from three to ten pesos per hectare and eliminate the production and machinery tax.[21]

These proposals offered a number of advantages to factory owners, but few to independent plantation owners. Only the second plan would have been beneficial to the landowner, although no industrialist would have sanctioned an increased production tax.

The new tax law passed in 1895 was not what the governor had expected, but was rather a compromise. It eliminated the machinery tax, yet kept both the production and land tax at the 1894 rate. This modified tax package benefited the factory owners and at the same time did not harm any other group. Although the new tax law would not yield as much income to the provincial treasury as the 1894 law, the tax change offered the best solution for all concerned. Even the province would benefit so long as the factory owners actually paid the production tax.[22]

The independent planters had protected themselves against additional taxation, and soon after they went one step farther to ensure their political and industrial interests. During a meeting of independent plantation owners on August 10, 1895 the Centro de Cañeros was formed. They initially created the group to "decide which methods were appropriate to defend themselves against the extremely low prices for sugar that serve as the base for the price of sugarcane." [23] Among the founders were six of twenty-three Tucumán legislators who had voted on the 1895 sugar tax law. [24] They did not see themselves as outspoken opponents of industrialists, but they wanted safeguards during moments of crisis. This Centro, along with strong representation in the local legislature, ensured the planters' interests.

By the time new tax law became effective market conditions had changed so much that it helped neither planter nor industrialist. The low sugar prices alluded to in the 1895 Centro de Cañeros statement had resulted from an unexpected bumper crop that caused the wholesale price of sugar to decrease by almost fifty percent from 1894 to 1895. The harvest as well as the price drop surprised industrialists who had calculated that they would not be able to meet all market demands until 1896. The surplus sugarcane affected alcohol production as well, and increased alcohol production caused the price to plummet. To survive this new crisis and maintain the profits necessary to pay taxes and mortgage payments, sugar industrialists had to shore up both the alcohol and sugar markets.

TABLE 6.1

PRICES OF SUGAR AND ALCOHOL IN TUCUMÁN, [25]
1889-1897

1889	3.48 m/n per arroba	1889	2.25 per barrel of 26 bottles
1890	3.59 of 12 kilos	1890	.19 per liter
1891	6.73	1891	.60 with .10 tax
1892	5.00	1892	.44 .10 tax
1893	5.69	1893	.49 .20 tax
1894	4.79	1894	.50 .20 tax
1895	2.84 per 10 kilos	1895	.55 .20-.30
1896	2.60[a]	1896	.50 .30
1897	2.54[a]	1897	.71 .35

[a] without impuesto interno

TABLE 6.2

PRICE OF REFINED SUGAR (Rosario)
1890-1895

	Average		Highest Price	
1890	5.32	10 kilos	8.50	10 kilos
1891	8.45		10.50	
1892	5.94		6.90	
1893	6.29			
1895	5.22		5.90	

SYNDICATES

Maintaining the price of sugar was no easy matter. First of all, different kinds of sugar sold for different prices and competed with each other. The Refinería Argentina's product had been widely accepted in the port area, but a lively demand for unrefined first-, second- and third-class sugar allowed Tucumán factories to continue to distribute their own products. In addition to the factory owner and independent Tucumán sugar merchants, other wholesalers from major domestic consumer markets all had a say in the going price for unrefined sugar. In contrast the Refinería had no domestic competition, and its ability to hoard refined sugar allowed the company to sell at a consistently high price. If Argentine sugar producers hoped to force a price increase, they had to make several decisions. It would be easier to eliminate the trade in unrefined sugar and concentrate on sales of domestic refined sugar. This course of action, however, was quite unacceptable to those associated with the unrefined trade. If producers insisted on marketing a variety of sugars, they would have to agree on controls for production and distribution. This was not an impossible task, as cartels in Europe and the United States had demonstrated. [26]

The immediate model for sugar market control came from the organization of the alcohol trade. Since alcohol had first been taxed, prices had fallen so low that the wholesale price in Tucumán was less than cost. Alcohol producers decided to bolster retail prices by removing excess grain and cane alcohol stocks. The impetus for this came from the grain distillers.

Otto Bemberg and three other alcohol distributors first salvaged corn alcohol. Bemberg's Distilería Franco Argentina, in association with other distributors, bought all corn alcohol stocks at high prices and then exported the excess quantities. Distillers promised in return to produce no more alcohol than the amount stipulated by their contracts. After their initial success in the littoral Bemberg and his associates went to Tucumán to offer similar conditions to cane alcohol manufacturers. [27]

Bemberg and Emilio Pellet arrived in Tucumán in 1895. *El orden* welcomed the prospect of higher alcohol prices and encouraged industrialists to sign the contract. By the end of April Bemberg purchased thirty million liters of cane alcohol at twenty centavos per liter, plus one-third share in the profits from the eventual sale of this alcohol. [28]

While Bemberg was in Tucumán to buy alcohol he also proposed the formation of a sugar cartel. Emilio Pellet explained the mechanics of cartels to those industrialists who had not attended recent meetings of the Centro Azucarero in which discussions of the sugar crisis had led to the formation of such an organization. The new cartel, called the Unión

Azucarera, did not intend to restrict sugar production, merely to regulate prices. The organization would be formed by stockholders whose sugar would be marketed by that group. Sugar would be purchased on consignment and warrants issued for the sugar once it was placed in a specified depository. These warrants could then be redeemed at banks where industrialists received seventy-five percent of the warrant's value. Once the Unión refined the sugar and either sold limited quantities in Argentina or exported it, industrialists would then be able to retrieve their warrants and cash them in for the other twenty-five percent. The effectiveness of the cartel would depend upon the complete cooperation by industrialists to sell their sugar only to the Unión and to accept the Unión's price. [29]

Emilio Pellet remained in Tucumán in April and May, hoping to persuade sugar producers to sign an agreement. But from the outset the Unión faced firm opposition from factory owners who opposed the increased control of the sugar market by merchants and industrialists from the littoral. The Unión demanded the sole authority to consign and market sugar. How could factory owners accept this condition when they still expected income from the sale of unrefined sugar? Such an agreement would eliminate regional trade based in Tucumán and relegate the province to the status of the agricultural supplier to the Refinería and the Unión Azucarera. Business had not yet deteriorated enough to justify such a drastic measure. With all these facts to be considered, few signed the first contract offering. [30]

Sugar prices continued to drop throughout 1895, especially after the new harvest. Since the Unión had not signed many contracts before the harvest, it could not stop the debacle. By early September the Unión publicly acknowledged its failure that year. [31] And as prices continued to fall, those affected most by the price collapse were the independent plantation owners and smaller factories.

Was a sugar cartel the only way to restore high sugar prices? European countries where sugar cartels operated provided other alternatives. The use of sugar bounties, for example, had great possibilities for Argentina. In both France and Germany national legislatures had authorized an export bounty to maintain beet sugar prices at home. This allowed French and German sugar to sell at very low prices abroad and still bring profits to manufacturers. [32] If the bounty were not considered, another possibility would be the limitation of production. This seemed to be the least desirable choice for sugar producers and was not considered until much later. Of the two choices, the bounty system had greatly appealed to producers. All they needed was a willing legislature.

Once industrialists decided to experiment with sugar bounties, they had to figure out which legislature, national or local, would be most likely to grant such a bounty. There seemed to be a lot of resistance to sugar protection in the national legislature. In contrast, Tucumán legislators had been discussing the possibility of a sugar bounty since 1887, and legislators were already acquainted with the issues. The only problem with a Tucumán-sponsored bounty was that it could not apply to sugar produced elsewhere. Nevertheless, Tucumán sugar producers tried to have such a law passed at the same time the Centro Azucarero pushed for a similar national law.

Early in December 1895 the Tucumán legislature debated the idea of a provincial bounty. At the same time, the Centro Azucarero took advantage of a temporary change in national presidents to push for a national law. President Uriburu had become too ill to carry on his duties. Accordingly, the president of the Senate took over, since there was no vice president. That Senate president was Julio Roca, who served as temporary president from October 28, 1895, until February 8, 1896, a period of one hundred days. [33] Shortly after Roca assumed the presidency, the Centro Azucarero sent him a petition that requested his support for a national sugar bounty law. [34] The acting president introduced in response the first proposal for a national sugar bounty to Congress in an official communiqué dated December 10, 1895, and presented on December 12. He proposed a four-centavo impuesto interno on all domestic sugar, while twenty-five million kilos of sugar could be exported and rewarded with a twelve-centavo bounty. [35] Such a system would allow Argentine sugar to sell on the world market without losses to the producer.

On December 13 the Tucumán Chamber of Deputies approved an identical provincial plan. People in Buenos Aires saw it as a form of coercion: Tucumán would protect the sugar market if the nation would not. *El orden* joined Porteño critics to assail the actions of the provincial legislature and warn that the provincial bill would endanger the Roca-sponsored bill. Three days later, on December 16, local legislators withdrew the bounty bill from consideration. [36]

Sugar industrialists were left with a presidential plan that was bitterly criticized. *La prensa* opposed the bill because it offered nothing for Tucumán; it merely helped the Unión Azucarera dump its sugar holdings. [37] *La nación* saw the presidential message as the act of a lackey toward "Big Business" and failed to note that the Union's stockholders included many small industrialists. [38]

From the outset many deputies opposed the bounty system. At first they simply objected to the idea of another tax on the consumer. Later they focused upon the role of political influence and criticized that. According to the British press, legislators associated this measure with others under consideration.

> Another measure, very much of a piece with the unification scheme, as it is unblushingly designed to favour the interests of a clique . . . at the expense of the community at large, has just been laid down before Congress by Dr. Romero. The sugar planters of Tucumán . . . some three dozen in number, [want] to get rid of this surplus at a profit to themselves, at the cost of the whole population.... It seems almost incredible that immediately on the heels of the defeat of his unification bill, Dr. Romero should have the effrontery to propose such a measure to the Legislature. Still it is to be regretted that General Roca should allow his *locum tenens* spell of office to be stained by such a nefarious proposal; but Tucumán is a very powerful political province, General Roca was born there, and it is to be feared that these factors have prevented his putting his heel on the proposal. . . . In Congress the bill is to be looked on ...with strong disapprobation, and only a political *mot d'ordre* from high quarters could insure its passing. The case is so outrageous that the chances are no such word will be spoken. [39]

If the controversial presidential bill displeased the press and Congress, the modified bill presented to the Chamber of Deputies by its finance committee, headed by Marco Avellaneda, disturbed them even more.

On January 10, 1896, the finance committee proposed to place the sale of excess sugar under the control of the Banco de la Nación. The Banco would buy 25,000 metric tons of sugar valued at 7.5 million pesos, export the sugar and thereby eliminate fears that a sugar syndicate might dump the surplus stock rather than export it. The drawback to this plan was that the Bank's constitution prohibited such activities. The statutes forbade the release of such a large sum and they also prevented the bank from performing industrial transactions. In addition, no one could guarantee that the bank could sell the sugar at a profit. If the bank were unsuccessful, it would have merely paid the losses suffered by the speculative Unión Azucarera.[40] The Chamber of Deputies rejected the entire proposal. To salvage the bill, legislators rewrote it excluding the Banco de la Nación and limited bounties to the 1896 crop.[41]

Sugar politicians accomplished the impossible by convincing the Chamber of Deputies that they needed an export bounty to save the sugar industry. They did not have the opportunity to test that influence in the Senate. Since the deputies had taken so long to settle their differences, they approved the bounty bill shortly before the 1895 congressional session ended. The Senate, also at the end of its session, had not yet passed the national budget. Consequently, the upper chamber decided not to discuss the sugar bill until the 1896 sessions began in May.

The Senate's decision left the sugar industry without assurances that the 1896 sugar market would be stabilized by the export of surplus sugar. Faced with the prospects of another bumper crop, thoughts turned once again towards a cartel. In January 1896 the Unión Azucarera reorganized and presented a new contract to Tucumán industrialists. El orden published the contractual provisions, along with the names of those who had already purchased membership shares. Even though some industrialists refused to sign the contract before March and others failed to sign at all, the Unión managed to buy up large supplies. The Unión's principal opposition came from Alfredo Guzmán who, dissatisfied with his contract, tried to back out of it. The Guzmán controversy, which resulted in a protracted legal battle, was cited by the Unión as the primary incident that kept the cartel from operating well.[42] From 1896 to 1900 the Unión Azucarera reformed each year and tried to get all sugar producers to sign its contracts. And each year one or another industrialist would ruin a perfect cartel by refusing to sign.

LUCAS CÓRDOBA AND THE SPIRIT OF COMPROMISE

The presence of a new governor in 1895 and 1896 helped Tucumán adjust to these tumultuous moments. Governor Aráoz died of a heart attack on November 28, 1895. By December 1 new meetings of the electoral college resulted in the election of Aráoz's Minister of Government, Lt. Colonel Lucas A. Córdoba as the next governor. Córdoba was uniquely qualified to bargain for aid to Tucumán. A friend of both Roca and Tornquist, Córdoba also had a strong base of local supporters by virtue of his efforts to please many groups. He seemed to conduct things his own way, apparently independent of obligations to national officials. The formation of a new Partido Provincial, the PAN in federalist disguise, allowed the governor to present himself as a new type of rebel. The party, along with many provincial reforms, brought peace again to Tucumán.

In many ways Córdoba's politics embodied the true spirit of the acuerdo. He went from group to group in search of a way to keep peace and assuage the suffering brought on by the sugar crisis. Throughout 1896 the governor tried frantically to improve industrial and political relations that had been strained by recent events. This meant more than catering to the large industrialist. The organized plantation owner and the small factory owner all found a friend in Don Lucas.

Changes in the Ley de Conchabos typified the governor's reformist philosophy. With his approval the legislature revoked the law in April 1896. Although many opposed the law because it was expensive to enforce and a moral outrage, the final decision to abolish it did not stem from these grievances.[43] Rather, it sprang from the anger of the small-time planter

or industrialist who had been aggrieved by the use of political patronage
to secure workers for the large-scale employers.   Now, in the time of
record harvests, planters wanted equal access to workers as well as the
right *not* to hire during economic crises.

Governor Córdoba, however, had no intentions of liberating the
working population from the control of the factory owner.   Consequently,
he granted a series of extensions to existing contracts.   Thereafter many
planters and industrialists continued to treat workers badly and used the
police in the same coercive way as before.   Contractual servitude disappeared in 1896, but in fact the system remained intact for many years.

Besides the new labor law, the governor did other things to help
those involved in the sugar industry.   He refused to foreclose a factory
and auction it off for back taxes or debts to the Banco Provincial, though
officials from the impuesto interno bureau sent more than one factory to
the auction block, as did the national banks.   Planters also benefited from
the governor's lenient policies.   When a cyclone destroyed a number of
plantations in 1897, the governor excused those landowners from paying
their taxes.[44]   With this kind of concilatory attitude Córdoba reduced
Tucumán's endemic political tensions, though he sharpened the provincial
economic crisis.

Though most of his measures decreased provincial income, Governor
Córdoba turned to matters he felt were more important. He knew that,
unless the national sugar crisis were resolved, Tucumán could never rise
above its current problems. With this in mind the governor received legislative permission in October 1896 to meet with his friends in Buenos
Aires. Córdoba remained in the Federal Capital until January 1897, when
Congress finally enacted the first national sugar bounty law.

Tucumán had not become a paradise during Don Lucas's first years
in office, and his trip to Buenos Aires clearly proved that point. While
he spent his time consorting with the Centro Azucarero and national politicians, many in Tucumán suspected that their governor had become
another lackey of the Unión Azucarera. Consequently, they passed a new
license law while he was away, a law that now listed "monopolizers of
sugar or alcohol, or their representatives" eligible for taxation.   They
would pay five pesos for every 1,000 pesos of goods purchased in Tucumán. *La prensa* interpreted the law to be an outright political maneuver:

> It is said that the license law is not exactly a fiscal
> measure, nor is it intended to harm the Unión Azu-
> carera. It is a way of conveying a message to the
> absent Governor, a warning of what could happen
> if his political negotiations take an undesirable
> course.[45]

The tax provision created additional expenses for the Unión Azucarera
and made everyone aware of the fact that the old disputes had not died
out in the new regime.

Tucumán's taxation of the Unión Azucarera, an organization that
included many Tucumán industrialists, once again emphasized the industrial and political cleavages of the sugar industry.   The resentment of
nonindustrialists associated with sugar complicated sugar politics in the
same way that Tucumán's selfish stance disrupted regional alliances.
Similarly, the outrageous proposals made in Congress to help the domestic industry seemed no less arbitrary than the campaigns devised to strike
back at the sugar industry.   The confusing claims and counterclaims
bandied about in Congress and the press only made the controversy more
unclear.

The question no one seemed to ask at this moment was which country could offer a market for Argentine sugar.   The fact that European
countries had devised the bounty system Argentines wanted to imitate

showed that overproduction was not just an Argentine phenomenon. Indeed, it was a worldwide problem from which Argentina had been shielded by tariff barriers. Thus the idea of exporting sugar would be an illusory remedy if there were no place to export to. Once local sugar industrialists recognized this dilemma they would learn still another lesson about the price all sugar producers had to pay for the progress that had brought periodic surpluses to the world sugar market.

ENDNOTES TO CHAPTER VI

1. *Revista azucarera*, May 1894, p. 5.

2. Ibid.

3. Ibid., pp. 7-8. Actually there were sixteen proposals, but these were the most important.

4. A substantial portion of all sugarcane processed in Tucumán came from independent plantations. As early as 1889 over 6,500 hectares of cane had been purchased by various sugar factories. At the usual calculation of 50,000 kilos of cane per hectare, that represented almost a third of that year's total sugar production if the average cane-to-sugar ratio were five percent. Rodríguez Marquina, *Memoria* 1889, II:179-180.

5. *Revista azucarera*, June 1894, pp. 59-60.

6. Ibid., July 1894, pp. 134-135.

7. Ibid., August 1894, pp. 158-162; *El orden*, July 5, 1894, p. 1.

8. José A. Terry, *Memoria presentada al Sr. Presidente de la República: Tucumán, Salta, Jujuy y Santiago* (Buenos Aires: n.p., 1894).

9. Quinteros testimony, in *Tarifas de Aduana, estudios y antecedentes para su discusión legislativa por la comisión revisora nombrada por el poder ejecutivo* (Buenos Aires: Cía. Sudamericana de Billetes de Banco, 1894), p. xcvii.

10. Ibid., p. cxv.

11. García Merou testimony, ibid., pp. cccv-cccvi.

12. De Bary testimony, ibid., pp. cccv-cccvi. This decision had been made in a board of directors meeting in January 1893. Refinería Argentina, "Libro de Actas," Libro No. 1, pp. 70-71, ACT.

13. See the *La prensa* series, August 1, 1894, p. 5; August 4, 1894, p. 3; August 27, 1894, p. 3; September 8, 1894, p. 3; a typical Aníbal Latino article can be found in *Revista azucarera*, September 1894, pp. 210-216.

14. Presidential message, Diputados, October 8, 1894, p. 59.

15. Ibid., November 9, 1894, pp. 489-490; November 22, 1894, p. 686.

16. Note from Contaduría General to Minister Sixto Terán, May 31, 1894, AH, Comprobantes de Contaduría, t. 212, f. 410.

17. Finance Minister to Intervenor Domingo T. Pérez, January 8, 1894, AH, Comprobantes de Contaduría, t. 212, f. 410.

18. Alfredo Bousquet to Minister of Finance, April 6, 1894, AH, Comprobantes de Contaduría, t. 212, ff. 317-319.

19. *El orden*, April 4, 1893, p. 1.

20. Ibid., June 12, 1894, p. 1.

21. Message from the governor to the legislature, November 3, 1894, *Compilación*, XVIII:392.

22. License Law, March 21, 1895, *Compilación*, XVIII:409-410.

23. *Revista azucarera*, September 1895, pp. 895-896.

24. Compiled from Cámara de Diputados, AH, Diputados, 1895, p. 3; *El orden*, August 12, 1895, p. 1; *Revista azucarera*, September 1895, p. 825.

25. Adapted from *Revista azucarera*, November 1898, p. 320. Carrasco, *La producción y el consumo del azúcar en la República Argentina*, pp. 52-53; Refinería Argentina, *Memorias 1889-1895* (Buenos Aires: Peuser, 1890-1896). After 1895 Refinería publications stopped listing refined sugar prices.

26. See Prinsen Geerlings, *The World's Cane Sugar Industry*, especially p. 26.

27. *Revista azucarera*, November 1894, p. 312; June 1895, pp. 682-683; *La prensa*, July 6, 1895, p. 6.

28. *El orden*, April 27, 1895, p. 1.

29. The various contracts offered to industrialists can be found in *Revista azucarera*, September 1895, pp. 797-801.

30. Ibid., August 1895, pp. 749-752; *La nación*, September 7, 1895, p. 3.

31. Ibid.; *El orden*, May 3, 1895.

32. Prinsen Geerlings, *The World's Cane Sugar Industry*, pp. 25-34.

33. José Arce, *Cronología de Roca*. Estudio VII (Buenos Aires: Ministerio de Educación y Justicia, 1965), pp. 105-109.

34. *El orden*, December 7, 1895, p. 1.

35. Presidential message, Diputados, December 12, 1895, pp. 650-651. This communiqué has been mistakenly attributed to President Uriburu in Emilio J. Schleh, *Compilación legal sobre el azúcar*, I (Buenos Aires: Ferrari, 1939): 35-36.

36. Discussion of provincial export law, December 13, 1895, AH, Diputados, pp. 90-92. *El orden*, December 13, 1895, p. 1; *La nación*, December 17, 1895, p. 5; *Revista azucarera*, January 1896, p. 1012.

37. *La prensa*, December 15, 1895, p. 3; December 17, 1895, p. 4.

38. *La nación*, December 13, 1895, p. 4; December 16, 1895, p. 4.

39. *The Economist* [London], 54:2733 (January 11, 1896): 40.

40. Diputados, January 15, 1896, pp. 1175-1177.

41. Diputados, January 15, 1896, p. 1186.

42. For details on the Guzmán-Unión Azucarera conflict see Guzmán y Compañía, *Réplica de los sres. Guzmán y Cía. al sindicato Unión Azucarera Argentina* (Tucumán: Talleres El Norte, 1896); Unión Azucarera Argentina, *La Unión Azucarera y los sres. Guzmán y Cía.* (Buenos Aires: Mariano Moreno, 1896); *Revista azucarera*, September and October 1896.

43. Governor Aráoz mentioned these aspects in his annual message of September 17, 1894, *Compilación*, XVII:180.

44. Governor's decree of August 28, 1897, *Compilación*, XXI:307.

45. *La prensa*, January 10, 1897, p. 4.

CHAPTER VII
The Quest for New Sugar Markets

*Chile and Uruguay are two principal markets that
Argentine sugar producers should explore. . . .
Other possible markets are Bolivia, Paraguay,
Peru. . . and a part of Brazil, . . . São Paulo,
Santa Catarina, Paraná and Río Grande.*

Estanislao Zeballos, 1896[1]

    If Argentina had begun to export sugar just a few years earlier than she did, she might have challenged Peru and Brazil for a share in the South American sugar trade. The Refinería Argentina, almost constantly under-utilized, could have worked full time and lowered the cost of refined sugar. Projected railroad lines from Tucumán to Bolivia could have lowered the transport costs to that market, and the western line that ultimately linked Mendoza to Santiago, Chile, could have served a similar purpose. Perhaps these were but idle pipe dreams of ardent nationalists and optimistic sugar producers. In fact, Argentina did not show a market surplus until 1895, and railroad construction proceeded much more slowly than anticipated. Argentina never should have gotten into the sugar export business to begin with. Although endowed with rich soil and some of the most modern processing machinery then available, the area suitable for sugarcane cultivation was too small, climatically too unpredictable and too far from a seaport to compete internationally. When Argentine sugar finally found its way to the international market, sugar exporters encountered an additional problem: Argentina was too weak diplomatically to negotiate favorable sugar sales with any country except Great Britain.
    But maybe these are the judgments of hindsight, for in the late eighties and early nineties unlimited expansion seemed to be a reality for the Argentine sugar industry. Land devoted to sugarcane in Tucumán increased from 12,000 hectares in 1884 to 22,000 in 1891, and to 40,606 in 1895.[2] New lands were turned over for sugarcane cultivation in Salta and Jujuy and the national Congress even encouraged beet sugar cultivation in the littoral.[3] Entrepreneurs built new processing factories in Tucumán and remodeled facilities there and elsewhere.
    One of the most successful factory builders and renovators was Ernesto Tornquist. He started off by renovating the Nueva Baviera factory and then worked quietly with Tucumán entrepreneur Pedro G. Méndez to extend his sugar empire. From 1891 to 1894 Méndez bought over 2,500 hectares of virgin forests, cleared the land, planted sugarcane, bought

machinery and installed it in the new La Florida factory.   Méndez also owned La Trinidad and Lastenia sugar factories.[4]

On April 10, 1895 the Compañía Azucarera Tucumán (CAT) came into existence, took over the operation of the Nueva Baviera, La Florida and La Trinidad factories and paid Tornquist and Méndez two million gold pesos for their factories.[5]   The first directorate of the CAT consisted of Tornquist associates and the Méndez family.[6]   The CAT also had a silent partnership in two more factories, Lastenia and San Andrés, ostensibly owned by a corporation under Méndez's control.   From 1898 to 1901 the CAT officially purchased these two factories from Méndez and by then the company produced one-quarter of all Tucumán sugar.   The grinding capacity of the five factories, however, was much greater than the supply of company cane, and the CAT thus became one of the main cane buyers in province.   Tornquist's CAT and Refinería Argentina immediately became close allies and major powers within the Unión Azucarera.

The CAT Refinería Argentina complex offered a more efficient alternative to the sugar industry than the traditional family-owned enterprises. The presence of such "big business" in Tucumán thus stimulated the purchase of company lands and consolidation of other sugar factories under corporate ownership.   The Gallo brothers, for example, tried to organize a string of factories like the CAT.   Already the owners of the Luján factory, in 1894 the Gallos bought the Contreras factory in Santiago del Estero and by 1899 had acquired the Colmenar, Buenos Aires and San Ramón factories in Tucumán.[7]   Most of these factories had been financially troubled when the Gallos purchased them, and the family then tried unsuccessfully to turn them into profit making enterprises.

Clodomiro Hileret also challenged the Tornquist group for a major role in the sugar industry.   In 1889 he had begun to construct his second factory, Santa Ana.   Located in the southern part of Tucumán, Santa Ana gradually dominated the sugar industry there by buying up available cane to keep it operating full time during the zafra.   By 1895 Santa Ana produced more sugar than any other factory (9,220 metric tons), as well as the largest quantity of alcohol (2.3 million liters).[8]   To sell this alcohol Hileret allied himself with Barón Portalis, and by January 1896 Hileret made the relationship a formal partnership.   This same year the Portalis Company, along with Pedro G. Méndez, became the principal sugar wholesalers in the Republic.[9]

The fierce competition among these and other men for control of the sugar business had helped make the sugar cartel a key issue for those who feared big business. At the same time, investment in land and machinery was too great to lose in squabbles caused by what appeared in 1895 to be a temporary crisis of overproduction.   Consequently it became more imperative that sugar prices be maintained even if a tight domestic cartel could not be formed.

The only other way to assure stable sugar prices was to export excess stocks, provided that the price received compensated for costs.   Thus the proximity of the receiving country as well as its sugar tariff would be key considerations unless a federal bounty compensated for low prices and high shipping costs.

Before 1890 Argentina could have sold her sugar to neighbors in South America.   By 1895, however, this was impossible.   The growth of the Argentine sugar industry, as well as transport systems to Chile and Bolivia, had proceeded too slowly to break Peru's commercial predominance in Chile and Bolivia.   When Argentina began to export in 1895, Peru had already resumed the exportation of sugar and her exports had increased from 40,000 metric tons in 1892 to 105,462 tons in 1897.[10]   Bolivia had been drawn into the Peruvian orbit by the construction of new roads and highways, although Argentina still managed to sell Bolivia significant quantities of sugar in 1898 and 1899.   Chile by 1898 had two sugar refineries to process foreign sugar, although she purchased no sugar from

Argentina since the two countries were on the verge of war. To the east, Uruguay posed other problems. There government officials refused to grant tariff concessions to Argentine sugar.[11] Brazil, already caught up in the world sugar crisis, had begun to concentrate on her southern provinces as a new consumer market.[12] The only other neighbor who wanted to buy Argentine sugar was Paraguay. But the Paraguayan sugar market was too small and uncertain to absorb the entire Argentine surplus.

Europe seemed to offer few prospects. After all, it had been European beet sugar that had forced international sugar prices to plummet while protected by government bounties until an international convention signed at Brussels in 1903 ended the bounty system. Non-sugar-producing countries like Great Britain could purchase cheap continental beet sugar as well as Caribbean cane sugar, both of which were less expensive than Argentine sugar. Although a significant portion of Argentine sugar went to England between 1895 and 1900, Argentines initially dismissed the possibilities of entering the British sugar market. The burden of purchasing Argentine sugar eventually fell upon Great Britain because of traditional trading relationships and because the United States refused to offer Argentine sugar special tariff concessions. This refusal, due largely to U.S. interest in Hawaiian and Cuban sugar and disinterest in Argentine trade, strained diplomatic relations between Argentina and the United States and drew Argentina closer to England. Yet for a while sugar politicians looked to diplomatic arrangements with the United States as a panacea.

For many years Argentine diplomats had expressed a disdain for the colossus of the north at international meetings and during bilateral trade negotiations. The United States, under the prodding of Secretary of State James Blaine, had tried during the eighties to obtain better terms of trade with Argentina and other Latin American countries through reciprocal trade agreements. Some of the specific problems with the Argentine-U.S. negotiations had been Argentine pride and U.S. refusal to grant tariff concessions to Argentine wool. Then a new U.S. tariff passed in 1894 placed wool on the duty-free list, but Argentines petulantly refused to reciprocate the gesture in their ensuing tariff revisions.[14] By the time Argentine sugar interests entered as a factor in U.S.-Argentine trade negotiations, the situation had become even more complicated.

While Europe and Argentina protected sugar with government bounties, the United States did its best to protect U.S. sugar refiners and those involved in the Hawaiian and Cuban sugar trade from the effects of bountied sugar. In 1894 the U.S. removed sugar from the free list and charged a 40 percent *ad valorem* duty on all sugar, in addition to a specific tax on refined sugar. Even more important, provisions had been made to discourage bountied sugar with another small specific duty.[15] The punitive tax on bountied sugar would become equal to the duty after the passage in 1897 of the Dingley Tariff. Argentine sugar exporters were well aware of North American intentions but believed that their sugar would receive special consideration from the United States after a reciprocal trade agreement could be worked out. Eventually the two nations became embroiled in a conflict over sugar bounties and Argentina had to make special arrangements for sugar bound for the U.S. market. In the meantime, however, prospects of a trade agreement allowed people like Carlos Pellegrini, Ernesto Tornquist, and Tucumán Governor Lucas Córdoba to test the power of sugar politics.

Carlos Pellegrini became involved in sugar politics on two separate occasions. The first time Pellegrini was invited by the Centro Azucarero to preside over a sugar congress that hopefully would encourage stockpilers to reach a marketing agreement. Pellegrini did his best to unite dissident groups, and he even tried to bring reassurances from the U.S. Minister to Argentina that sugar exported to the United States would pay special tariffs. Despite additional entreaties from Tornquist, Governor

TABLE 7.1

EXPORT OF ARGENTINE SUGAR, 1892–1900 (kilos) [13]

Destination	1892	1893	1894	1895	1896	1897	1898	1899	1900
Africa						96,146			
Belgium					10,000				
Bolivia	25	100		602	175	13,252	60,071	63,000	9,000
Brazil					974	530	2,034		5,000
Chile									
USA				24,629	6,386,758	2,320,986			
France							18,156		49,000
Paraguay	1,865	18,088		5,000		234,097	68,553	21,000	
S. Vicente (?)					2,282,402	18,590,702	2,205,914	3,215,000	
G. Britain				47,931	12,749,893	19,220,158	13,476,468	19,416,000	15,207,000
Uruguay			8,100	5,000	361,425	593,570	4,988,382	3,986,000	
Other countries				500	234,700	664,460			

Córdoba and other Argentine government officials, the U. S. Minister could not get his country to guarantee a reciprocal trade agreement. U.S. reluctance, along with mutual distrust on the part of Argentine sugar industrialists, thwarted all attempts at industrial accord. The sugar congress ended in failure, the Unión Azucarera limped on and Pellegrini devised other plans to enhance his political reputation.

Unfortunately for sugar politicians Pellegrini turned to the alcohol industry for his next political campaign and thereby created more uncertainty for them. Struck by evidence of widespread tax fraud and aware of Argentina's need to uncover new fiscal resources, Pellegrini designed to plan to turn alcohol tax collection into a great profit-making venture. Though his plans for a state alcohol monopoly might have reaped new revenues for the national treasury, it threatened the alcohol industry with possible expropriation or rigid surveillance. As if these prospects weren't dismal enough, the proposed government monopoly later became linked with a tax farming scheme to guarantee the repayment of a new government loan. This quixotic effort neither comforted the unstable sugar industry nor enhanced Argentina's treasury.

SUGAR BOUNTIES

To fully understand the new directions in sugar politics, we must backtrack to the passage of national sugar bounties in January 1897, the event that marked the beginning of a new round of sugar politics. After the Senate had refused to debate the 1895 bounty proposal and effectively prevented further discussion until May 1896, enemies of the sugar producers had encouraged the Chamber of Deputies' budget committee to propose a new bill that eliminated any bounty but retained a two-centavo impuesto interno. To counteract the budget committee Governor Córdoba had gone to Buenos Aires to introduce a Tucumán petition of protest and a new bounty bill sponsored by the Centro Azucarero. Aided by the efforts of Tucumán Deputy Eliseo Cantón and President of the Chamber of Deputies, Marco Avellaneda, the deputies sanctioned a six-centavo impuesto interno on each kilo of domestic sugar in existence after January 1, 1897, along with a twelve-centavo bounty for the export of 35 percent of the new crop.

Once the Senate took up the matter sugar politicians successfully sought additional favors. This time Tucumán Senator Francisco L. García introduced an amendment that exempted all sugar stocks left over from previous crops from the six-centavo impuesto interno. Instead, the old sugar would pay a one-centavo tax and in turn 25 percent of that sugar could be exported with a four-centavo bounty. García justified the modifications because they would make sure the older stocks disappeared from the warehouses.[16] The new provisions clearly had the Unión Azucarera in mind, and such blatant privileges were quickly recognized as a way to subsidize the dumping abroad of the Unión's 100,000 tons of sugar. The bill did nothing for industrialists who did not belong to the Unión and had already sold their sugar, nor for the planters and workers whose plight never seemed to matter. In response to the García amendment, one senator suggested that Congress would better serve the nation by legislating to limit sugar cultivation in order to keep production in line with domestic consumption and thus avoid the dilemmas of the world sugar trade.[17] At the moment, however, no one pushed this particular suggestion, and the amended bill passed the Senate and became law in January 1897.

Instead of ending the controversy the sugar bounties raised new questions. Would the Unión Azucarera be the only stockpiler allowed to export sugar? Who would buy Argentine sugar? If these questions could not be answered quickly, all the advantages of bounties would disappear. As the 1897 harvest season approached, the Centro Azucarero tried to unite the dissident industrial groups so that they would at least join the Unión Azucarera. During the May 8 meeting of the Centro its president, Mauricio Mayer, suggested that three industrialists meet with Carlos Pellegrini and invite him to preside over a sugar congress that would try to resolve internal industrial conflicts. [18]

The Centro chose Pellegrini because it knew he approved of taxing national industry and also sanctioned the idea of bounties. If Pellegrini's presence could help industrialists unite, it would also benefit the industry by befriending another powerful political figure. [19] In response, Pellegrini seemed eager to accept the invitation to preside over a special May 24 meeting.

THE SUGAR CONGRESS

As presiding officer Pellegrini made several demands. If industrialists wanted his cooperation, they in turn had to work in unison. This meant that representatives of all the sugar producing provinces had to be consulted, not just the most powerful. Pellegrini therefore requested that a new commission be organized to represent the sugar industry. Those selected--Ernesto Tornquist, Lídoro Quinteros, Mauricio Mayer, Martín Berho, Brígido Terán, Vicente Gallo, Federico Carlisle and Pedro Alvarado--then set out to meet Pellegrini's second demand: to work out industrial problems in a manner agreeable to all. In their search for industrial harmony the new group sought to write up a new Unión Azucarera purchasing contract to replace three already suggested by various Porteño and Tucumán groups. [20]

The new committee met the following day and from the outset the individual members stood firm in their efforts to make sure that no one dominated the debates. Ernesto Tornquist opened the session by asking whether it was more important to limit production or to continue manipulating the market, thereby allowing sugar production to increase unfettered. [21] The question immediately precipitated sharp disagreement, especially among those hostile to the Tornquist empire. Anti-Tornquist industrialists feared that any method to control the planting and harvesting of sugarcane would be used against them. Thus Tornquist could not pursue the question. Instead, the committee returned to its original plan to consider a new sugar sales contract.

The committee had hoped ideally to blend the three existing proposals. The first, or "Nougués" plan, had been drawn up by Miguel Nougués. The second, or "Tucumán" project, was backed by independent sugar merchants and non-Tornquist-associated factories. The basic difference between the first two proposals was the second plan's provisions to revive the trade in unrefined sugar. The third plan, or the "Buenos Aires" plan, was sponsored by the Centro Azucarero, the Unión Azucarera and the Refinería Argentina. This version offered the lowest guaranteed prices for sugar and obliged the Refinería Argentina to process sugar only for the Unión Azucarera. [22]

Like the suggestion to limit sugarcane cultivation, no consensus could be reached regarding the contract. With the prospects that the closed meetings would end without any progress, Pellegrini directed the group's attention to a third issue--the need for a guaranteed market--and unveiled a detailed plan consisting of pursuing diplomatic negotiations that would lead to a reduction in United States tariffs for Argentine sugar. Groundwork for such an arrangement had already been covered. On the Argentine side, representatives of the Unión Azucarera had petitioned for help from Finance Minister Escalante. [23] Pellegrini, meanwhile, had approached U.S. Minister William Buchanan and found the diplomat eager to improve trade relations between his country and Argentina. In fact, long before Pellegrini had approached him Buchanan had suggested to his superiors that special concessions for Argentine sugar might do wonders for trade.[24] Buchanan's initial interest in sugar had been further heightened by a series of private meetings with Tornquist and Escalante and by correspondence with his dear friend, Governor Lucas Córdoba.[25]

In response to Minister Buchanan's inquiries the U.S. State Department in April 1897 passed on a suggestion brought forth by Treasury Secretary William Gage that:

> An offer of reciprocal privileges by the Argentine Republic to the products of the United States would entitle the sugars of that Republic to a reduction in the event of the bill [the Dingley Tariff] becoming law in its present shape may be profitably brought to the attention of the Argentine government in such an informal way as the pending character of the proposed measure may permit.[26]

Buchanan informed Pellegrini of the dispatch shortly before the sugar congress convened, and this information encouraged Pellegrini to write his own memorandum to the industrialists.

The memorandum stated that the industrialists' last recourse was the United States market. Surplus sugar could be sold there profitably if the Presidents of the United States and Argentina could make an executive agreement in accordance with previous U.S. offers of reciprocal trade:

1. That the [U.S.] President decree that imported sugar from the Argentine Republic up to the amount of 70,000 tons per year be granted a 92 percent reduction in import taxes.

2. In exchange for this concession the Argentine Republic could favor the industry and commerce of the United States in the following way:

   a. Grant an annual subsidy of 100,000 or 150,000 gold pesos for a monthly express steamship line between New York and Buenos Aires [this subsidy would be paid out of sugar tax revenues];

   b. Place a specified minimum tax on the import of certain articles almost exclusively produced in America, such as:
   1. Kerosene and its related products;
   2. Dried apples. . ., etc.

With such a presidential agreement, the sugar industry could resolve its problems in two years.[27]

As with every other plan the sugar commission appeared to be impressed with Pellegrini's idea but dismissed it as impractical. Success depended upon the reactions of two presidents and involved issues unrelated to sugar politics. Not even sugar politicians could force an Argentine president or a U.S. president to reverse long-standing tariff policies and antagonisms. Besides, Pellegrini could not guarantee that his conversations with the U.S. Minister would lead to the initiation of executive negotiations.

After Pellegrini and his select sugar committee failed to agree on any issues, the sugar congress began to disband. In the final session of May 28 Pellegrini reported that the congress had indeed been a failure and predicted a dismal fate for the northwest and for the sugar industry.[28]

With opposition to the Unión Azucarera still strong, independent industrialists had a chance to export bountied sugar on their own. The harvest had already begun and bounties had encouraged a number of factory owners to refrain from selling their sugar to the Unión. Juan Posse, the feisty politician, led the opposition by claiming that he would lose 60,000 pesos if he sold his sugar to the syndicate. Heartened by Posse's resistance, other industrialists held out.[29] Interprovincial rivalry also figured in the contract stalemate. In Tucumán severe frosts had diminished the projected sugar production for 1897. Industrialists from Salta and Jujuy, unaffected by the frosts, wanted to hold on to their sugar, since they felt market problems would be alleviated by natural disaster.[30]

While the industrialists bickered over sugar contracts, Ernesto Tornquist and the Centro Azucarero continued to seek diplomatic intervention for sugar. On June 20, 1897 Tornquist wrote a Mr. Burns, owner of a steamship line in the United States:

> Partly in consequence of the natural increase of trade and partly in connection with the Dingley-Tariff Bill the commercial relations between Argentina and the United States are one of the topics of the day just now--and amongst others a scheme is talked of regarding a new *direct steamship line* between the two countries with a substantial *subsidy* on the part of the Argentine government. I know steps have been taken with Mr. Buchanan, U.S. Minister at Buenos Aires, in order to get the scheme furthered as far as it may depend on the American side. . . .
>
> The particular advantage to which my firm is looking forward consists in the cheap sugar freights we expect to get through the line. . . .
>
> My second enquiry is, what are the prospects of the so-called *Merchant Marine Bill,* by which a reduction of duty should be granted to any merchandise imported on a ship belonging to the U.S.? If such a bill became law, the establishment of a direct line would naturally grow in importance for our own sugar trade.[31]

Tornquist concluded his letter by offering Mr. Burns the opportunity to get this U.S.-Argentine steamship concession, "as I believe I have sufficient influence with the Argentine Congress and Government to secure in all probability the preference of my candidate."[32]

Tornquist, along with Pellegrini and Argentine Minister of Foreign Relations Alcorta, continued the push for a subsidized steamship line to the United States--something the U.S. had suggested in 1891.[33] At that time Argentina had expressed little interest. Now the tables had turned. The Argentines were interested, but U.S. officials were cool to the idea. For this reason Buchanan gave Pellegrini and others little encouragement for a steamship line, especially if it were tied to tariff concessions.[34] Even though Tornquist probably knew of Buchanan's position, he still sent the letter to Burns, hoping that the Merchant Marine Bill would provide benefits that would make a reciprocal trade agreement unnecessary.

Mr. Burns, however, was not at all interested in the steamship concession and gave Tornquist no hopes of making a deal. [35]

While Tornquist awaited Burns's response, the Centro Azucarero and Lucas Córdoba again wrote Minister Buchanan hoping to arouse his help. The Centro proposed that the United States reduce the sugar tariff for 50,000 tons of Argentine sugar as a gesture for the Argentine sugar industry. [36] Governor Córdoba wrote Buchanan in July and expressed his faith that the United States would come to the aid of the Tucumán sugar industry:

> Beside the English, we have no other clients than you, and you are the only ones who can save us.
>
> I know that the Dingley Tariff is about to be passed and will establish new high tariffs for all sugars imported to the United States. We need the law to leave an open door, or half-open door: let our sugars be admitted with a good advantage over the others--a 92 percent [reduction] for example, as Dr. Pellegrini thought, or at least 75 percent. [37]

Buchanan did his best to advance the cause of Argentine sugar, but few North Americans cared about the Argentine sugar industry. Buchanan not only conveyed all inquiries and requests to the State Department; he also sent explanations of why Argentines thought their sugar industry should receive such preferential treatment from the United States. [38] Aware of the political influence of Argentine sugar industrialists, Buchanan feared that reprisals against U.S. products might result from an unfavorable stand on sugar. When the United States finally passed the Dingley Tariff in the fall of 1897, Congress ignored Buchanan's pleas.

U.S. indifference to the Argentine sugar industry triggered a wave of anti-American sentiment, which in turn provoked temporary sympathy for the domestic sugar industry. Indeed, only Buchanan's constant pleas for moderation prevented the Argentine Congress from passing anti-U.S. customs legislation for 1898. Instead, Congress added a special clause to the 1898 impuesto interno law that excused all Argentine products from impuestos internos as well as bounties when the products were exported. This contradictory provision gave sugar stockpilers two choices: they could pay production taxes and sell to the domestic market or to countries where bountied sugars entered unpenalized, or they could export to the United States untaxed and unbountied. [39] Until this law went into effect all sugar was subject to production taxes, but exporters who sent their sugar to the U.S. obtained affidavits certified by Argentine customs that they had received no bounties. In return, the United States government agreed to charge the Argentine sugar a lower tariff. [40] This legal maze allowed Argentine sugar to compete in the U.S. market (although after 1897 no sugar was sent to the U.S.), but only by making the entire bounty system seem ludicrous.

Even after the complicated bounty arrangements had been worked out for 1898, sugar producers still had no assurances that surplus sugar would always be exported. To ensure this and remove competition in the sugar export business, the Unión Azucarera joined forces with the Refinería Argentina in January 1898 and cornered the sugar market. This time the Refinería, instead of the Unión Azucarera, offered to buy all sugar stocks at a set price, export 80,000 bags of sugar and stabilize domestic sugar prices. To enhance the bargain the Refinería offered three pesos per ten kilos, whereas the Unión Azucarera had recently offered only 2.25 pesos. The offer was too attractive to refuse, so holdouts from the earlier contracts sold out. This arrangement resulted in the

Refinería becoming the second major stockpiler. Later the Unión Azucarera exported the sugar purchased by the Refinería.[41] Tranquility
reigned until the next harvest.

THE ALCOHOL MONOPOLY

Shortly after the abortive sugar congress disbanded, Pellegrini
revealed his alcohol monopoly scheme, one that kept the alcohol and sugar
industries under public scrutiny. The new plan became public knowledge
in July 1897 when Pellegrini published an article in *La biblioteca*, Paul
Groussac's fashionable Porteño journal. In this article Pellegrini suggested that the national government take over the Bemberg alcohol cartel
and tighten the procedures used to collect alcohol taxes. The best way
to supervise the taxation and sale of alcohol would come from expropriat-
ing grain distilleries and offering a guaranteed price to cane distillers.
The sugar-based alcohol industry could not be expropriated, he reasoned,
because it existed as a subsidiary of the sugar industry. Grain distilleries, in contrast, functioned as independent entities.[42] This mixed
monopoly would allow the government, instead of Bemberg, to limit alcohol
production and keep alcohol prices high, while also increasing government revenues.

Since a monopoly already existed, Pellegrini felt that the idea of
government monopoly should not offend any alcohol producer. Those
subject to expropriation would be well compensated, and those subject to
close federal regulation would at least have the certainty of minimum
prices. At the same time, increased national revenues could be used to
pay off Argentina's outstanding debts after expropriation costs had been
paid. He also took care to disagree with those who felt that alcohol taxes
could prevent alcoholism or who believed that alcoholism was such a social
problem that it warranted government control. The only reason that
alcohol should be taxed was to make money.[43]

One year after the *La biblioteca* article appeared, a Porteño deputy
introduced a bill to create a government alcohol monopoly. Deputy Miguel
Morel presented his monopoly bill on July 1, 1898, in conjunction with a
bill to authorize an internal loan of 15,000,000 pesos. The loan would be
guaranteed by the income produced from the alcohol monopoly, and the
funds would be used to compensate those distillers forced to close their
factories and those who decided to sell out to the national government.
In his initial presentation Morel claimed that:

> The Alcohol Monopoly would harm no one in private
> industry. For a while now a powerful syndicate has
> existed that monopolized the alcohol market. All
> distilleries were controlled by it. For this reason
> an alcohol monopoly would not harm anyone or the
> capital invested in the industry. Instead of having
> a private company the state will from now on take
> care of it.[44]

He also defended the legislation by pointing out that rumors of possible
conflict with Chile might materialize and lead to war. Argentina needed
new armaments and a defense fund, all of which might come from the
alcohol monopoly's profits. Thus the close government control of alcohol
production would benefit the country in a patriotic as well as a remunerative sense, even though the government had to first pay out 15,000,000
pesos to grain distillers.[45]

Although Morel tried to make the bills palatable by appealing
patriotism, the expropriation costs and the possible political repercussions staggered the imagination. Expropriation might take twenty-five

years, thereby increasing instead of diminishing government debts. In the meantime no one knew how Bemberg and his group would react to the summary takeover of the alcohol trade. Another person to be considered was the incoming president, General Julio Roca. If Roca did not fully endorse the bills, they had little chance of success.

After Roca officially took office in October 1898, he hesitated to give full support to Pellegrini and Morel, but he also refused to make open criticism. In the meantime Tucumán industrialists feared that Pellegrini's widespread influence could force the passage of the alcohol legislation. Consequently, in October 1898 Tucumán alcohol producers petitioned the Centro Azucarero for help in the matter. The Centro's president reassured the petitioners that:

> For the time being, any negotiation would be premature since, according to reliable sources, the national government has decided to postpone until next year all decisions related to a monopoly. [46]

Finally on November 8, 1898, to the embarassment of the Centro Azucarero, President Roca outlined his own alcohol legislation. He began his message by noting that, as the alcohol tax had increased, the number of liters taxed had decreased along with anticipated revenues. In 1895 when the tax had been fifteen centavos, 33,249,011 liters had tax stamps placed on them. In 1897 when the tax rose from thirty-five centavos to sixty centavos, only 29,486,807 liters had been stamped. Now that the alcohol tax had been recently increased to one peso, the president had grave doubts that further tax fraud could be prevented unless extreme measures were taken to close down illegal operations and make sure that other distilleries paid taxes on their total production.

To deal with these problems Roca advised Congress that he, as President, should be empowered to track down and close all clandestine distilleries, to prohibit the construction of new ones with capacities of less than twenty hectoliters and to punish tax evaders. He also wanted to create a special office to supervise alcohol tax collections and devise new penalties for defrauders and delinquent industrialists. Finally the new bill authorized the President to award tax farming privileges to a private group under certain conditions. The group had to advance the national government an unspecified amount of gold pesos to pay off the foreign debt. In return the group would collect alcohol taxes, up to one-half of which could be used to repay the principal and interest on the loan, while the other half was turned over to the national government for unspecified use. After the principal and interest had been repaid, the group would lose the privilege of tax collection. [47]

Roca's new plan directly challenged the Pellegrini-Morel bill by eliminating both the state monopoly and the forced expropriation. Yet it still retained the notion that alcohol revenues would be dedicated to paying off Argentina's foreign obligations. His plan also removed government-guaranteed alcohol prices, although it opened the door for Bemberg or other interested parties to lend the government money. Finally, to make the legislation more palatable to alcohol producers, Roca included provisions to reward a government bounty equal to the production tax for each liter exported. [48]

Although the president had the power to push his bill through Congress, certain aspects of the legislation would be difficult to justify. No one denied that the government had the right to supervise collection of alcohol taxes in an efficient manner, but critics claimed that it was unconstitutional to limit the size of distilleries:

Limitation of productive capacity for the sake of easier tax collection is inadmissible because the Constitution guarantees liberty of industry and commerce. Why should residents of Jujuy, Catamarca, Chubut or Neuquén. . . be forced to consume alcohol made in large distilleries that can operate in large centers?[49]

As with all legislation Roca's new bill had to pass the scrutiny of the Deputies' budget committee. It eventually emerged as two separate bills. The first one related to industrial restrictions and tax collection procedures. The second one turned the unspecified loan into one with a ceiling of thirty million pesos. The group that lent the money would still be able to collect taxes, and up to four million gold pesos would be used each year to repay the loan's principal and interest. When the loan was repaid the lenders would relinquish their tax farming privileges.[50]

Once the budget committee divided the legislation in two bills and showed how much alcohol revenues could be tied to the government loan, it became evident to the Argentine press how demeaning tax farming could be to the national image, especially if a foreign group offered the loan. "It is backwards, it means selling national sovereignty. It is a renunciation of all the triumphs of human progress in the last generation. It is, thus, something that Africa or Asia would do, something beneath the consideration of *South America*."[51] This comment from *La prensa* was echoed in Tucumán's *El orden*, and soon public indignation was directed at the two presidential bills.[52]

Like all the other revised presidential alcohol legislation, the two bills had an easy time passing the two chambers, although the *Spirits Loan*, as it soon became known, was worded in general terms that guaranteed its repayment without tax farming. When defenders of Pellegrini's monopoly plan tried to revive interest in a state-controlled monopoly that actually ran grain distilleries, Roca's Finance Minister José María Rosa quickly rose to the defense of the presidential version and thereby effectively squelched potential opposition.[53]

The eventual fate of the alcohol loan further strained relations between Roca and Pellegrini, especially after the latter took it upon himself to secure the loan. Pellegrini zealously, almost fanatically, tried to work out an arrangement with European bankers, both English and German, but Argentina's credit abroad discouraged favorable proposals. On January 30, 1899 *The Economist* reported on the progress of the alcohol loan:

> The latest advices from Europe to bankers and leading commercial men here are by no means favourable as to the prospects of the £6,000,000 Spirits Tax Loan being launched. Some of the advices say that it will be impossible for Argentina to raise a loan *en règle* in Europe, either in London or on the Continent, till some stronger proof be given by both the Government and congress that the promises of retrenchment are really meant than has been afforded during the session just closed. The syndicate that is nibbling at the loan, it is stated, are asking such usurious terms that they virtually amount to a refusal to lend.[54]

As of April 1899 no syndicate would make an offer to the Argentine government. Meanwhile back at home, all the new federal regulations designed to eliminate fraud were never effectively enforced and rumors arose again that a state monopoly would be imposed.[55] When President Roca delivered his annual message the following month, he publicly ac-

knowledged that he had given up hopes of working out loan terms acceptable to the national government:

> The first attempts made to contract the thirty
> million gold peso loan authorized by Congress did
> not appear to be meritorious, indicative of the
> costs of re-establishing credit, once it is lost. . .
> Thus I believe it prudent to suspend further at-
> tempts. . . . The loan will be contracted only
> under conditions that honor Argentine credit. [56]

Unlike Roca, Pellegrini did not lose hopes of working out arrangements to farm out alcohol taxes and possibly expropriate the grain distillers. Even the cane distillers, earlier opposed to a state monopoly,
felt it would be better than the uncertainty that now characterized the
alcohol trade. Roca's silence and Pellegrini's persistence in this matter
foreshadowed the later open rift between the two politicians. [57]

From a fiscal point of view the new alcohol laws were a distinct
failure. The Bemberg monopoly still dominated the alcohol market, thereby skimming profits that could have entered the national treasury under
Pellegrini's plan. Roca had calculated that the increased alcohol taxes
and new collection procedures would bring 20,000,000 pesos into the
national coffers in 1899. Instead, the receipts for that year only came to
13,625,599 pesos. [58] Though the press placed the blame upon the release
of stockpiled alcohol that had not been subject to increased taxes, the
fact remained that both large and small alcohol producers continued to
evade successfully tax payments. [59]

The strict surveillance of alcohol production may not have reduced
fraud, but it did raise the ire of Tucumán alcohol producers and encouraged them to reconsider the government monopoly. The new regulations
hindered smooth and efficient production by forcing chemical analysis at
inconvenient moments. Special equipment and government inspectors were
supposed to monitor this process, and the national government wanted
the industrialist to pay for both. Yet regardless of who paid for them,
fraud continued along with low alcohol prices.

By the turn of the century the search for market stability for sugar
and alcohol had led industrialists to see how far they could go to get government protection for their products. These efforts had caused the two
industries to become pawns of international diplomacy, as seen in the case
of United States-Argentine trade negotiations and the Spirits Loan. Such
experiences helped define the boundaries of government protection of
national industries and the political costs of such aid.

To assess the state of the sugar industry in 1900, as well as its
prospects for the future, one had to look at the various sectors within
the sugar industry--industrialists, planters and workers, as well as other
pressure groups that affected sugar politics: national politicians, presidents, cartels, the national treasury and the provinces involved in sugar
cultivation. The rewards and pitfalls of the sugar business were unevenly
distributed, and many claims to success or failure, favoritism and exploitation, turned out to be publicity rather than actual fact. Despite their
loud wailings about taxes, big business and the international sugar market, some sugar and alcohol industrialists found themselves among the
richest men in Argentina. Others joined the ranks of impoverished elites.
Though the government continued to complain about the costs of bounties
and poor tax collections, sugar and alcohol taxes still provided a major
source of government income. The two industrial cartels did manage to
manipulate prices to their benefit although the profits from such machinations, at least in the sugar industry, did not seem to be very great.

As for the future, the outlook for the sugar industry after 1900 depended greatly upon which group was under consideration and how uncontrollable factors like weather conditions and international price movements would limit general industrial progress.

ENDNOTES TO CHAPTER VII

1. Estanislao S. Zeballos, *La concurrencia universal y la agricultura en ambas Américas*; 2nd ed. (Buenos Aires: Peuser, 1896), p. 277. Another version of this chapter was presented to the Twelfth Annual Meeting of the Asociación Argentina de Estudios Americanos, Universidad del Belgrano, Buenos Aires, September 23, 1978.

2. Guy, *Politics and the Sugar Industry in Tucumán, Argentina, 1870-1900*, Appendix Table B1, p. 326.

3. Law #2907 to encourage beet sugar cultivation, December 6, 1892, Diputados, pp. 821-822.

4. Centro Azucarero Argentina, *Cincuentenario*, pp. 33, 57; *Revista azucarera*, September 1894, p. 206.

5. Pillado, *Anuario Pillado de la deuda pública y sociedades anónimas establecidas en la República Argentina para 1899*. (Buenos Aires: La Nación), pp. 193-194.

6. *Cincuentenario de la S.A. Compañía Azucarera Tucumana, 1895-1945* (Buenos Aires: Peuser, 1945), unpaginated.

7. Páez de la Torre, "Personajes en el olvido," *La gaceta*, August 10, 1970.

8. Centro Azucarero Argentina, *Cincuentenario*, pp. 97-98; *El orden*, October 9, 1891, p. 1.

9. *Revista azucarera*, February 1896, p. 1073.

10. Ibid., September 1900, p. 252.

11. Ibid., May 1900, p. 124; *South American Journal*, 41:9 (August 29, 1896):220.

12. Eisenberg, *The Sugar Industry in Pernambuco*, pp. 221-222.

13. Centro Azucarero Argentina, *La industria azucarera; informes, legislación y estadística* (Buenos Aires: Centro Azucarero, 1903), p. 17. The entry of S. Vicente represents an intermediate stop. Consequently it is impossible to discern the ultimate disposition of that sugar.

14. Frederick W. Taussig, *The Tariff History of the United States*. 6th ed. (New York and London: G. P. Putnam's Sons, 1907); McGann, *Argentina, The United States, and the Inter-American System, 1880-1914*, p. 174.

15. Taussig, *The Tariff History of the United States*, pp. 312-313.

16. Senado, January 13, 1897, pp. 892-893.

17. Ibid., pp. 895-896.

18. Centro Azucarero Argentina, "Industria azucarera de la República Argentina; Trabajos para un acuerdo entre los fabricantes," Suplemento al No. 38 de la *Revista azucarera* (Buenos Aires: J. Carbone, 1897), p. 3; *Revista azucarera*, June 1897, p. 1805.

19. At the time, however, *El orden* questioned the selection of Senator Pellegrini. *El orden*, May 14, 1897, p. 1.

20. Centro Azucarero Argentina, "Industria azucarera de la República Argentina; Trabajos para un acuerdo entre los fabricantes," p. 28.

21. Ibid.

22. Ibid., pp. 32-44.

23. *South American Journal*, 42:20 (May 15, 1897):545.

24. Buchanan to Secretary of State Richard Olney, Despatch No. 308, February 13, 1897, NA/M69-29.

25. Buchanan to Olney, Despatch No. 310, February 16, 1897, NA/M69-29.

26. Acting Secretary of State John Sherman to William Buchanan, Despatch No. 211, April 2, 1897, NA/77-12.

27. Centro Azucarero Argentina, "Trabajos para un acuerdo," pp. 46-48.

28. *Revista azucarera*, June 1897, pp. 1777-1780.

29. *El orden*, July 22, 1897, p. 1.

30. *Revista azucarera*, June 1897, pp. 1777-1780.

31. Unsigned, handwritten copy of letter dated June 20, 1897, "Carpeta de Borradores, 1896-1897," ACT.

32. Ibid.

33. McGann, *Argentina, the United States, and the Inter-American System, 1880-1914*, p. 171.

34. Buchanan to Olney, Despatch No. 359, June 15, 1897, NA/M69-29.

35. Tornquist to Burns, August 26, 1897, "Carpeta, 1896-1897," ACT.

36. Note of June 26, 1897, published in *Revista azucarera*, August 1897, pp. 1884-1886.

37. Letter of July 18, 1897, ibid., pp. 1886-1887.

38. Buchanan to Secretary of State John Sherman, Despatch No. 394, September 15, 1897, NA/M69-30.

39. Impuesto Interno Law #3681, Article 19, Diputados, 1897, pp. 1021-1022.

40. Buchanan to Sherman, Despatch No. 395, September 18, 1897, NA/ M69-30; Sherman to Buchanan, Telegram, November 8, 1897, NA/ M77-12.

41. *Revista azucarera*, January 1898, pp. 7-10; *El orden*, January 14, 1898, p. 1; *La prensa*, March 15, 1898; April 22, 1898, p. 5; *South American Journal*, 44:23 (June 4, 1898):625.

42. Carlos Pellegrini, "El estanco de alcohol," *La biblioteca*, 2:5 (July-September 1897):33-34.

43. Ibid., pp. 11, 37. For a sharp response to Pellegrini's views on the social consequences of alcoholism see Fermín Rodríguez, "Alcoholismo y suicidio en Buenos Aires," pp. 443-466.

44. Diputados, July 1, 1898, p. 297.

45. Ibid., p. 296.

46. *Revista azucarera*, November 1898, p. 323.

47. Presidential message, Diputados, November 9, 1898, pp. 168-171.

48. Ibid.

49. *La prensa*, November 13, 1898, p. 3.

50. Ibid., November 19, 1898, p. 3.

51. Ibid., November 23, 1898, p. 3.

52. Ibid.; *El orden*, November 14, 1898, p. 1.

53. Diputados, December 13, 1898, pp. 383-384.

54. *The Economist*, 57:2897 (March 4, 1899):311.

55. Ibid., 42:2908 (April 19, 1899):723; see also *South American Journal*, 47:12 (September 16, 1899):317.

56. Annual Message, May 1899, Roca, *Documentos*, III:13.

57. For the details of the later rift, see José María Bustillo, "Estudio preliminar," in Carlos Pellegrini, *Discursos y escritos* (Buenos Aires: Ediciones Estrada, 1959), pp. cxxxvi-cxxxix; Noberto D' Atri, *Del 80 al 90 en la Argentina. Datos para una historia política* (Buenos Aires: A. Peña Lillo, 1973), p. 176.

58. See Chapter V, Table 5.1, Alcohol Tax Receipts.

59. *The Economist*, 47:2908 (May 20, 1899):723.

CHAPTER VIII
The End of an Era

By the beginning of the twentieth century the basic goals of the Generation of Eighty had been accomplished. The nation had been unified economically and politically. Previously isolated regions of the Republic now had direct contact with the populous coastal area. The city of Buenos Aires, earlier the bastion of local wealth and privilege, was now the seat of the national government and the pride of the nation. There the ruling elites kept a close watch over the country to make sure that their plans proceeded smoothly. [1]

From the vantage point of Buenos Aires the disturbing events of the nineties had only been temporary setbacks. Economic depression had given way to prosperity, and Argentine leaders no longer had to consider such humiliating plans as tax farming to straighten out the government's financial affairs. A period of austerity and retrenchment enabled Argentina to repay her foreign debts earlier than scheduled. These actions, along with a reorganization of the national banking and monetary systems, helped restore the nation's honor and credit. [2]

But from the viewpoint of the interior provinces, the events of the nineties had been symptomatic of a serious malady that could only bring further deterioration. Unlike the coastal area whose cattle and cereal industries and prosperous urban centers had encouraged immigrants and further growth, the interior's wine and sugar industries and other economic pursuits had barely managed to stave off economic stagnation. For most of Argentina the Generation of Eighty's successful programs of nation building did not bring about all the changes anticipated by the politicians of the time. Most importantly, instead of eliminating the differences between the interior and the littoral, the programs of this political group had in fact accentuated and widened the gap.

Regional industries recovered from the post-1890 depression but at a much slower pace than those in the littoral. Part of this lag was due to specific industrial problems, but part of it was also due to the reluctance of the national government to encourage nonexport activities. Consequently, regional industries after 1900 found themselves in an extremely ambiguous situation. They were desperately needed to sustain and encourage further economic development in the interior, yet they were incapable of financing such diversification. At the same time, those industries that had been aided by favorable tariffs and political favoritism were selected to bear special taxes and criticized for their earlier successes.

For these reasons national fiscal policies in the 1890s did little to
help the interior. While impuesto interno revenues filled up the national
coffers, they drained the interior of capital at a very critical moment.
Meanwhile, the national government failed to spend these new revenues
on projects that would help the interior. The end result of such policies
was to discourage the new industries there. After all, if some new non-
export activity became as successful as wine or sugar, it too would be
added to the tax rolls. Such prospects contrasted sharply with those of
the new meat-packing plants that had been specifically exempted from
production taxes. No wonder native and foreign investor alike looked to
place his money in either land or export ventures. About the only regional industry that attracted substantial investments after 1900 was the
quebracho wood industry in the northeast--an export industry.[3]

Just how did the sugar industry fit into this picture? How did the
national government benefit from sugar? After all, sugar exporters received government bounties from 1897 to 1905. Nevertheless, the treasury still retained from 1,500,000 to more than 3,000,000 pesos m/n per
year from sugar impuestos internos:[4]

TABLE 8.1

SUGAR IMPUESTOS INTERNOS, 1897-1905

Year	Tax per Kilo	Bounty	Taxes Collected	Bounties Paid	Amount Retained by Treasury
1897	0.06	0.04*	4,384,363.80	718,302.98	743,253.57
	0.01	0.12*	1,461,556.55	2,868,070.43	1,516,293.37
1898	0.06	0.16	4,765,862.64	2,947,843.68	1,818,018.96
1899	0.06	0.16	6,200,345.44	3,875,621.92	2,324,723.52
1900	0.06	0.16	5,958,890.14	3,714,666.40	2,244,223.74
1901	0.06	0.16*	9,507,530.52	6,231,208.68	3,276,321.84
1902	0.06	0.16*	7,599,024.78	5,091,570.16	2,507,454.62
1903	0.06	0.16	7,704,048.20	5,127,135.84	2,576,912.36
1904	0.06	0.16	7,419,873.39	4,877,075.68	2,542,797.71
1905	0.06	0.16	2,146,373.21	---------	2,146,373.21
			57,147,868.67	35,451,495.77	21,696,372.90

The 21,696,372.90 pesos, added to the taxes paid by sugar producers on
their alcohol, represented sugar profits taken by the national government
to be used elsewhere. In this way the national government managed to
skim the sugar industry of surplus capital in the same way it siphoned
off income from other interior industries nurtured during the eighties.

In a strictly political sense the national government also benefited
from other aspects of the sugar controversies of the nineties. Though
national leaders had great difficulties controlling the sugar business,
they found that sugar politics had its rewards. They learned how to
make alliances based upon the sugar question and then exploit these alliances for other purposes. Strong politicians like presidents Roca and
Pellegrini had used sugar politics to advance personal ambitions. Weaker
politicians like Uriburu and Sáenz Peña also found uses for sugar. They
learned that raising alcohol taxes and calling for investigations of the
sugar industry could enhance their public image. The advantages of
sugar politics were not reserved for presidents. A number of senators,
deputies and ministers of the treasury and interior all found that from
time to time sugar controversies offered them a way to gain favorable
publicity.

The fact that the national government had exacted its tribute from the sugar industry did not mean that no one got rich from the sugar business. Tornquist and his friends, Hileret, Nougués and several other Tucumán factory owners emerged from the sugar crisis as rich men. It did, however, intensify the long-standing battles over who would get more of sugar's profits. It also encouraged a growing conservatism among industrialists who wanted to keep their share of the sugar business. Before 1900 sugar producers had tried a variety of technological, political and business maneuvers that demonstrated their willingness to experiment and their awareness of what other sugar producers had done under similar circumstances. The Argentine sugar producer had explored almost every conceivable way to improve his sugar and locate new markets. The crises of the nineties had shown him that many problems associated with sugar would ultimately affect the future expansion of the industry. With this in mind, sugar producers after 1900 changed their focus. Aware of the prospects for the future, they became less interested in the technological progression of the industry and more in its distributive aspects.

Conflicts over distribution first afflicted the sugar industry during the fight over the importation of Brazilian sugar. These kinds of disputes soon stimulated other forms of industrial dissension. The Unión Azucarera attempted to monopolize sugar sales and pitted the Tornquist empire and its allies against independent sugar producers. The Centro Azucarero successfully blamed the independent plantation owners for high sugar prices and thereby won sympathy for the factory owner. The province of Tucumán lost needed revenues in order to prevent more legislative fights over which sugar group in the province would pay a greater portion of taxes. At first glance it seemed that these battles left the most powerful groups in the best position to deal with future problems. This, however, was not always true, particularly in the long run. Thus, in order to see who would be best prepared to face the post-1900 sugar battles, we must first see how different sugar groups survived the conflicts of the nineties.

LOBBIES AND CARTELS

Once the sugar industry became "big business" in the 1890s, industrialists decided to band together and help each other in times of political and industrial crisis. The formation of the Centro Azucarero theoretically guaranteed that all sectors of the sugar business would be heard. This organization, financed entirely by dues assessed its members, became a permanent feature of the sugar industry.

The Centro survived the first sugar crisis in good financial order. Its dues allowed the organization to maintain considerable cash reserves at all times--even when member factories and plantations were on the auction block. It had paid for the Terry excursion to Tucumán in 1894 and for the sugar congress in 1897. Its secretary, José Ceppi, kept the public well aware of issues that affected sugar. Even though such activities cost a lot, the Centro was so financially secure that in 1898 members voted to reduce annual fees by 50 percent. [5]

Despite the reduced fees, the Centro still had enough money to continue its role as a lobby both inside Congress and outside. In Congress it offered its own version of legislation that involved the sugar and alcohol industries and presented petitions signed by the Centro's adherents. Outside Congress the Centro involved itself in a number of issues unrelated to sugar. In March 1898, for example, the Centro Azucarero contributed 20,000 pesos towards the purchase of a new gunboat. At that moment war with Chile seemed inevitable and Argentina was forced to ask for private donations in order to modernize the navy. Of course, the Centro publicized its contribution as much as possible, pointing to the patriotism of the sugar industry. Because of the Centro's actions the sugar industry became one of the few national industrial groups that would or could contribute towards the war effort. [6]

The following year the Centro Azucarero made another gesture to help identify sugar with national issues. In this case the Centro responded to a request from the Committee for National Production to join the group. The object of this committee was to defend national industries against unfair legislation. The Committee had suggested in its letter that the sugar lobby commit itself to a membership fee of 100 pesos per month, In response, the Centro gallantly offered to double the suggested dues and further promised to purchase 3,000 pesos worth of stock in Carlos Pellegrini's new newspaper, El país, whose goal was also to defend national industry. [7] These efforts did much to give sugar favorable publicity and win friends among other industrial groups.

Another function of the Centro Azucarero consisted of mediating internal squabbles. In this effort the Centro failed. After its 1894 publicity campaign the Centro could not enlist the membership of many independent planters. Thereafter the Centro only paid lip service to the many complaints sent in by planters about factory owners. [8] Within the industrial sector the Centro also played favorites. It continually backed the Tornquist group and the Unión Azucarera over the protests of other sugar producers. In 1900 the Centro finally recognized its inability to persuade certain Tucumán factory owners to join the Unión Azucarera. Fearful that it would lose its influence in Tucumán as a result of this admission, the Centro set up a special office there to keep close tabs on the situation. This move did nothing to satisfy the dissidents, and a number of them actually dropped their Centro Azucarero membership that year to protest the partiality of the organization. [9] As for sugar producers outside Tucumán, their share of the business was so small that within the Centro they had to choose between alliances with the Tornquist group or the Tucumán dissidents rather than form an independent group.

Like the Centro Azucarero, the Unión Azucarera provoked strong reactions within the sugar sector. Although viewed by the press and by sugar producers as some sort of impersonal force that intended to grab all of sugar's profits for itself, the Unión in fact was merely a group of sugar producers and wholesalers bound together by contract. If there was any conspiracy, it came from the sugar industry. Any profits reaped by the Unión Azucarera thus represented additional income for part of the industrial and commercial sectors.

The other cartel that affected the sugar industry, the alcohol cartel, was much more circumspect about its financial situation and therefore more difficult to assess. The organization evidently did not publish financial statements, and the constant barrage of public criticism and publicity encouraged this group to maintain a low profile. Almost everyone who manufactured alcohol, with the glaring exception of Clodomiro Hileret, sold his alcohol to the cartel. Yet there must have been a considerable degree of dissatisfaction with this arrangement within the ranks of both cane and grain distillers. Before Roca ended the practice of changing the alcohol tax in mid-year, many alcohol distillers had lost substantial sums by having sold their product too early. After that, Pellegrini's monopoly plan, along with Roca's modifications, deeply disturbed the alcohol trade. For these reasons a group of grain or cane distillers would periodically come up with their own plans for an official monopoly.

Within the sugar sector the alcohol cartel enjoyed the support of the Centro Azucarero so long as cane distillers could be assured a sales price that covered basic production expenses. The close political relationship between sugar and alcohol politics also tended to reinforce the Centro's alliance with the alcohol group. Finally, the presence of Otto

Bemberg as a moving force in both organizations further cemented the bonds between the two organizations.

THE REFINERÍA ARGENTINA-COMPAÑÍA AZUCARERA TUCUMANA

Like the lobby and cartels associated with sugar the Tornquist enterprises found ways to overcome problems that stumped other groups in the sugar industry. The first segment of the empire, the Refinería Argentina, had a government guarantee of seven percent profit that could have subsidized the establishment for fifteen years if business had been bad. The Refinería was so successful, however, that it only collected government subsidies during the first year of operations.[10] From 1891 to 1900 the company reported earnings of 8 to 10 percent per year on preferred stocks.[11] Remaining profits were then poured back into the company or occasionally paid out in dividends on common stock. Besides profits and dividends the Refinería's yearly statements noted purchases of additional machinery and land, the issuing of new debentures in Europe and other observations of how well the company functioned. These reports also showed how the officers of the Refinería perceived their ability to protect the firm from industrial instability.

As far as its officers were concerned, the Refinería's major asset consisted of the ability to remove the company from business fluctuations by operating only on consignment. In 1898 they reiterated their decision to restrict operations to refining, since it had "had the double advantage of keeping the refinery completely outside market fluctuations while guaranteeing us positive benefits with absolutely no risks involved."[12] Few industries in Argentina could make such boasts during the difficult years of the nineties.

Like the Refinería Argentina the Compañía Azucarera Tucumana had managed a way to turn a profit even during the worst years of the sugar crisis. While the CAT gradually expanded to five factories, it also paid its regular stockholders 8 percent in 1895, 10 percent in 1896-1897, 5 percent in 1898, 6 percent in 1899 and 7 percent from 1900 to 1901.[13] Equally important, Tornquist's European connections had been as helpful to the CAT as to the Refinería. The CAT had also been able to sell debentures in Europe that helped expand the company's capital-- a prospect rarely available to Tornquist's competitors.[14]

NON-CAT TUCUMÁN FACTORIES

Unlike the Tornquist factories, the fate of other Tucumán sugar factories was extremely uncertain. Although people still talked about the lavishness of the Hileret plantation chalet at Santa Ana, not all sugar industrialists lived in the lap of luxury. An anonymous industrialist submitted a list of unsuccessful sugar ventures to the 1907 Tariff Review Commission as testimony to the precarious conditions in Tucumán:[15]

Amalia factory	Changed hands three times, twice owners went bankrupt
Cruz Alta	The owner died heavily indebted
Lastenia	Changed hands five times for lack of operating capital
La Invernada	The founder went bankrupt
Luján	The founder committed suicide because of bad business

Nueva Baviera	. . . . . .	The founder lost his money and had to settle with creditors
El Paraíso	. . . . . .	Twice the founder had to settle claims with creditors
Reducción	. . . . . .	The second owner went bankrupt, factory closed
Caspinchango	. . . . . .	Two proprietors went bankrupt, factory closed
San Felipe	. . . . . .	The proprietor went bankrupt
San Vicente	. . . . . .	The founder went bankrupt
San Andrés	. . . . . .	The founder went bankrupt, thereafter ownership changed twice due to lack of operating capital
San Ramón	. . . . . .	The founder went bankrupt
Unión	. . . . . .	The founder went bankrupt, factory closed
San Germán (Santiago)	. . . . . .	The founder went bankrupt, committed suicide
Concepción	. . . . . .	Turned over to creditors

The industrialist who presented this memorandum wanted to show the Review Commission how bad the sugar business had become for factory owners, so he painted as bleak a picture as possible, even to the inclusion of the melodramatic and unconfirmed suicides of two industrialists. He mixed events of the eighties with those of the nineties. He also failed to disclose how many factories were left at the end of the disaster to carry on sugar production. Finally, the industrialist gave no explanation for these particular business failures. Even if all this information had been included, the commission still could have concluded that only the shrewdest industrialists came out of the depression of the nineties in good condition. [16]

How did a clever entrepreneur cope with the uncertain sugar market? Eudoro Avellaneda and Brígido Terán's successful Los Ralos factory showed how a modest enterprise could actually flourish amidst adversity provided that the owner had the proper connections. Business was so good for this company that its holdings actually expanded rather than contracted in the late 1890s.

To accomplish this they combined sound business decisions with help from influential people. Their business acumen was revealed when they decided to keep up their ranches rather than concentrate solely on sugar. When they needed money they mortgaged the ranches rather than the factory. In this way, Los Ralos was never threatened with foreclosure like so many other factories. Good friends in high places also helped Avellaneda and Terán avoid the mortgaging of their factory. The two owners had enough influence in the banks to secure ranch loans that could only be considered extremely reasonable. The Banco Hipotecario Nacional branch in Tucumán gave at least two loans to them. In January 1888 the bank granted a 12,000 peso mortgage on the Humaita ranch. After the 1890 crash banker Vicente Padilla, an obvious friend, granted Avellaneda and Terán a ten-year moratorium on the payment of the loan. About the same time the Banco Hipotecario Nacional revised the payment schedule on a 25,000 gold peso loan so that Terán would have twenty-eight years to repay the loan. [17] These generous bank terms certainly

made business much easier for these men, since they removed obstacles
that had stopped many industrialists.

Maintaining a diversified business enterprise also helped the Nougués family, owners of the San Pablo factory. Like Los Ralos San Pablo
was a modest sugar factory, although it could produce twice as much
sugar as Los Ralos.[18] Like Avellaneda and Terán the Nougués brothers
had purchased lands for both plantation and ranching. By 1895 the San
Pablo company controlled 35,000 hectares of land, and between 1892 and
1905 the Nougués brothers spent at least 2.3 million pesos on nine additional land purchases.[19] Several parcels of land had been mortgaged to
the company by impoverished planters prior to the final sale. Most of the
land purchases, however, consisted of forests and pastures. They also
purchased the Bouvier sugar factory in Formosa.[20] With these parcels of
land the Nougués brothers never faced any real danger of losing their
sugar factory.

Perhaps as important as the rural properties purchased by the
Nougués brothers during this time were the urban properties acquired
both within and outside Tucumán. These properties, along with stocks
in businesses located throughout the republic, provided still another
source of capital in case of emergencies. An initial examination of the
San Pablo yearly financial statements suggests that such investments,
along with constant use of short-term bank loans both within and outside
Tucumán, helped the sugar business through its difficult moments.[21]
Thus, like Avellaneda and Terán, the Nougués family met the problems of
the time with a combination of sound tactics.

The Padilla brothers, owners of the Mercedes factory, found out
how important it was to have additional capital to help their factory
through the sugar crisis. The Padillas had spent all their money on
plantation lands and machinery for their factory. Consequently, their
factory controlled even more land than San Pablo (37,497 hectares) and
produced 300 percent more sugar in 1895.[22] While the Padillas built up
their sugar business, they also accumulated extensive debts that after
1895 became burdensome. They owed money to several banks, to the CAT,
to Porteño sugar wholesalers and to other sugar men.[23] Unlike the Nougués the Padillas had no other properties to sell off or mortgage. According to Ernesto Padilla, then a law student living in Buenos Aires, his
father and uncles finally decided to close the factory and live off the sale
of their sugarcane. In this way they avoided further indebtedness in the
form of provincial production taxes along with the national taxes on sugar
and alcohol. Instead, they signed a contract with the Compañía Azucarera
Tucumana, one of their creditors, to sell all their cane to the Florida factory for six centavos per ten kilos for three years. Ernesto later claimed
that the contract represented a great sacrifice for the company but saved
the business.[24]

Alfredo Guzmán's actions during the sugar crisis offer one more
example of the kind of ingenuity and utilization of resources that helped
save some Tucumán industrialists from business failure. Guzmán had
purchased the Concepción factory in 1887 and from that time on worked
alone and with business partners to modernize his factory. In 1895 Concepción had manufactured more than seven million kilos of sugar and one
million liters of alcohol. That same year Guzmán decided to expand his
business in another way: he installed a small refinery adjacent to his
factory. He did this to break the monopoly of the Refinería Argentina
and to retain his share of the wholesale sugar trade.[25]

Guzmán's decision to enter the refining business opened up new
opportunities for those with enough capital to follow his lead. Though
most industrialists lacked both the money and the desire to construct
refineries, Avellaneda and Terán did so in 1898, and in 1900 the CAT
installed a refinery in Lastenia. Subsequently, a number of other industrialists followed suit both in Tucumán and in other provinces.

The various ways Tucumán industrialists responded to the problems facing the sugar industry in the 1890s had a definite impact on the future of the sugar industry. Whether an industrialist decided to purchase new machinery, expand his holdings or enter the refining business, all these decisions required immense amounts of capital. This meant that, along with whatever profits might accrue from sugar sales, industrialists would still need credit. This demand would then encourage more infighting among sugar industrialists as well as prevent local banks from lending money for other industrial purposes.

The need for large amounts of credit could be measured in a number of ways. The first would be the extent of indebtedness of Tucumán entrepreneurs, and we have two such estimates by public officials. In his 1894 report to President Sáenz Peña, Finance Minister José Terry claimed that Tucumán inhabitants, primarily sugar industrialists and planters, owed more than fifteen million pesos m/n to the following banks:[26]

To the Banco Nacional	8,695,000 m/n
Banco Hipotecario Nacional	3,031,000
For overdue service payments	131,000
converted gold cédulas	982,000
other overdue service charges	45,000
To the Banco de la Nación	2,123,000
	15,007,000

This figure did not include loans to private individuals. In 1898 a congressional investigation committee calculated the amount of Tucumán indebtedness including private loans at 21,000,000 pesos, a sum that excluded monthly interest payments that ranged two and one-half to five percent:[27]

To private individuals	13,585,830 m/n
the Banco Provincial	973,316
Banco Hipotecario Nacional	4,464,404
Banco Nacional	2,827,361
Banco de la Nación	7,571
	21,858,482

The investigative committee attributed the large amount of private loans to the reduced activities of state banks.[28] Though these calculations lacked uniformity and precision, they did reveal the problems that accompanied a continuing need for large amounts of credit that at high interest rates sustained the sugar industry in Tucumán during a deflationary period.

The second way to measure the importance of credit would be the amount of political pressure that might be applied to secure bank loans or to increase the number of public lending institutions--something that is extremely difficult to measure. Yet the fact that some loans were renegotiated while others were not and thus led to foreclosure, indicated a selectiveness that might be interpreted as political in nature. A survey of which factories were sold off by national banks reinforced this impression. The Colmenar, San Andrés, Reducción, Perseverancia and San Vicente factories were auctioned to cover the debts incurred with either the Banco Nacional or Banco Hipotecario Nacional. The owners of these factories, along with those prosecuted by the impuesto interno offices, had all been identified with Liberal, Mitrista or Radical political activities. With PAN officials still in control of the national banks in the 1890s, it was probably more difficult for non-PAN-affiliated industrialists both to secure loans and refinance them than it was for PAN members.[29]

Restricted credit facilities of national banks along with the political selectivity being used to deal with debtors led Tucumán industrialists to seek new provincial lending institutions. For the moment it was impossible to attract to Tucumán branches of private banks operating in cities like Buenos Aires. In the meantime the Tucumán legislature amended the statutes of the Banco Provincial so that it could function like a land mortgage bank. These revisions, passed in March 1900, marked the realization of the Portalis project of 1889.[30] Though the province would not be able to subsidize large-scale loans to industrialists through the Banco Provincial, it would still be able to provide moderate loans to both industrialists and planters. Thus, in their own way, planters again managed to find ways to use politics to help their situation in the sugar industry.

The tremendous capital demands of the sugar industry after the 1890s led to another consequence: the increased number of factories legally organized as joint stock companies (*sociedades anónimas*). The CAT was first formed in this way in 1895. Later, Concepción, Luján, Santa Bárbara, Reducción and Santa Lucía factories were all reorganized as sociedades anónimas between 1900 and 1905 as new owners set out to improve these establishments.[31] This change in legal status encouraged smaller investors to place money in sugar without having to bear the total financial responsibilities of a sugar factory. Even one-family operations would eventually resort to this kind of protection and divide the shares among relatives. The realities of the sugar industry hastened the demise of business practices that dated back to colonial times.

Factory owners in Tucumán met the challenges of the nineties in a variety of ways. Tornquist, Padilla, Hileret and Guzmán tried to increase business to take advantage of economies of scale; the Nougués and Avellanedas and Teráns kept their sugar business at a moderate level while investing sugar profits in land, cattle and urban properties. Aided by friends in influential places and reasonable business decisions, at least nineteen out of thirty-two non-CAT factories in Tucumán withstood the first sugar crisis.[32]

OTHER SECTORS OF THE TUCUMÁN SUGAR INDUSTRY

As for the nonindustrial sectors of the Tucumán sugar industry, the independent planter, the renter and the laborer did not enjoy extensive economic and political privileges. They received nothing from national sugar bounties since they never had any sugar to sell. Similarly, the alcohol and sugar cartels helped the industrialist without providing relief to other sectors of the sugar industry. In general the industrialist had profited at the expense of the agricultural sector.

Besides being left out of most of the important sugar deals of the nineties, the agricultural sector benefited least from the great technological advances that revolutionized the manufacture of sugar. The adaptation of new varieties of sugarcane in Tucumán came rather slowly and by necessity rather than choice. The use of fertilizers and irrigation was limited to plantations that belonged to a few industrialists.[33] No changes whatever aided the laborer who still had to bend and cut the cane with a machete, much the same way it had been done in the sixteenth century. Thus the lack of change in agricultural practices contrasted sharply with new industrial techniques.

The people outside the more modern phases of the sugar industry far outnumbered the industrialists and factory workers. According to the 1895 national census, 2,605 plots of land covering 53,086 hectares had been planted with sugarcane in Tucumán. Of the farmers who worked these lands, 563 rented their property from others. Most of the cane planters owned or worked plots of land between one and fifty hectares, since about 79 percent of all Tucumán farmers at that time worked properties of that size.[34]

During the crisis years a number of farmers temporarily switched to other cash crops such as tobacco and fruit because low cane prices made sugar unprofitable for them. By 1899 the amount of sugarcane planted in Tucumán had been reduced to 38,870.5 hectares.[35] This trend reversed itself only after 1904, and by 1914 the national census reported that Tucumán had 90,848 hectares devoted to sugarcane. At that time the number of sugarcane plantations had increased to 4,684, 4,229 of which had plots of less than 50 hectares, while 11 were plantations that ranged from 5,000 to 25,000 or more hectares.[36] Most of these extensive land-holdings belonged to industrialists. At the same time, the number of renters and sharecroppers working any crop in the province increased to 1,224 and joined the growing numbers of *minifundistas* (cultivators of tiny plots).[37] Thus as a number of industrialists purchased additional lands for their companies, they apparently bought some moderate-sized plantations and then rented out land. After prosperity returned to the sugar industry in the twentieth century, even those with unproductive *minifundios* or rented lands wanted to grow cane. In this way the Tucumán sugar industry, unlike that in other Argentine provinces as well as in other countries, encouraged a landholding pattern of both latifundios and minifundios.

By far the greatest number of people associated with the agricultural sector consisted of men, women and children who worked in the fields. They also had the dubious distinction of being the most exploited and the least powerful economically and politically. It is impossible to calculate exactly how many people worked on sugar plantations in any given year, since most of the labor force was composed of migrant workers. The congressional committee that studied the sugar industry in 1898, however, claimed that close to 70,000 people depended directly upon the Tucumán sugar industry for their livelihood. Most of them are unskilled, illiterate and poor.[38]

Like the independent plantation owner the worker found relief from exploitation by more powerful groups only through the efforts of provincial legislators. The repeal of the Ley de Conchabo in 1896 had been hailed as a great moral victory as well as the end of special privileges for industrialists. Yet 1896 also marked the beginning of very bad years for sugarcane cultivators, years when they were short of cash and probably trying to use fewer workers in the fields. Without the work laws, the province of Tucumán had no legal compulsion to hire the unemployed. Police did not have to enforce the ban on corporal punishment that had been part of the old law. Thus, what appeared at first to be a political move in favor of the working class actually removed the worker from the protection of the law.

In economic terms the depression in the sugar industry struck at the workers most deeply. They depended upon the four-month seasonal salaries of 25 pesos per month to sustain them for the whole year. Yet many workers still never saw cash and instead received the tokens to be used in the plantation store. When Juan Bialet Massé visited Tucumán in 1904 to examine the status of the sugar industry's work force, he noted that salaries had not improved since the 1890s, although by this time a number of factory owners offered workers fringe benefits such as medical facilities, schools and recreational sites. Bialet Massé's trip coincided with a strike among sugar workers for higher pay and the closing of company stores, goals that were not fully achieved until many years later.[39]

THE PROVINCE OF TUCUMÁN

The various sectors of the sugar industry were not the only parts of the Tucumán economy affected by the fall of sugar prices in the 1890s.

Indeed, the entire province felt the repercussions of bad business conditions. On an official level the provincial treasury found that the one-half centavo production tax collections became erratic and tended to diminish:[40]

TABLE 8.2

RECEIPTS FROM ONE-HALF CENTAVO SUGAR TAX

1894	362,264.35 m/n
1895	554,112.27
1896	677,590.68
1897	469,457.35
1898	293,711.56
1899	342,491.26

Besides the sugar industry only commercial enterprises in the city provided significant revenues. These businesses, however, were overtaxed and depressed by conditions in the sugar industry. The tax burden for merchants and other businessmen became so onerous that they petitioned the legislature in 1897 to reduce taxes or face the imminent collapse of these businesses.[41] Because the commercial situation was so grave, legislators reconsidered an earlier plan to raise these taxes. A combination of unstable sugar revenues and the inability to increase the tax burden elsewhere kept the provincial treasury threadbare during the 1890s.

By 1899 other indications of the effect of the sugar crisis on the provincial economy appeared. Following what had earlier been an informal procedure, the Tucumán Minister of Finance officially reduced the salaries of all provincial employees by 10 to 20 percent. He exempted only schoolteachers, already notoriously underpaid. This pay cut was maintained in 1900.[42] Though such economies helped to trim the provincial budget considerably, the province still had to default on its financial obligations. In the mid-1890s Tucumán province had contracted another public loan, this time to finance the installation of water pipes so that San Miguel could have running water. The current provincial revenues made the payment of that loan impossible, and legislators saw no hopes of change until the sugar business had improved.

THE LEY DE MACHETE OF 1902

The Tucumán government found that its political ties to the sugar industry could be as stifling as its economic dependence. This became obvious in 1902, when provincial officials tried to solve sugar's problems by decree. In that year Ernesto Tornquist approached Governor Lucas Córdoba, then serving his second term of office, and asked him to force sugar producers to limit sugar production according to a quota system. Assisting in these negotiations were President Julio Roca and ex-President Carlos Pellegrini.[43]

The provincial law of July 14, 1902 represented the only alternative never before tried by sugar producers. Tornquist had suggested production limitation on several occasions, but no one supported the idea. The quotas he devised with the governor's help explained why: the decree clearly benefited Tornquist and his friends. The CAT factories alone received 35 percent of the total sugar quota. Known Refinería-CAT associates--the Nougués, the Methvens (Azucarera Argentina) and the Padillas, as well as Tornquist's principal competitor Clodomiro Hileret--received another 27 percent. The other factories were supposed to content themselves with the remaining 38 percent. According to the law each kilo of sugar produced within a specified limit would pay the usual one-half centavo tax. Each kilo over the limit would be taxed 40 centavos, which could be reclaimed only if the sugar were exported.[44]

The Ley de Machete only covered Tucumán sugar, since it would be impossible for the province to tax sugar produced elsewhere. The law contained no provisions to enable disgruntled industrialists to protest their share of the total quota, although it did include provisions to pay indemnities to planters forced to plow under their unsold cane. Finally, the law never considered the fate of the already depressed labor force and, since production would be reduced by one-third, many cane cutters would lose their jobs. Although many people were angered by the terms of the law, only Clodomiro Hileret, the Nougués brothers and the Rougés family responded with legal suits. Hileret's lawsuit proved to be the most important, since he took the case to the Argentine Supreme Court, where the law was declared unconstitutional. In response to the court's decision the Tucumán government rescinded the Ley de Machete on October 13, 1903.[45]

Nevertheless, the law accomplished its basic task. Since more than a year and two harvests had passed before the Supreme Court rendered its decision, many planters had simply stopped tending their fields. After 1903 they started to plant cane again, but it took several years for the stalks to mature.

Economic frustration and political conservatism for the sake of sugar took its toll on the province of Tucumán after 1900. True, sugar had saved the province from the kind of subsistence economy that sustained its neighbors. Sugar had also financed substantial urban and rural growth not found in other parts of the northwest. Yet the costs of maintaining the sugar industry often exceeded the advantages sugar offered. The provincial government still had to pay for the irrigation projects designed to bring water to the plantations. After 1900 this specifically meant the construction of El Cadillal dam.[46] The police force, even though excused from its earlier task of registering peons and domestic servants, still worked as much for the factory and plantation owner as for the government by rounding up the unemployed and keeping them in line.

Even the educational system became subverted by the sugar industry. At the lower levels, the paucity of the provincial treasury as well as the lure of the zafra prevented workers' children from receiving adequate education. At the college level the eventual foundation of the Universidad Nacional de Tucumán was prompted as much by the need to train sugar engineers as by the desire to make a liberal education available to students in the north.[47] This monopolization of political, economic and social resources by the sugar industry was not a vestige of some kind of colonial tradition that seemed suitable for sugar magnates to perpetuate. Rather, the necessities of the modern sugar industry created a new world in Tucumán.

THE SUGAR INDUSTRY IN PROVINCES OUTSIDE TUCUMÁN

The other group that must be included in any discussion of what happened to the sugar industry in the 1890s consisted of those involved in sugarcane cultivation and processing outside Tucumán. Throughout this study mention has been made of these establishments without devoting detailed treatment to them or to their owners. Yet these factories, especially those in Salta and Jujuy, would play an important role in the twentieth-century sugar industry.

Industrialists in Santiago del Estero, Formosa, the Chaco and Misiones found that difficult weather conditions hindered the continued expansion of the sugar industry there. After an initial spurt in sugarcane cultivation that began in 1879, Santiago entrepreneurs recognized the fact that the province's barren salt-crusted land, even with the aid of irrigation, simply could not produce enough sugar to feed the factories. By 1889 there were six factories in operation fed by 2,925 hectares; by 1895 only two factories remained in operation and only 796 hectares of cane existed to supply them.[48] In the other provinces, diametrically opposite conditions had similar implications for the sugar industry. Constantly wet weather, along with spongy soil, prevented sugarcane from growing properly. A number of the factory owners in these provinces tried to concentrate on alcohol rather than on sugar production, and for a while these factories continued to function on a small scale.[49]

Lack of railroad facilities, rather than climatic conditions, impeded the expansion of sugar in Salta and Jujuy. Unlike the other areas just discussed, these two provinces had better cane growing conditions than those in Tucumán. Yet Tucumán was served by three railroad lines, while the more northern provinces had only one to rely upon. The Salta-Tucumán section of the North Central did not open until 1891, and its extension to Jujuy was not finished until several years later. By that time the sugar industry was in full crisis and there was little impetus to expand the one factory in Salta and three in Jujuy.[50]

Besides the more favorable environment for sugar growing in Salta and Jujuy, industrialists in these provinces had a number of advantages over their competitors in Tucumán that could not be utilized until the twentieth century. First of all, they faced little industrial competition within their respective provinces. Neither Salta nor Jujuy had groups of powerful merchants and small entrepreneurs like those present in Tucumán since the 1840s. Consequently, the land and capital resources had remained in the hands of traditional elites along with a small number of trusted outsiders. Second, there were less political competitors among whom sugar industrialists would have to divide government favors and resources. This meant that questions of taxes, control of the labor force and public irrigation projects could be settled among the factory owners with little outside interference. Third, these industrialists had access to inexpensive labor sources unavailable to Tucumán entrepreneurs. Bolivian Indians as well as certain Argentine Indians could still be recruited by *agentes de conchabo* hired by the four factory owners from the north. Such Indians were more easily exploited than the Creole worker in Tucumán and were paid much less. When sugar producers could finally begin to expand sugarcane cultivation in Salta and Jujuy, lower labor costs would become a highly significant factor.

CONCLUSION

The situation of the sugar industry in Argentina after 1900 was anything but static. Although Argentine sugar had been closed out of international markets in the nineties, the domestic market continued to expand. Between 1895 and 1914 the population of Argentina doubled from 4,000,000 to 8,000,000, while the per capita intake of sugar increased from 22 to 27 kilos per year.[54] To meet the needs of the expanding consumer market the forty-two Argentine sugar factories doubled their production of sugar and increased the capital value of their land and machinery from 15,417,984 gold pesos to 71,876,936 gold pesos, or an increase of more than 450 percent.[52] As long as there was a need for more sugar, internecine warfare within the sugar industry was kept at a minimum. The Unión Azucarera faded away after the Argentine government eliminated sugar bounties in 1905. The Refinería Argentina found that it had enough business to keep the machines operating despite the existence of several refineries in Tucumán. Even the federal government managed to derive advantages from the prosperous sugar business. The

Saavedra Lamas law, passed in 1912, established a gradual way to lower the duty on imported sugar while guaranteeing the sugar producer a minimum price. [53]

By the 1920s, however, sugar production began to keep pace with the rate of consumption and conflict again hit the industry, especially in Tucumán. The first major fight broke out between factory owners and independent plantation owners over the price of sugarcane. Whereas prior to this time industrialist-planter disputes had been contained within the province, the increasing role of the national government in the regulation of the sugar industry encouraged the intervention of national officials. The *Laudo Alvear* of 1928, a presidential decree, fixed the relative share of sugar profits between the industrialist and the planter until new laws in the 1940s supplanted this early legislation. [54] By that time political conditions within the sugar industry and within Argentina had changed enough to allow the workers to participate in industrial and political decisions.

As the various groups within the sugar industry became incorporated into the industrial and political power structures, the shape of the sugar industry itself changed. The Unión Azucarera and the Ley de Machete were at first replaced by more informal and then by national government-controlled industrial agreements for marketing and price fixing. New refineries were installed, including a large Porteño establishment founded by a descendant of Hileret in 1923. Confronted by fierce competition from factories that utilized more modern equipment, the Refinería Argentina closed its doors in 1932 and most of its equipment was transported to Tucumán and incorporated into facilities there. [55]

Within the factory sector the newer factories in Tucumán, Salta and Jujuy enjoyed advantages similar to the new refineries. More efficiently operated and less burdened by long-standing debts, the newer factories began to exert the kind of industrial and political power previously wielded by the older Tucumán establishments. Their effort to command a significant role in the Argentine sugar industry was aided immeasurably by a series of national decrees from 1966 on that closed down a number of older factories in Tucumán.

Within the agricultural sector workers after 1943 won the right to organize unions on plantations and they, along with the independent plantation owners, formed crucial pressure groups. Peronism found strong support among rural proletariats who had long felt the impact of industrialism in the countryside. Tucumán sugar workers became more militant than those in the far north, and in this way the labor situation reinforced developments in the industrial sector.

Although the relative importance of groups associated with the sugar industry tended to change over time, the relationship of the sugar industry to the northwestern part of Argentina remained the same. Without sugar the northwest would never have fit into the vision of Argentina constructed by the Generation of Eighty. The sugar industry had allowed the northwest to survive the process of national unification. At the same time, however, the sugar industry tended to generate its own patterns of conflict that ranged from national to class issues. Neither local nor national politicians could resolve the conflicts to the satisfaction of all interested parties, nor could they envision some sort of alternative to the sugar industry. Haunted by this dilemma, Tucumán and its sugar industry would continue to bother political leaders.

ENDNOTES TO CHAPTER VIII

1. For a detailed treatment of the city of Buenos Aires and its evolution at this time see James R. Scobie, *Buenos Aires, Plaza to Suburb, 1870-1900* (New York: Oxford University Press, 1974).

2. Williams, *Argentine International Trade Under Inconvertible Currency, 1880-1900,* pp. 148-162; A. G. Ford, "British Investment and Argentine Economic Development, 1880-1914," in *Argentina in the Twentieth Century,* David Rock, ed. (Pittsburgh: University of Pittsburgh Press, 1975), pp. 12-40.

3. Ricardo Mazorati, *La industria del extracto de quebracho en la Argentina frente al "HOLDING" internacional* (Buenos Aires: privately printed, 1960), pp. 32-33; Gastón Gori, *La Forestal (la tragedia del quebracho colorado)* (Buenos Aires: Proyección, 1974), pp. 51-53.

4. García, *La industria azucarera argentina y las consecuencias de su protección,* pp. 145-146. The asterisks indicate the years when partial bounties were offered for old sugar.

5. *Revista azucarera,* March 1898, p. 83.

6. Ibid., April 1898, pp. 128-130.

7. Ibid., December 1899, pp. 681-683.

8. Ibid., April 1898, p. 131.

9. For the list of Centro Azucarero delegates in Tucumán see Centro Azucarero, *Cincuentenario,* pp. 19-20; *El orden,* January 17, 1900, p. 1.

10. *Ernesto Tornquist,* p. 23n. This occurred in 1892, the first year of full-time operations.

11. Pillado, *Anuario Pillado de la deuda pública y sociedades anónimas establecidas en la República Argentina en el año 1899,* passim, states that the dividends paid on preferred shares amount to 4 percent in 1891, 5 percent in 1892, 7 percent in 1893, 7 percent in 1894, 8 percent in 1895, 10 percent in 1896, 8 percent in 1897, and 10 percent in 1898, all of which agree with Refinería reports. Refinería Argentina, *Primera a Undécima Asambleas Generales Ordinarias* (Buenos Aires: Peuser, 1888-1898). Later reports from the Refinería Argentina quoted profits of 8 percent in 1899, 10 percent in 1900, 9 percent in 1901, 9 percent in 1902, 10 percent in 1903, 10 percent in 1904, and 10 percent in 1905. Remaining profits were destined to expand reserve funds and provide additional capitalization. Occasionally small dividends of 2 to 4 percent were also paid to holders of ordinary shares. Refinería Argentina, *Duodécima á 18a Asambleas Generales Ordinarias* (Buenos Aires: Peuser, 1899-1905).

12. Refinería Argentina, *Undécima Asamblea General Ordinaria* (Buenos Aires: Peuser, 1898), p. 5.

13. Tilmant, "Ernesto Tornquist," pp. 271-274; Pillado, *Anuario Pillado.* 1899, pp. 193-195. Besides these dividends, substantial reserve funds were also augmented and debentures were guaranteed 6 percent interest.

14. Ibid.; *The Argentine Year Book, 1902* (Buenos Aires: John Grant and Son, 1903), p. 439.

15. Argentine Republic, Cámara de Diputados, Comisión Revisora de las Leyes Aduaneras, *La cuestión azucarera; Informe da la subcomisión especial encargada de su estudio* (Buenos Aires: n.p., 1907), p. 61.

16. For additional information on these business failures see Schleh, *Noticias históricas sobre el azúcar en la Argentina*, pp. 256-267; Centro Azucarero, *Cincuentenario; La industria azucarera*, noviembre 1955, pp. 476-478.

17. These data are available through the generosity of the Avellaneda family of Tucumán. The conclusions are based upon a series of deeds, a payment receipt for a loan on the Humaita ranch, a payment booklet for Banco Hipotecario Nacional loan No. 68/3144, Series C and other pertinent documents located in the private archives of the Avellaneda y Terán and Santa Lucía Companies, AAT.

18. Guy, *Politics and the Sugar Industry in Tucumán, Argentina, 1870-1900*, Appendix A, pp. 316-325.

19. This statement is based upon the collection of deeds and contracts in the Nougués Hermanos archives. Carpeta Marrón series, ASP.

20. Schleh, *Noticias históricas sobre el azúcar en la Argentina*, p. 362.

21. This statement is based upon studies of San Pablo Inventories conducted by Jorge Balán and the author. Inventarios, I-II, 1875-1896, ASP.

22. Guy, *Politics and the Sugar Industry in Tucumán, Argentina, 1870-1900*, Appendix A, pp. 316-325.

23. A number of letters in Ernesto E. Padilla archives, now in the possession of Ernesto E. Padilla (h), refer to a series of debts contracted by the Padilla brothers. Ernesto E. Padilla to José Padilla, to José Padilla, Buenos Aires, October 29, 1895, AEEP; Ernesto E. Padilla to José Padilla, Buenos Aires, February 22, 1896, AEEP; Ernesto E. Padilla to José Padilla, Buenos Aires, March 9, 1896, AEEP; José Padilla to Ernesto E. Padilla, Tucumán, December 27, 1897, AEEP; José L. Ocampo to José Padilla, Buenos Aires, September 15, 1898, AEEP; Ernesto Tornquist to Ernesto E. Padilla, Mar del Plata, March 16, 1899, AEEP.

24. Ernesto E. Padilla, *Un tercer cuaderno* (Tucumán: Universidad Nacional de Tucumán, 1960), pp. 107-111.

25. *Revista azucarera*, September 1894, pp. 218-220; ibid., November 1900, pp. 317-320; Centro Azucarero, *Cincuentenario*, p. 67.

26. Terry, *Memoria*, pp. 8-9.

27. Argentine Republic, Congreso, Cámara de Diputados, Comisión de Agricultura y Colonización, *Investigación parlamentaria sobre agricultura, ganadería, industrias derivadas y colonización; ordenada por la H. Cámara de Diputados en resolución de 19 de junio de 1896. Anexo G:* Tucumán y Santiago del Estero por Antonio M. Correa. Revisado y aumentado por Emilio Lahitte (Buenos Aires: Tip. de la Penitenciaría Nacional, 1898), pp. 17-18.

28. Ibid., pp. 18-19.

29. Guy, *Politics and the Sugar Industry in Tucumán, Argentina, 1870-1900,* Appendix A, pp. 316-325.

30. Law of March 5, 1900, *Compilación,* XXIII:279-280.

31. Guy, *Politics and the Sugar Industry in Tucumán, Argentina, 1870-1900,* Appendix A, pp. 316-325.

32. Ibid.

33. According to the 1895 census, of all the lands devoted to sugarcane cultivation, only six utilized fertilizers and 776 had private irrigation facilities. *Segundo Censo Nacional,* III:LXII.

34. Ibid., p. 187; Correa and Lahitte, Anexo G, p. 12.

35. Guy, *Politics and the Sugar Industry in Tucumán, Argentina, 1870-1900,* Appendix Diagram B-2, p. 327.

36. *Tercer Censo Nacional,* V:201.

37. Ibid., pp. 802-803.

38. Correa and Lahitte, *Anexo G, Tucumán y Santiago del Estero,* pp. 156-157. This figure included people working in any kind of activity basically dependent upon the sugar industry.

39. Bialet Massé, *El estado de las clases obreras a comienzos del siglo,* pp. 500-510, 522-539.

40. Governor Lucas Córdoba, Message to the Legislature, September 10, 1898, *Compilación,* XXII:229; Tucumán Province, *Anuario estadístico de la provincia de Tucumán correspondiente al año 1899* (Tucumán, 1900), p. 158.

41. Commercial petition, January 30, 1897, *Compilación,* XX:410-412.

42. *La prensa,* June 13, 1899, p. 5; Decree, Governor Próspero Mena, February 6, 1900, *Compilación,* XXIII:267-268.

43. *Ernesto Tornquist,* pp. 27-28; García, *La industria azucarera argentina y las consecuencias de su protección,* pp. 107-111.

44. Ibid., *Compilación,* XXV:123-156 contains the legal antecedents to the law and its eventual annulment.

45. Ibid.

46. This project was first suggested by Governor Lucas Córdoba in 1904.

47. Enrique Kreibohm, *Un siglo de cultura provinciana; aportaciones históricas alrededor de la vida de una institución tucumana de la "Sociedad Sarmiento" a nuestra universidad* (Tucumán: UNT, 1960), pp. 96-103.

48. Gancedo, *Memoria descriptiva de Santiago*, pp. 190-196; Schleh, *Noticias históricas sobre el azúcar en la Argentina*, pp. 365-366.

49. Schleh, pp. 360-363. Sugarcane was also cultivated on a small scale in Santa Fe and Corrientes.

50. Wright, *British-Owned Railways in Argentina*, p. 52.

51. *Tercer Censo Nacional*, VII:544.

52. Ibid., p. 541.

53. Ministerio de Comercio e Industria, Instituto de Investigaciones Económicas, *Problema azucarero argentino* (Buenos Aires: Ministerio de Comercio e Industria, 1956), p. 7.

54. Ibid., pp. 9-10.

55. Schleh, *Noticias históricas sobre el azúcar en la Argentina*, pp. 359-360; Centro Azucarero, *Cincuentenario*, p. 215.

APPENDIX

TABLE A.1

NATIONAL PRODUCTION AND IMPORTATION OF SUGAR
1870-1900

	National Production (M. Tons)		Importation (M. Tons)		
Year	Tucumán	Other Provinces	Refined	Non-refined	Total
1870	1,000	------	8,184	11,415	19,599
1872	1,200	200	11,278	13,439	24,717
1877	3,000	------	11,413	11,858	23,271
1880	9,000	------	11,548	9,080	20,628
1881	9,000	------	17,569	8,726	26,295
1884	24,152	------	28,595	6,315	34,910
1889	40,843	8,478	33,031	1,435	34,466
1890	41,000	------	26,428	3,113	29,541
1891	41,000	5,366	11,199	1,637	12,836
1892	53,475	4,221	18,324	1,447	19,771
1893	50,000	12,000	9,884	083	9,967
1894	75,083	9,917	12,062	3,090	15,152
1895	109,253	20,747	5,620	031	5,651
1896	135,605	27,395	2,071	003	2,074
1897	90,785	20,831	946	------	946
1898	66,697	8,841	440	------	440
1899	76,680	13,588	456	000.2	456.2
1900	100,267	16,942	458	000.2	458.2

Diagram based upon *La industria azucarera*, no. 546 (April 1939),
311 and 320; and published in *The Americas*, 32:4 (April 1976), 574.

TABLE A.2

CURRENCY USED IN TUCUMÁN 1870-1900

1870-1881

Bolivian peso: silver coins of 25 or 20 grams.
Peso fuerte: gold and silver pesos of varying weights issued
prior to 1881.

Official Exchange Rates

June 1876	25 gr.	.92 ps. ftes
	20 gr.	.74 ps. ftes
March 1877	25 gr.	.88 ps. ftes
	20 gr.	.69 ps. ftes
January 1879	25 gr.	.82 ps. ftes
	20 gr.	.65 ps. ftes
September 1879	25 gr.	.99 ps. ftes
	20 gr.	.79 ps. ftes
November 1881	25 gr.	.84 m/n
	20 gr.	.72 m/n

1881-1900

Peso nacional: gold, silver and copper coins. 1 gold peso = 1.6219
grams = .967 pesos fuertes of 1875 = $.965 U. S. = 5 francs.
After 1883 the gold peso was used exclusively for international
transactions, while paper pesos (moneda nacional, or m/n) became the official domestic currency. The value of the paper
peso was determined by a gold premium:

Gold Premium on Paper 1883-1900

1883	par	1892	232
1884	par	1893	224
1885	37%	1894	257
1886	39	1895	244
1887	35	1896	196
1888	48	1897	191
1889	91	1898	158
1890	151	1899	125
1891	287	1900	131

Sources: Juan Álvarez, *Temas de historia económica argentina*, Junta
de Historia y Numismática, Biblioteca de Historia Argentina y
Americana, vol. II (W.M. Jackson, Inc.: Buenos Aires, 1929),
pp. 111, 117, and 118.

Argentine Republic, *Tercer Censo*, X:395.

TABLE A.3

PRINCIPAL TUCUMÁN SUGAR FACTORIES

Name	Founder	Proprietor in 1895
Amalia	Ezequiel Molina (1870)	Delfín Jijena
Azucarera Argentina	David Methven (1882)	Corporate ownership
Bella Vista	Manuel García Fernández (1882)	García Fernández family
Buenos Aires	Catellano and Casalius (ca. 1883)	not operating
El Colmenar	Astoul, Mata and Dubourg (1884)	Julio Dubourg
Cruz Alta	Simón García (1824)	María Luísa García
Concepción	Juan José García (1840)	Alfredo Guzmán, Eduardo Leston and Lídoro Quinteros
Esperanza	Wenceslao Posse (1845)	Posse family
Caspinchango	Juan Recalt (ca. 1882)	Leudesdorf Bros.
La Florida (CAT	Pedro G. Méndez (1890)	Compañía Azucarera Tucumana
Nueva Baviera (CAT)	Francisco Duport (1879)	Compañía Azucarera Tucumana
La Trinidad (CAT)	Juan Manuel Méndez (1878)	Compañía Azucarera Tucumana
Lastenia (CAT)	Evaristo Etchecopar (1840)	Ingenios Río Salí
San Andrés (CAT)	Domingo García (1860)	Herman Tullström
Industria Argentina	Roque Pondal (1870)	Posse y Pondal
La Invernada	Enrique Erdman (ca. 1882)	Ramón Ferreira
Luján	Santiago Cardozo (1858)	Gallo Bros.
Lules	Clodomiro Hileret and Juan Dermit (1879)	Hileret, Emilio Rodrigue Víctor Negri
Santa Ana	Hileret (1889)	Hileret
Mercedes	Miguel M. Padilla (1858)	Padilla family

TABLE A.3 (continued)

Name	Founder	Proprietor in 1895
El Manantial	Garnaud Bros. (1883)	Juan Videla
El Paraíso	Vicente José García (1835)	García family
Perseverancia	Javier Usandivaras (1870)	not in operation
La Providencia	S.A. Córdoba del Tucumán (1882)	S.A. Córdoba del Tucumán
Los Ralos	Eudoro and Marco Avellaneda, Brígido Terán (1876)	Avellaneda and Terán
Reducción	Vicente Posse (1852)	Salazar and Leudesdorff
San Felipe	Felipe Posse (1870)	Melitón Rodríguez and I. Sosa
Santa Bárbara	Jorge Vergnes (1884)	Jorge Vergnes
San Felipe de las Vegas	Felipe Bernan (1882)	Felipe Bernan
San José	José Frías and Sons	Frías family
San Juan	Juan Posse and Leocadio Paz (1870)	Paz and Posse families
San Miguel	Belausteguí and Co. (ca. 1882)	Francisco Bustamante
Santa Lucía	Gerado Constanti (1883)	José Federico Moreno
Santa Rosa	León Rougés (1889)	Leon Rougés y Cía.
San Pablo	Juan Nougués (1827)	Nougués Bros.
San Vicente	Manual Posse and Son (1882)	Abraham Medina
Unión	Gaspar Taboada	Taboada and Dode

Abbreviations Found in Endnotes

AH	Archivo Histórico de Tucumán
NA	National Archives (USA)
AAT	Archivo Avellaneda y Terán
ACT	Banco Tornquist, Casa Tornquist Papers
ADR	Archivo Dardo Rocha
AFH	Archivo Federico Helguera
AGN	Archivo General de la Nación
AHL	Archivo de la Honorable Legislatura de Tucumán
AJC	Archivo Juárez Celman
APG	Archivo Próspero García
ASP	Archivo San Pablo
AVP	Archivo Victorino de la Plaza
AWP	Archivo Wenceslao Posse
AEEP	Archivo Ernesto E. Padilla

BIBLIOGRAPHY

ARCHIVES

Archivo de la Honorable Legislatura de Tucumán [AHL]
  Actas de la Legislatura, 1880-1884.
  Cámara de Diputados, 1884-1900.
  Cámara de Senadores, 1884-1900.

Archivo General de la Nación [AGN]
  Archivo Victorino de la Plaza [AVP], Sala VII, Miscellaneous
    Correspondence, 1891-1897.
  Archivo Próspero García [APG], Sala VII, Private and Official
    Correspondence, 1890-1894.
  Archivo Juárez Celman [AJC], Sala VII, Private and Official
    Correspondence, Telegrams, 1880-1890.
  Archivo Dardo Rocha [ADR], Sala VII, Private Correspondence,
    1880-1886.

Archivo Histórico de Tucumán [AH]
  Sección Administrativa, 1870-1900.
  Comprobantes de contaduría hacienda, 1870-1900.

National Archives (United States of America) [NA]
  Despatches from United States Ministers to Argentina, 1896-1898.
    Microcopy No. 69, Rolls 29-30.
  Diplomatic Instructions of the Department of State, 1801-1906.
  Argentina. Microcopy No. 77, Roll 12.

PRIVATE PAPERS

Archivo Ernesto E. Padilla [AEEP]; Miscellaneous Correspondence.

Archivo Federico Helguera [AFH]; Books I and II.

Archivo San Pablo [ASP]; Carpeta Marrón Series; Inventarios I and II,
  1876-1895; Lardière Correspondence; Miscellaneous Correspondence.

Archivo Wenceslao Posse [AWP]; Copybooks I and II

Banco Tornquist, Casa Tornquist Papers [ACT]; Libro de Actas,
  Refinería Argentina; Memorias, Refinería Argentina; Primera á 18^a
  asambleas generales ordinarias, Refinería Argentina; Carpeta de
  Borradores.

Los Ralos, S.A.; Avellaneda y Terán; Santa Lucía, S.A. [AAT];
  Tucumán; Miscellaneous land deeds, company papers.

Rodríguez Marquina, Paulino. *Memoria descriptiva de Tucumán. Su industria, su presente, pasado y porvenir estadística.* 3 vols.
  Unpublished manuscript.

NEWSPAPERS AND JOURNALS

Boletín de la Unión Industrial Argentina, 1887-1900.

Boletín del Departamento Nacional de Agricultura, 1878-1897.

La capital [Rosario], 1885.

El condor [Tucumán], 1877–1878.

The Economist [London], 1870–1900.

El independiente [Tucumán], 1877–1898.

Impuestos internos, 1900

La industria azucarera [Successor to Revista azucarera], 1903–

El industrial, 1881–1887.

La nación, 1870–1900.

El orden [Tucumán], 1883–1900.

La prensa, 1870–1900.

La razón [Tucumán], 1872–1873.

El republicano [Tucumán], 1881–1882.

Review of the River Plate, 1892–1900.

Revista azucarera, 1894–1903.

South American Journal and Brazil and River Plate Mail [London], 1863–1900

Sud América, 1891–1892.

La tribuna nacional, 1886.

OFFICIAL PUBLICATIONS

Argentine Republic. Bancos y Moneda. Recopilación de leyes y decretos, 1854 a 1890. Buenos Aires: Publicación Oficial, 1890.

Argentine Republic. Banco Hipotecario de la Nación. Memoria y balance, 1887–1891. Buenos Aires, 1888–1892.

Argentine Republic. Cámara de Diputados. Comisión Revisora de las Leyes Aduaneras. Estudios e informes. Buenos Aires, 1907.

Argentine Republic. Cámara de Diputados. Comisión Revisora de las Leyes Aduaneras. La cuestión azucarera; informe de la subcomisión especial encargada de su estudio. Buenos Aires, 1907.

Argentine Republic. Cámara de Senadores. Diario de Sesiones, 1854–. Buenos Aires: Imprenta del Congreso de la Nación.

Argentine Republic. Comisión Directiva del Censo. Primer Censo de la República Argentina. Verificado en los días 15, 16, y 17 de septiembre de 1869. Buenos Aires: El Porvenir, 1872.

Argentine Republic. Comisión Directiva del Censo. *Segundo Censo de la República Argentina.* [El 10 de mayo de 1895]. 3 vols. Buenos Aires: Taller Tipográfico de la Penitenciaría Nacional, 1898.

Argentine Republic. Comisión Directiva del Censo. *Tercer Censo Nacional de la República Argentina.* Levantado el 10 de junio de 1914. 10 vols. Buenos Aires: G. Pisce, 1917-1919.

Argentine Republic. Congreso. Cámara de Diputados. Comisión de Agricultura y Colonización. *Investigación parlamentaria sobre agricultura, ganadería, industrias derivadas y colonización;* Ordenada por La H. Cámara de Diputados en resolución de 19 de junio de 1896. Anexo G. Tucumán y Santiago del Estero por Antonio M. Correa. Revisado y aumentado por Emilio Lahitte. Buenos Aires: Tip. de la Penitenciaría Nacional, 1898.

Argentine Republic. Congreso Nacional. Cámara de Diputados. *Diario de Sesiones, 1854- .* Buenos Aires: Imprenta del Congreso de la Nación.

Argentine Republic. Congreso Nacional. Cámara de Diputados. *El Parlamento argentino, 1854-1947.* Buenos Aires: Imprenta del Congreso, 1948.

Argentine Republic. *Registro Nacional de la República de Argentina, 1887.* Buenos Aires: Ministerio de Justicia e Instrucción Pública, 1887.

Argentine Republic. *Tarifas de Aduana.* [Estudios y antecedentes para su discusión legislativa por la comisión revisora nombrada por el poder ejecutivo.] Buenos Aires: Cía. Sudamericana de Billetes de Banco, 1894.

Castro, Antonio P. *Epistolario entre Sarmiento y Posse, 1845-1888.* [Aclaraciones y biografía por Antonio P. Castro.] Archivo Histórico Sarmiento, Serie V; Archivo Museo, No. 1, 2 vols. Buenos Aires: Archivo Histórico Sarmiento, 1946.

Cordeiro, Ramón; Carlos Dalmiro Viale; Horacio Sánchez Loria; y Ernesto del Moral, eds. *Compilación ordenada de leyes, decretos, y mensajes del período constitucional de la provincia de Tucumán que comienza en el año 1852.* 33 vols. Tucumán: Prebisch y Violeto, 1915-1919.

Ministerio de Comercio e Industria. Instituto de Investigaciones Económicas. *Problema azucarero argentino.* Buenos Aires: Ministerio de Comercio e Industria, 1956.

Museo Roca. *Publicaciones del Museo Roca: documentos.* 7 vols. Buenos Aires: Ministerio de Educación y Justicia, 1966-1967.

Santiago del Estero Province. *Recopilación de leyes, decretos y resoluciones de la provincia de Santiago del Estero.* 6 vols. Buenos Aires: Peuser, 1897-1910.

Tucumán Province. *Anuario estadístico de la provincia de Tucumán.* Tucumán, 1895- .

Tucumán Province. *Boletín oficial, 1873, 1882.*

Tucumán Province. *Registro estadístico correspondiente al año 1882.* Buenos Aires: Coni, 1884.

BOOKS AND ARTICLES

Adamson, Alan H. *Sugar Without Slaves: The Political Economy of British Guiana, 1838-1904*. New Haven: Yale University Press, 1972.

Agote, Pedro. *Report on the Public Debt, Banking Institutions and Mint of the Argentine Republic, and on the National and Provincial Estimates and Taxation Laws*. Trans. by L. B. Trant. Book IV. Buenos Aires, 1887.

Agulla, Juan Carlos. *Eclipse de una aristocracia; una investigación sobre las élites dirigentes de la ciudad de Córdoba*. Buenos Aires: Ediciones Libera, 1968.

Álvarez, Juan. *Las guerras civiles argentinas*. Colección Siglo y Medio, no. 94. 3rd ed. Buenos Aires: EUDEBA, 1966.

_____. *Temas de historia económica argentina*. Junta de Historia y Numismática, Biblioteca de Historia Argentina y Americana, Vol. II. Buenos Aires: W. M. Jackson, Inc., 1929.

Arce, José. *Cronología de Roca*. Estudio VII. Buenos Aires: Ministerio de Educación y Justicia, 1965.

The Argentine Year Book, 1902. Buenos Aires: R. Grant and Son, 1903.

Avellaneda, Nicolás. *Discursos de Nicolás Avellaneda, I. Oraciones cívicas*. Biblioteca Argentina No. 27. Buenos Aires: La Facultad, 1928.

_____. *Escritos y discursos*. 12 vols. Buenos Aires: Compañía Sudamericana de Billetes de Banco, 1910.

Balestra, Juan. *El noventa; una evolución política argentina*. 4th ed. Buenos Aires: Luis Fariña, Editor, 1971.

Barba, Fernando E. "La crisis económica de 1873-1876." *Trabajos y comunicaciones*, 14 (1965):47-60.

Bialet Massé, Juan. *El estado de las clases obreras argentinas a comienzos del siglo*. 2nd ed. Córdoba: Universidad Nacional de Córdoba, 1904, 1968.

Bliss, William Horacio. *Del virreinato a Rosas, ensayo de historia económica argentina*. Tucumán: Editorial Richardet, 1959.

Bosonetto, Julio C. "Distribución de los ingenios azucareros tucumanos." In *Geographia una et varia: Homenaje al doctor Federico Machatschek con motivo de sus bodas de oro con el doctorado 1899--5 de noviembre de 1949*. Instituto de Estudios Geográficos, Publicaciones especiales II. Tucumán: UNT, 1951. pp. 43-55.

Bousquet, Alfredo. *Estudio sobre el sistema rentístico de la provincia de Tucumán de 1820 a 1876*. Tucumán: La Razón, 1878.

Burgin, Miron. *Economic Aspects of Argentine Federalism*. Cambridge: Harvard University Press, 1946.

Burmeister, Hermann. *Descripción de Tucumán*. Tucumán: Universidad Nacional de Tucumán, 1916.

Canton, Darío. *El Parlamento argentino en épocas de cambio: 1890, 1916 y 1946.* Buenos Aires: Editorial del Instituto di Tella, 1966.

Carranza, Arturo B. *La cuestión capital de la República 1826 a 1887.* 6 vols. Buenos Aires: L. J. Rosso, 1926.

Carrasco, Gabriel. *La producción y el consumo del azúcar en la República Argentina.* Buenos Aires, 1894.

Centro Azucarero Argentina. "Industria azucarera de la República Argentina; Trabajos para un acuerdo entre los fabricantes." Suplemento al No. 38 de la *Revista azucarera.* Buenos Aires: J. Carbone, 1897.

_____. *La industria azucarera; informes, legislación y estadística.* Buenos Aires: Centro Azucarero, 1903.

Centro Azucarero Argentina. *Cincuentenario del Centro Azucarero Argentino, desarrollo de la industria en medio siglo 1880-1944.* [by Emilio J. Schleh]. Buenos Aires: Centro Azucarero, 1944.

Cincuentenario de la S. A. Compañía Azucarera Tucumana, 1895-1945. Buenos Aires: Peuser S. A., 1945.

"Confronting Theory and Practice." *Latin American Perspectives,* 2:1 (Spring, 1975). Special Issue No. 4.

Cornbilt, Oscar E., Ezequiel Gallo (h), y Alfredo A. O'Connell. "La generación del 80 y su proyecto; antecedentes y consecuencias." In Torcuato S. Di Tella, Gino Germani, *et al., Argentina, sociedad de masas.* 3rd ed. Buenos Aires: EUDEBA, 1968. pp. 18-58.

Cutolo, Vicente Osvaldo. *Nuevo diccionario biográfico argentino.* Vols. I-3. Buenos Aires: Elche, 1968- .

Daireaux, Émile. *La vie et les moeurs à la Plata.* 2 vols. Paris: Hatchette, 1888.

D'Atri, Noberto. *Del 80 al 90 en la Argentina. Datos para una historia política.* Buenos Aires: A. Peña Lillo, 1973.

Deerr, Noel. *The History of Sugar.* 2 vols. London: Chapman and Hall, Ltd., 1949.

del Pont, Augusto Marcó. *Roca y su tiempo; cincuenta años de historia argentina.* Buenos Aires: L. J. Rosso, 1931.

di Tella, Torcuato, Gino Germani, Jorge Graciarena, *et al. Argentina, sociedad de masas.* 3rd ed. Buenos Aires: Jorge Álvarez, 1966.

di Tella, Torcuato S., y Tulio Halperín Donghi, comps. *Los fragmentos del poder de la oligarquía a la poliarquía argentina.* Los Argentinos, vol. 9. Buenos Aires: Jorge Álvarez, 1969.

Dorfman, Adolfo. *Historia de la industria argentina.* 2nd ed. Buenos Aires: Solar-Hachette, 1970.

Dussaut, Alejandro. *La colonia francesa en el Río de la Plata, conferencia pronunciada con motivo del centenario el 13 de mayo de 1966.* Buenos Aires: privately printed, n.d.

Eichner, Alfred S. *The Emergence of Oligopoly. Sugar Refining as a Case Study.* Baltimore, Md.: Johns Hopkins Press, 1969.

Eisenberg, Peter L. *The Sugar Industry in Pernambuco; Modernization Without Change, 1840-1910.* Berkeley: University of California, 1974.

Ernesto Tornquist, 1842-1942; Estudio biográfico de su vida publicado con motivo del centenario de su natalicio. Buenos Aires: Compañía Impresora Argentina, 1942.

Etchepareborda, Roberto. *Tres revoluciones: 1890-1893-1905.* Buenos Aires: Pleamar, 1968.

Ferns, Henry. *Britain and Argentina in the Nineteenth Century.* Oxford: Oxford University Press, 1960.

Ferrer, Aldo. *The Argentine Economy.* Translated by Marjory M. Urquidi. Berkeley: University of California, 1967.

Ford, A. G. "British Investment and Argentine Economic Development, 1880-1914." In David Rock, ed., *Argentina in the Twentieth Century.* Pittsburgh: University of Pittsburgh Press, 1975. pp. 12-40.

Fúrlong Cárdiff, Guillermo. *Ernesto E. Padilla, su vida, su obra.* [Prólogo de Gustavo Martínez Zuviría. Epílogo de Manuel Lizondo Borda.] 2 vols. Tucumán: UNT, Facultad de Filosofía y Letras, 1959.

Galíndez, Bartolomé. *Historia política argentina: la revolución del 80.* Buenos Aires: Coni, 1945.

Gallenga, Antonio. *South America.* London: Chapman and Hall, 1880.

Gallo, Vicente C. *La presidencia Avellaneda: una página de historia institucional y política; conferencia pronunciada por el doctor Vicente C. Gallo.* Buenos Aires: L. J. Rosso, 1918.

_____. "Recuerdos de juventud. Mi primera actuación pública en la política. [Tucumán hace 55 años.]" *Sustancia,* 1:3 (diciembre 1939): 339-350.

Gamboni, Olga. "La rebelión del oeste y sus proyecciones en el norte." *Trabajos y comunicaciones,* 13 (1965):75-110.

Gancedo, Alejandro. *Memoria descriptiva de la provincia de Santiago del Estero.* Buenos Aires: Stiller and Laass, 1885.

García, Tubal C. *La industria azucarera argentina y las consecuencias de su protección.* Tesis presentada para optar al grado de Doctor in Ciencias Económicas. Buenos Aires: Universidad Nacional de Buenos Aires, Facultad de Ciencias Económicas, 1920.

García de Saltor, Irene, Ana María Musso Coloma de Risco, Mirta Elena Oliva, Nilda Esther Hernández, y Felicidad María Carreras. "Crónica de la epidemia del cólera en Tucumán." *Cuadernos de Humanidades; Aportes para la historia de Tucumán* [Universidad del Norte "Santo Tomás de Aquino," Facultad de Humanidades], 1:2 (n.d.):5-103.

García Soriano, Manuel. "La condición social del trabajador en Tucumán durante el siglo XIX." *Revisión histórica:*1 (mayo 1960):7-46.

_____. "El trabajo de los indios en los ingenios azucareros de Tucumán." *Revista de la Junta de Estudios Históricos de Tucumán*, 2:2 (julio 1969):109-129.

Gargaro, Alfredo. "Antecedentes de la Guerra del Paraguay y reacciones en las provincias." *Trabajos y comunicaciones*, 10 (1963):83-91.

Glade, William P. *The Latin American Economies, a Study of their Institutional Evolution*. New York: American Book Company, 1969.

Gori, Gastón. *La Forestal (la tragedia del quebracho colorado)*. Buenos Aires: Proyección, 1974.

Graham, Richard. *Britain and the Onset of Modernization in Brazil 1850-1914*. London: Cambridge University Press, 1968.

Granillo, Arsenio. *Provincia de Tucumán, 1872*. 2nd ed. Series V, vol. 1. Tucumán: Archivo Histórico de Tucumán, 1947.

Groussac, Paul. *Los que pasaban: José Manuel Estrada, Pedro Goyena, Nicolás Avellaneda, Carlos Pellegrini, Roque Sáenz Peña*. 2nd ed. Buenos Aires: Editorial Sudamericana, 1919, 1939.

Groussac, Paul, Alfredo Bousquet, Inocencio Liberani, Dr. Juan M. Terán, y Dr. Javier Frías. *Memoria histórica y descriptiva de la provincia de Tucumán*. Buenos Aires: M. Biedma, 1882.

Gunder, Frank, André. *Capitalism and Underdevelopment in Latin America; Historical Studies of Chile and Brazil*. New York: Monthly Review Press, 1967.

Guy, Donna J. *Politics and the Sugar Industry in Tucumán, Argentina, 1870-1900*. Unpublished dissertation, Indiana University, 1973.

_____. "The Rural Working Class in Nineteenth-Century Argentina: Forced Plantation Labor in Tucumán." *Latin American Research Review*, 13:1 (Spring 1978):135-145.

_____. "Tucumán Sugar Politics and the Generation of Eighty." *The Americas*, 32:4 (April 1976):566-584.

Guyot, Yves. *The Sugar Question in 1901*. London: H. Rees, Ltd., 1901.

Guzmán y Compañía. *Réplica de los sres. Guzmán y Cía. al sindicato Unión Azucarera Argentina*. Tucumán: Talleres El Norte, 1896.

Hat, Roberto. *Almanaque, guía de Tucumán para 1884*. Buenos Aires: Guillermo Kraft, 1885.

Heins, Guillermo [Capitán Nemo]. *América industrial y comercial*. Buenos Aires: Pan América, 1936.

Heras, Carlos. "La rebelión del oeste a través del Archivo de Marcos Paz (nov. 1886-feb. 1867)." *Trabajos y comunicaciones*, 10 (1963):93-120.

Huret, Jules. *En Argentine: de Buenos-Aires au Gran Chaco*. Paris: E. Fasquelle, 1911.

Imaz, José Luiz de. *Los que mandan (Those Who Rule)*, trans. and with an introduction by Carlos A. Astiz and Mary McCarthy. Albany: State University of New York Press, 1970.

In Memoriam: Ernesto Tornquist. Buenos Aires: privately published, 1908.

Kossok, Manfred. *El virreinato del Río de la Plata, su estructura económica social*. Buenos Aires: La Pléyade, 1972.

Kreibohm, Enrique. *Un siglo de cultura provinciana; aportaciones históricos alrededor de la vida de una institución tucumana de la "Sociedad Sarmiento" a nuestra universidad*. Tucumán: UNT, 1960.

Labougle, Alfredo. *Carlos Pellegrini: un gran estadista. Sus ideas y su obra*. Academia de Ciencias Económicas, Ediciones Especiales No. 14. Buenos Aires: El Ateneo, 1957.

Lahitte, Emilio. *Informes y estudios de la Dirección de Economía Rural y Estadística*. 2 vols. 2nd ed. Buenos Aires: Ministerio de Agricultura, 1916.

_____. *La industria azucarera. Apuntes de actualidad*. Buenos Aires: Europea de M. A. Rosas, 1902.

Laks, J. *La verdad sobre la cuestión azucarera*. Buenos Aires: Editorial Documentos, 1960.

Lanzetti, Raquel, Norma Pavoni, y Norma D. Riquelme de Lobo. "Aportes para el estudio de tres intervenciones a la provincia de Tucumán (1887-1893-1905)." *Cuaderno de la Cátedra de Historia Argentina*, Serie 1, No. 2. Córdoba: Universidad Nacional de Córdoba, 1968.

Lázaro, Orlando. "Tres aspectos del gobierno de Lucas A. Córdoba." *Revista de la Junta de Estudios Históricos de Tucumán*, 1:1 (marzo 1968):9-45.

Leoni Pinto, Ramón. "La historiografía del Tucumán moderno, notas y comentarios sobre una contribución." *Revista de la Junta de Estudios Históricas de Tucumán*, 2:2 (julio 1969):145-166.

Lizondo Borda, Manuel. *Historia de Tucumán; siglo XIX*. Facultad de Ciencias Culturales, Instituto de Historia XIV, Publicación 452. Tucumán: UNT, 1948.

Mabragaña, Heraclio. *Los mensajes: historia del desenvolvimiento de la Nación Argentina; redactada cronológicamente por sus gobernantes, 1810-1910*. 6 vols. Buenos Aires: Compañía General de Fósforos, 1910.

Martínez, Pedro Santos. *Las industrias durante el virreinato, 1776-1810*. Buenos Aires: EUDEBA, 1969.

Mazorati, Ricardo. *La industria del extracto de quebracho en la Argentina frente al "HOLDING" internacional*. Buenos Aires: privately published, 1960.

McGann, Thomas Francis. *Argentina, the United States and the Inter-American System, 1880-1914*. Cambridge: Harvard University Press, 1957.

Mulhall, Michael George, and Edward T. Mulhall. *Handbook of the River Plate; Comprising Buenos Ayres, the Upper Provinces, Banda Oriental, and Paraguay*. Vol. 1. Buenos Aires: Standard Printing Office, 1869.

_____. *Handbook of the River Plate; Comprising Buenos Aires, the Provinces of the Argentine Republic, and the Republics of Uruguay and Paraguay*. London: Edward Stanford. Buenos Aires: M. G. and E. T. Mulhall, 1875.

_____. *Handbook of the River Plate; Comprising the Argentine Republic, Uruguay and Paraguay*. 5th ed. Buenos Aires: M. G. and E. T. Mulhall, 1885.

Nicolau, Juan Carlos. *Industria argentina y aduana, 1835-1854*. Buenos Aires: Devenir, 1975.

Padilla, Ernesto E. *Un tercer cuaderno*. [Introducción de Sisto Terán.] Tucumán: UNT, 1960.

Padilla, Vicente. *El norte argentino. Historia política, administrativa, social, comercial de las provincias de Tucumán, Salta, Jujuy, Santiago y Catamarca*. Buenos Aires: Ferrari, 1922.

Páez de la Torre (h), Carlos. "El Gobernador Celedonio Gutiérrez y sus relaciones con los 'salvajes unitarios,' 1841-1852." In Academia Nacional de Historia, *Primer Congreso de Historia Argentina y Regional*. [Celebrado en San Miguel de Tucumán de 14 al 16 de agosto de 1971.] Buenos Aires: Academia Nacional de Historia, 1973. pp. 765-782.

_____. "Personajes en el olvido." *La gaceta*, 1967- .

Pagés, Pedro. *La industria azucarera en el norte de la república*. Buenos Aires: Imprenta del Departamento Nacional de Agricultura, 1888.

Pellegrini, Carlos. *Discursos y escritos*. [Selección y estudio preliminar de José María Bustillo.] Buenos Aires: Ediciones Estrada, 1959.

_____. "El estanco de alcohol." *La biblioteca*, 2:5 (julio-septiembre 1897):5-43.

_____. *Obras (1846-1906)*. [precedidas de un ensayo biográfico por Agustín Rivero Astengo]. 5 vols. Buenos Aires: Coni, 1941.

Peña, David. *Viaje político del Dr. Bernardo de Irigoyen al interior de la República (julio, agosto, y septiembre de 1885)*. Buenos Aires: A. Moën, 1885.

Pillado, Ricardo. *Anuario Pillado de la deuda pública y sociedades anónimas establecidas en la República Argentina para 1899*. Buenos Aires: La Nación, 1899.

Platt, Desmond Christopher St. Martin. *Latin America and British Trade, 1806-1914*. New York: Barnes & Noble, 1973.

Prinsen Geerlings, Hedrick C. *The World's Cane Sugar Industry, Past and Present*. Manchester: N. Rodger, 1912.

Quesada, Vicente [Víctor Gálvez]. "Recuerdos de Tucumán y Salta. Las ciudades del interior hace 30 años." *La nueva revista de Buenos Aires*, 20 (1884):443-466.

Quintero, Eduardo. *Ocho días en Tucumán*. Buenos Aires: M. Biedma, 1877.

Refinería Argentina. *Memorias, 1889-1900*. Buenos Aires: Peuser, 1890-1901.

_____. *Primera a 18ª asambleas generales ordinarias*. Buenos Aires: Peuser, 1899-1905.

Ricci, Teodoro Ricardo. *Algunas consideraciones sobre la economía de Tucumán*. Facultad de Filosofía y Letras, Departamento de Geografía, Serie monográfica 19. Tucumán: UNT, 1971.

_____. *Evolución de la ciudad de San Miguel de Tucumán*. Colección del Sesquicentenario de la Independencia Argentina. Tucumán: UNT, 1967.

Rickard, Francis Ignacio. *The Mineral and Other Resources of the Argentine Republic in 1869*. London: Longmans, Green and Co., 1870.

Rippy, J. Fred. *British Investments in Latin America, 1822-1949. A Case Study in the Operations of Private Enterprise in Retarded Regions*. Minneapolis: University of Minnesota Press, 1959.

Rodríguez, Fermín. "Alcoholismo y suicidio en Buenos Aires." *La biblioteca*, 2:5 (julio-septiembre 1897):443-466.

Rodríguez, Marquina, Paulino. *La mortalidad infantil en Tucumán*. Tucumán: El Orden, 1898.

Saksonoff Velarde, Atilio. "Historia de las instituciones bancarias de la provincia." *Primer Congreso de Historia de los Pueblos de la Provincia de Tucumán*. Tucumán: Ministerio de Gobierno, Subsecretaría de Cultura, 1953, pp. 259-272.

Samson, Ing. "Proyecto para una sociedad anónima para la elaboración y refinación de azúcar en la provincia de Tucumán." *Boletín del Departamento Nacional de Agricultura*, 4 (1880):311-315.

Santamarina, Estela Barbieri de. "Los límites de la provincia de Tucumán: históricos, actuales, fisio y antropogeográficos." In Estela Barbieri de Santamarina, María A. Moreno, y Enrique de Jesús Setti. *El área jurisdiccional del Tucumán, su representación cartográfica y sus derroteros*. Cuaderno de Humanitas, No. 27. Tucumán: UNT, Facultad de Filosofía y Letras, 1968. pp. 9-33.

Sanucci, Lia E. M. *La renovación presidencial de 1880*. Departamento de Historia, Colección de Monografías y Tesis. Buenos Aires: Universidad Nacional de la Plata, 1959.

Schleh, Emilio J. *Compilación legal sobre el azúcar*. I. Buenos Aires: Ferrari, 1939-1950.

_____. *La industria azucarera argentina; pasado y presente*. Buenos Aires: n.p., 1910.

_____. *La industria azucarera en su primer centenario, 1821-1921:* Buenos Aires: Ferrari, 1921.

_____. *Noticias históricas sobre el azúcar en la Argentina.* Buenos Aires: Centro Azucarero Argentina, 1945.

Scobie, James R. *Argentina, a City and a Nation.* 2nd ed. New York and London: Oxford University Press, 1971.

_____. "Buenos Aires as a Commercial-Bureaucratic City, 1880-1910: Characteristics of a City's Orientation." *American Historical Review,* 77:4 (October 1972):1035-1082.

_____. *Buenos Aires, Plaza to Suburb, 1870-1900.* New York: Oxford University Press, 1974.

_____. *La lucha por la consolidación de la nacionalidad argentina, 1852-1862.* Buenos Aires: Solar-Hachette, 1964.

Smith, Peter H. *Argentina and the Failure of Democracy. Conflict among Political Elites 1904-1955.* Madison: University of Wisconsin Press, 1974.

_____. *Politics and Beef in Argentina. Patterns of Conflict and Change.* New York: Columbia University Press, 1969.

Sommariva, Luis H. *Historia de las intervenciones federales en las provincias.* 3 vols. Buenos Aires: El Ateneo, 1929.

Sommi, Luis V. "La estructura económico-social de la Argentina en 1890." *Revista de historia,* 1:1 (1957):18-35.

Sosa, Ismael A. *Historia constitucional de Tucumán (período 1820-1884).* Facultad de Derecho y Ciencias Sociales, Publicación No. 379. Tucumán: UNT, 1945.

Spalding, Jr., Hobart A. "Education in Argentina, 1890-1914: the Limits of Oligarchical Reform." *The Journal of Interdisciplinary History,* 3:1 (Summer 1972):31-61.

Stein, Stanley and Barbara. *The Colonial Heritage of Latin America; Essays on Economic Dependence in Perspective.* New York: Monthly Review Press, 1967.

Taussig, Frederick W. *The Tariff History of the United States.* 6th ed. New York and London: G. P. Putnam's Sons, 1907.

Terry, José A. *Memoria presentada al Sr. Presidente de la República: Tucumán, Salta, Jujuy y Santiago.* Buenos Aires, 1894.

Tilmant, Jules. "Ernesto Tornquist et le commerce anversois." In *In Memorium: Ernesto Tornquist.* Buenos Aires, 1908. pp. 251-299.

Tjarks, Germán O. E., Olga G. d'Agostino, Hebe G. de Bargero, Laura B. Jany, Ana E. Magnavacca, María Haydee Martín, Elena Rebok, y María Susana Stein. "Aspectos cuantativos del estado económico y social de la ciudadanía argentina potencialmente votante (1860-1890)." *Boletín del Instituto de Historia Argentina 'Dr. Emilio Ravignani',* 11:18-19 (1969):26-100.

Tomaso, Dr. Antonio E. *El monopolio de azúcar. Un caso típico de proteccionismo criollo.* Buenos Aires: Lotito y Barberis, 1915.

Torres, José Luis. *Los "Perduellis".* Buenos Aires: Editorial Freeland, 1973.

Unión Azucarera Argentina. *La Unión Azucarera y los sres. Guzmán y Cía.* Buenos Aires: Mariano Moreno, 1896.

Wauters, Carlos. *El riego en Tucumán a través de los siglos desde la fundación de la ciudad hasta la sanción de la ley vigente. 1686 a 1897.* Publicación ordenada por la Junta Superior de Irrigación bajo la presidencia del ingeniero Carlos Wauters. Tucumán: Talleres de la Provincia, 1904.

Williams, Eric. *Capitalism and Slavery.* Chapel Hill: University of North Carolina, 1944.

Williams, John Henry. *Argentine International Trade Under Inconvertible Paper Money, 1880-1900.* Cambridge: Harvard University Press, 1920.

Wilmowski, Máximo. *Guía comercial de la provincia de Tucumán para 1893.* Tucumán, 1893.

Wright, Winthrop R. *British-Owned Railways in Argentina, Their Effect on Economic Nationalism, 1854-1948.* Latin American Monographs No. 34. Austin: University of Texas Press, 1974.

Zeballos, Estanislao S. *La concurrencia universal y la agricultura en ambas Américas.* 2nd ed. Buenos Aires: Peuser, 1896.

Zinny, Antonio. *Historia de los gobernadores de las provincias argentinas.* 5 vols. Buenos Aires: La Cultura Argentina, 1920-1921.

INDEX

Railroads, 2, 10, 33-34, 49, 135;
Buenos Aires-Rosario line, 50;
Córdoba-Tucumán line (North
Central) 3-4, 15, 19-21, 30-31,
37, 49-50, 63, 135; freight
rates, 51, 91; Northwest Argentine, 37, 135.

Refinería Argentina, 47, 52-56,
90-92, 95, 105-106, 110, 113-114,
127, 129, 133, 135; See also
Ernesto Tornquist, Centro
Azucarero, sugar bounties
and Unión Azucarera.

Roca:
Ataliva, 9-10.
Julio, 4, 21-22, 32-35, 37-40, 63,
64-68, 75, 77, 79-82, 85, 96,
98, 115-116, 126, 133; See also
Generation of Eighty, federal
intervention in Tucumán,
Miguel Nougués, Refinería
Argentina.

Rocha, Dardo, 62; See Tucumán
political factions.

Rodríguez Marquina, Paulino, 37,
65.

Sáenz Peña:
Luis, 79, 81, 82-84, 89, 91-92,
124, 130; See Tariff Review
Commission.
Roque, 79.

Salta, 12, 14, 20-21, 33, 112, 134-
136.

San Miguel de Tucumán, 11, 15, 37,
49, 83-84.

Santiago del Estero, 10-11, 14, 33-
35, 50, 52, 106, 134-135; See
also Taboadas, Tucumán tax
system, Bartolomé Mitre.

Sarmiento, Domingo F., 10, 27-28,
32.

Spirits Loan, 114-117.

Sugar:
bounties, 96-99, 109, 124.
Brazilian, 55-56, 105-107.
congress, 110-114, 125.
Peruvian, 21, 105-106.

Sugar factories:
Formosa: Bouvier, 129.
Misiones: San Juan, 48.
Sante Fe: Mercedes, 53.
Santiago del Estero: Contreras,
106; San Germán, 128.
Tucumán: Amalia, 127; Azucarera
Argentina, 54, 133; La Banda-
Lastenia, 49, 93, 106, 127, 129;
Buenos Aires, 106; Colmenar,
106, 130; Concepción, 71, 128-
129, 131; Cruz Alta, 127;
Esperanza, 16; La Florida, 70,
106, 129; La Invernada, 127;
Los Ralos, 29, 128-129; Luján,
106, 127, 131; Lules, 49; Manan-
tial, 76; Mercedes, 70,129;
Nueva Baviera, 48, 105-106, 127;
Paraíso, 128; Perseverancia, 130;
Providencia, 50; Reducción, 16,
128, 130-131; San Andrés, 16,
93, 106, 130; San Pablo, 19-21,
52, 129; San Ramón, 106; Santa
Ana, 49, 70-71, 106, 127; Santa
Bárbara, 131; Santa Lucía, 50,
131; Santa Rosa, 49; San Vicente,
93, 130; La Trinidad, 106;
Unión, 128.

Taboada brothers, 10, 32, 35.

Tariff:
Dingley (U.S.), 107, 112-113.
general discussion, 4, 22, 80, 89,
92.
Review Commission, 89-92, 127-128.
Sugar, 4, 51-55, 81, 90-92.

Terán, Brígido, 29, 110, 128-129.

Terry, José A., 90-92, 125, 130;

Tornquist, Ernesto, 48, 52-53, 78,
81, 85, 92, 98, 105-107, 110-113,
125-130, 131, 133; See Tucumán
sugar factories, Refinería Argentina, Sugar Congress, Ley de
Machete.